Corporate Financial Risk Management

Corporate Financial Risk Management

A Computer-based Guide for Nonspecialists

Roy L. Nersesian

PRAEGER

Westport, Connecticut
London

Library of Congress Cataloging-in-Publication Data

Nersesian, Roy L.
  Corporate financial risk management : a computer-based guide for nonspecialists / Roy L. Nersesian.
       p.   cm.
  Includes bibliographical references and index.
  ISBN 0–56720–584–4 (alk. paper)
  1. Corporations—Finance.   2. Risk management—Computer programs.   3. Electronic spreadsheets—Computer programs.   I. Title.
  HG4026.N474   2004
  658.15′5′02855369—dc21   2002193027

British Library Cataloguing in Publication Data is available.

Copyright © 2004 by Roy L. Nersesian

All rights reserved. No portion of this book may be
reproduced, by any process or technique, without the
express written consent of the publisher.

Library of Congress Catalog Card Number: 2002193027
ISBN: 0–56720–584–4

First published in 2004

Praeger Publishers, 88 Post Road West, Westport, CT 06881
An imprint of Greenwood Publishing Group, Inc.
www.praeger.com

Printed in the United States of America

The paper used in this book complies with the
Permanent Paper Standard issued by the National
Information Standards Organization (Z39.48–1984).

10 9 8 7 6 5 4 3 2 1

To my brother Dick and his wife, Olga

Contents

Introduction		ix
1	Risk: It Is All in the Tail	1
2	What Rate to Compensate for Risk?	25
3	Managing Risk in a Project Financing	55
4	Risk in Financing General Corporate Credits	93
5	The Risk of Running Out of Cash	121
6	Evaluating Risk Inherent in Product Development	141
7	A Not-So-Random Walk Down Wall Street	153
8	Hedging with a Swap	177
9	Insuring Against Business Risks	201
Suggested Reading		231
Index		233

Introduction

Risk is encompassing in nature; everything we do is fraught with risk. In this book, risk is defined in a rather narrow fashion as an excessive financial loss of a type that can be analyzed on a Microsoft Excel spreadsheet. Risk is presented from the perspective of a businessperson who, with a problem at hand, turns it over for analysis by a corporate planning staff. The corporate planning staff response is to be in a straightforward manner utilizing standard business terminology without resorting to esoteric mathematical concepts.

Certain risks that can create excessive financial losses are endogenous, that is, under management's control. Corporate managers bear the risk of selecting the wrong business strategy for a company, of implementing the right strategy wrongly, of not making the correct operational, marketing, and financial decisions to accomplish business objectives. There are also exogenous risks over which we have little or no control. Two such risks are the price and volume of the goods we make and the services we provide. Some say that companies do set the price for the goods they make and determine the volume they sell. Those who maintain this delusion must not be experienced in business. While it is true that there is some leeway in setting prices, the marketplace allows for little discretion. If this observation were not true, then prices would be at levels that generate high gross profit margins. With rare exceptions, we don't see "grossly gross" profit margins. Moreover, sales volume is set not by the productive capacity of factories but by the number of buyers. It is true that some companies are better at tapping the pool of available buyers than others. It is true that the characteristics and quality of the product and its price relative to the competition are under management control and do influence sales. Thus, management can take actions that expand or contract its market share, although management does not control what its competitors are doing. No matter how much competitors squabble over market share, the aggregate number of buyers willing to buy a product is set by economic conditions, customer preferences for other products, public perception of the desirability of the product, changes in a product's life cycle, demographics, government regulations, and a host of other matters beyond the control of managers.

If sales volume were under the control of companies, then we would sell all we produce. This is patently untrue. Books on quality management have been written telling us that all we have to do to take over a market is manufacture attractively priced, high-quality products. If you believe that, call up the cell phone manufacturers with your attractively priced, high-quality cell phone and ask them why they are having such hard times. Or call Japan.

The first two chapters provide an introduction to @Risk software by dealing with the kind of risk we are most apt to think about—the risk of a catastrophe, in this case, the risk of a house burning to the ground. Premiums are derived for insuring the total value of a small number of houses versus insuring a small value of a large number of houses. Whereas the average loss rate is identical for both situations, management actually has control over the shape of the risk-loss profile through diversification. Thus, management is not without tools in determining how risk affects a company.

Chapter 3 examines the risk of financing a project. A project is a single product or single service entity for which there is no outside credit support other than what is produced or provided by the investment. The example under consideration is a factory where the price and volume of sales are not known with certainty. The risk of price and volume not generating sufficient revenue to support operations including debt servicing is analyzed from the perspective of a bank financing the new factory. Risk is measured in terms of the necessity of drawing down on a solvency loan, an unlimited line of credit to ensure the solvency of the factory. The risk of project financing can be managed by controlling the minimum working capital requirement and the role of equity and debt in financing the factory. Both the borrower as owner and the lending institution sit on the same side of the table in the sense of wanting to avoid the risk of insolvency that can lead to bankruptcy. An equity owner can utilize the same methodology presented in Chapter 3 to judge the profitability of a project and to establish the role of working capital and equity for financing the project to guard his or her interests as can a lending institution to protect its interests.

Chapter 4 examines the risk of a corporation in a hundred different activities of generating insufficient funds flow. A radically different approach has to be taken to evaluating risk for a company with many diverse activities than for a project financing where there is a single line of business. As it is impossible to scrutinize a company's many different activities on an individual basis, an aggregate approach is taken to analyze the adequacy of funds flow. Funds flow is more encompassing than cash flow. Cash flow is the after-tax profits net of debt repayment, which results from the ongoing activities of a company. Funds flow is cash flow net of capital expenditures and dividends. Capital expenditures are necessary for maintaining the competitiveness and enhancing a company's productive capacity plus opening

INTRODUCTION   XI

up new lines of business. A company with a positive cash flow can have a negative funds flow, which means that the company must tap outside sources of equity and debt in order to continue as an ongoing concern. This chapter offers a means for managers to determine the need for outside sources of capital under conditions of uncertainty.

The risk of a company running out of cash because of vagaries between cash inflows and outflows is examined in Chapter 5. The major difference between corporate and personal cash management is that personal cash management focuses on maintaining a minimum balance adequate to meet our needs. Corporate cash management is concerned with maximum balances. Cash management can be costly if too much money is being kept in the corporate checking account, forcing the company to utilize more expensive sources of cash, such as borrowings, to fund capital expenditures. This chapter provides a methodology for determining the optimal maximum amount of money to be dedicated to corporate cash and short-term investment accounts to handle the vagaries of cash inflows and outflows.

Chapter 6 looks at the risk associated with product development. The risk is associated with proceeding with a project that may or may not materialize and that, if it does materialize, may not be profitable. While it is understandable why some companies would shy away from such ventures, it is to our benefit that others don't. Companies at the forefront of technological development must wrestle with deciding whether to proceed with a research and development (R&D) project. R&D and product development projects are inherently risky because there is no assurance of success, and failures can be costly. While evaluating the potential of success or failure of R&D and product development projects is inherently frustrating, the act of trying to quantify probabilities of success and costs associated with success and failure is useful as a tool for aiding in the management decision on whether to proceed.

Evaluating swaps and other means of protection against adverse price changes requires a future price. Chapter 7 discusses the challenge of forecasting. The chapter creates a (not-so) random price generator that is utilized in Chapter 8 to evaluate the use of swaps to protect against an adverse price change. The situation under scrutiny is built around a copper-mining company that is exposed to the exogenous risks of a low copper price and an adverse currency exchange rate. While the benefit of a swap in protecting against a low price of copper and an adverse currency exchange rate is clear, the cost in terms of profits foregone is not so clear. The decision on the appropriate swap volume is based on a cost-benefit analysis that provides the appropriate degree of protection for the least cost in foregone profits.

Chapter 9 expands on Chapter 8 by examining the use of commercial insurance to protect against the triple exogenous risks of a low copper price, an adverse currency exchange rate, and a high floating interest rate as an alternative to swaps. Here the reward of an imponderable, such as a high copper price, can compensate for an adverse currency exchange rate and a high interest rate. The payment of insurance is contingent on the three exogenous factors having values that create a negative cash flow. The chapter ends with a minicase on determining the appropriate insurance premium for protecting against high heating oil costs for a school district.

It is the hope of the author that there is sufficient "meat on the bone" for corporate planning staffs to take perhaps a different look at protecting a corporation against exogenous risks. The methodology is restricted to conventional spreadsheet formulations with a heavy dose of plain business common sense. The mathematical underpinnings are those normally associated with financial spreadsheets. Although at times the formulation looks daunting, on second look, it really isn't. The spreadsheets are set up for specific situations to aid in discussion and provide a guide for modeling actual situations faced by companies. Success in writing this book can be measured by the degree that the thoughts expressed herein are utilized by planning staffs.

1
RISK: IT IS ALL IN THE TAIL

SYNOPSIS

It is not the average loss rate that is of concern, but the loss profile. We can live with the average loss rate, but the potential for horrendous losses is hidden from view in the tail of a probability distribution. This chapter deals with the subject of risk, the danger that lurks in the tail of the risk profile distribution, and how diversification affects a risk profile without affecting the degree of risk itself.

Is life a series of random events, or is there evidence of intelligent design? This is a hotly debated subject among evolutionists and creationists. Daily sales in a store or the price of a commodity is influenced by events, but the probability distributions used to describe daily sales or price of the commodity can be generated from random numbers. Random numbers can be used to establish a probability distribution that is then used to predict sales being below the breakeven for operating a store or the price of a commodity either rising or falling to levels that present a financial risk to a consumer or the producer of the commodity. Whether daily sales in a store and the price of a commodity are truly random events is not the question; the point is that they can be modeled with probability distributions based on randomness. This chapter also covers spreadsheet modeling details and @Risk software features that help in evaluating a risk profile.

RISK—IT IS FOREVER WITH US

What is the risk? Apparently, there is no real agreement on a formal definition of risk. It may be that it is difficult to define something that inundates our lives. We run the risk of not being alive one second from now, of not marrying the right spouse, of not selecting the right career, of being in the wrong place at the wrong time. The tragic events on September 11, 2001, have awakened in everyone an increased awareness of risk, the fragility of life, the uncertainty of the times. Defining risk in all its encompassing forms is a challenge. Here we narrow the scope of risk to the potential of not just losing money but losing too much money.

RISK IS IN THE EYE OF THE BEHOLDER

Risk is highly personal. For a company that consumes gold, risk takes the form of a rising price of gold. If the rising price of gold can be passed on to the consumers, then there is little risk other than a possible falloff in business. However, if this falloff in business is severe enough, then a high price of gold carries a risk of a contracting volume of business that may lead to a financial crisis.

On the other hand, a gold-mining company relishes the prospects of higher gold prices. That's why gold-mining companies are in business. Risk to a gold-mining company takes the form of a falling price. A small decline in the price of gold may represent the annoyance of decreased profitability but not risk. A major decline in the price of gold may mean the potential bankruptcy if its debt from developing relatively high-cost properties can no longer be serviced. For a low operating cost mine with no debt, a low gold price may mean cessation of operations but not bankruptcy. Thus, there is a different threshold of pain for every gold-mining company with regard to the price of gold depending on operating costs and financial obligations. The threshold of pain occurs when net cash flow turns negative or exceeds a certain limit. Risk can be defined by the circumstances that lead to a nonsustainable financial loss.

RISK IN MUNDANE MATTERS

Why do we buy fire insurance for our home? One reason is that the mortgage holder requires us to do so because we may not be eager to continue making mortgage payments on a burned-out shell or may be unable to do so as we are now obliged to find alternative housing. Another reason is that most of us cannot sustain the financial loss of our home in a fire even without a mortgage. So what do we do? We essentially deposit money, called insurance premiums, in a collective pot run by fire insurance companies. The companies issue policies for a premium based on the history of houses destroyed by fire plus an add-on to cover their operating costs.

When we buy fire insurance, we are essentially insuring each other's homes on a collective basis. The risk of fire has not been mitigated; the chances of a house being burned to the ground have not changed. What has changed is the risk of loss that is now spread over all the policyholders rather than being borne by a few individuals. Insurance does not affect the nature of risk, although many insurance companies take an interest in reducing the risk of whatever they insure. Fire and casualty insurance companies inspect their insured properties to suggest or mandate actions to correct hazardous conditions. Automobile insurance companies promote legislation that increases driver safety. Life insurance companies publish brochures on how to improve one's personal health. While insurance companies may appear as benefactors to society, reducing the risk of loss does happen to enhance their profitability.

Fire insurance companies have reserves to back up potential claims. The reserves are actually a small part of what is insured. A company that insures 100 houses at $100,000 each does not have $10 million in reserves, although that would be its maximum loss. Suppose that the company has an average loss record of ½% per year, or $50,000 on a $10 million portfolio of fire insurance policies. Clearly, having $10 million in reserves is excessive. Suppose the company has $100,000 in reserves. This is obviously sufficient if the average loss record is a precise ½% per year. It may also seem sufficient if losses vary between 0% and 1%. The worst one can do as long as history repeats itself is having annual claims of $100,000.

How much money can a fire insurance company make? Simple—take the premium income of insuring 100 houses, add in the income from the reserves being invested in financial instruments, subtract the claims and the administrative costs of running an insurance company, and voilà, the profit.

This calculation depends on the history of claims repeating itself. But history repeating itself does not absolve an insurance company from having an actual loss that exceeds the expected loss. Suppose the insured houses are in a single development nestled in the midst of a pine forest. There is a risk of a forest fire burning up the entire development. Bankruptcy takes care of the insurance company with $100,000 in reserves and claims totaling $10 million. Bankruptcy may also take care of some of the policyholders who owe a substantial amount of money to the bank for a burned-out shell covered by a worthless policy.

DIVERSIFICATION—KEEPING THINGS FROM GETTING WORSE

This problem of a single disaster financially destroying an insurance company can be handled by diversification. Diversification of risk has a long history going back hundreds of years. An early example of diversification of risk is Chinese merchants moving cargoes down the Yangtze River. They knew that some of the riverboats would be lost passing through the rapids. The merchants would stop upstream of the rapids and distribute their cargoes among different boats. Thus, a boat did not carry the cargo of a single merchant but cargoes of several merchants. The risk of the loss of a boat was not affected by distributing the cargoes. But if a boat were lost, one merchant did not suffer an irretrievable loss; rather, several merchants suffered sustainable losses.

Another example of diversification took place in Renaissance London with the idea of individuals buying shares in a shipping venture. Huge price spreads for products in various parts of the world made trade very profitable. These spreads existed because there was so little movement of goods. A ship that completed the voyage in buying silk and spices in China, where they were plentiful, and selling them in Europe, where they were scarce, would make a lot of money. That is why

European traders and seafarers risked their lives to sail to China. The only problem was that they might not make it back. Therefore, it was more prudent for financial backers to purchase shares in several shipping ventures than to put all their money into a single shipping venture. Having an interest in several shipping ventures greatly reduced the risk of a total loss of investment. The risk of the loss of a vessel was not mitigated, just the extent of the losses that one would face. The shares were liquidated when the vessel returned at a value reflecting the venture's profitability. Issuing shares in a temporary venture was the precursor for issuing shares in a permanent venture, the publicly owned corporation. These examples of diversification are alive today. Modern investment philosophy advises not putting one's eggs all in one basket but in a portfolio of investments—a lesson learned on the Yangtze River and in Renaissance London.

To diversify its portfolio of fire insurance policies, an insurance company could insure two houses per state and not worry about all their insured houses burning down simultaneously. Diversification of risk is the purpose of reinsurance. Rather than one fire insurance company insuring the value of 100 houses, the underwriting company could sell a portion of each policy to a reinsurer who might purchase a 1% slice of a portfolio of 10,000 existing fire insurance policies. This could be repeated with other reinsurers. This assuming of the responsibility to cover a small portion in many individual fire insurance policies is the best way to have the actual loss reflect the expected loss.

REINSURERS

This process can be taken one step further by breaking down insurance companies into two different businesses. One underwrites and administers fire insurance policies and then sells small portions of the portfolio of the policies to reinsurers. The other reinsures or assumes the risk for small portions of many fire insurance policies. The remuneration for the originating insurance company in selling the policies and handling the administrative details is the difference between the insurance premiums received from the policyholders and those paid to the reinsurers. The originating insurance company can reinsure its entire portfolio of policies, removing all risk of loss. The remuneration for the reinsurers is the premiums received from the originating insurance company net of claims payments. Their business decisions are based on the history of losses and on the competitive attractiveness for providing such insurance. The reinsurers issue reinsurance policies or buy bits and pieces of existing policies if they perceive that the premiums received will be higher than the potential claims net of their administrative charges.

ULTIMATELY POLICYHOLDERS PAY ALL CLAIMS

The insurance premium is based on expected losses plus competitive factors and administrative costs. The reserves of insurance companies are drawn down if actual losses exceed expected losses. Insurance companies with depleted reserves are no longer quite so generous in quoting new business. All policyholders, through higher insurance rates, eventually share in a catastrophic loss until the insurance companies rebuild their reserves. After the reserves have been replenished, then competition for the more lucrative areas of underwriting eventually forces insurance rates back to their previous levels.

Who will pay for the destruction of the World Trade towers and several buildings in the area that have collapsed or have to be razed plus other liabilities, which, in the months following the catastrophe, were estimated to be somewhere between $30 and $100 billion? First, the reserves of the originating insurance companies and the reinsurers are drawn down. Depleted reserves make the insurance companies and reinsurers more aggressive in quoting rates on renewal policies. It was estimated in late 2001 that insurance rates on office buildings would climb between 30% and 50% when up for renewal. Ultimately, the bill for the World Trade towers will be paid by the policyholders of office buildings throughout the world in the form of higher insurance rates in order to replenish insurance company reserves. There is no free lunch in business.

THE PROBLEM IS NOT IN THE AVERAGE, BUT IN THE TAIL

If we know that the loss is ½% on a portfolio of $100,000 fire policies written on 100 houses, there would be no risk. Each year we would be guaranteed claims of $50,000. Presumably, reserves of $50,000 would be sufficient charging ½% premium rate plus something to cover administrative costs including our salaries, bonuses, and the annual shareholder meetings in Bermuda.

Assuming that a fire results in a claim of $100,000 (no partial coverage), then we have a problem. It is impossible to have an average claim of $50,000. Claims are either none or $100,000 if losses are limited to 0% or 1% per year. The average loss of ½%, or $50,000, is achieved by claims being zero half the time and $100,000 the other half. In our minds, we automatically think in terms of a claim every other year. Nothing could be further from the truth.

Suppose that you are rolling a die and rolling an odd number means that one house is destroyed by fire. What is the chance of having a claim the first year? It is 50%. We collected $50,000 in premium income and have to pay out $100,000 in claims. But rolling an odd number with the first roll of the die doesn't mean that the second will necessarily be even. There is still a 50% chance of rolling another odd number, which means another $100,000 claim. True, the chance of rolling two odd numbers in a row is not 50%, but 25% (50% * 50%), but it can happen. This means we received $100,000 for two years of premium income and paid out $200,000 in claims. Maybe we can't afford our annual meeting in Bermuda.

But even though the average is $50,000 in claims per year, we can still have $100,000 in three consecutive years with a probability of 12.5% (50% * 50% * 50%) or 1/8. The chance of this happening four years in a row is 1/16, five years 1/32, six years 1/64, seven years 1/128, eight years 1/256. This, by the way, is the same probability of having no claims for eight consecutive years. That means we have collected eight years of premiums or $400,000 with no claims. This is the time to be in the insurance business. But we are dealing not with the potential to make money but with the risk of losing money. While the average tells us that claims will be $50,000 per year, it is entirely possible, although remote, that we can have claims of $100,000 for eight consecutive years, or $800,000. It is true that if we can stay in business long enough, there ought to be a period of time when claims will be zero in order to maintain the average of $50,000, but will we be around to enjoy the bonanza?

Figure 1.1 is the risk profile for having consecutive annual losses of $100,000 in a period of eight years. This is not an all-encompassing risk profile such as three years of no claims interspersed with five years of claims.

Risk is defined here as an excessive loss that threatens the viability of an enterprise. Suppose that reserves total $150,000, that we are collecting premiums of $50,000 per year, and that a house burns down each of three consecutive years. At the end of three years, we have collected $150,000 in premiums, paid out $300,000, and, in so doing, exhausted our reserves. An unacceptable risk awaits us in the fourth year if a house burns down in that we cannot cover the claim. The probability of a house burning down four years running is one chance in 16, which becomes a measure of risk.

THE NORMAL CURVE AS A MODEL OF RANDOMNESS

The normal distribution is commonly used in business applications. Daily sales over a period of time can follow a normal distribution. If daily sales can be modeled with a normal distribution whose mean is 100 and whose standard deviation is 10,

Figure 1.1
Risk Profile for Consecutive Claims

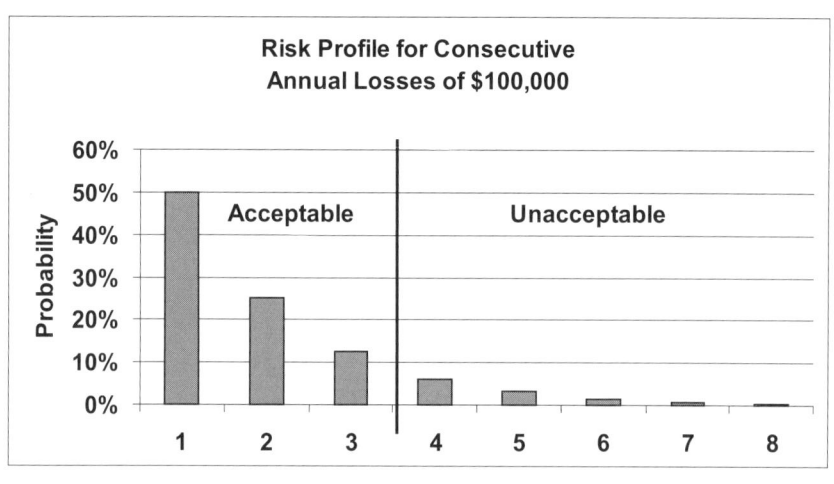

then average sales are 100 units per day and fall within the range of 90 to 110 units two-thirds of the time and between 80 and 120 units 95% of the time. This same observation holds for the price of a commodity that seems to follow a normal distribution.

But a normal distribution based on actual data can also be created from random numbers and therefore be used to model random events such as daily sales or the price of a commodity. Random numbers have values between 0 and 1 with equal probability. The chance of a random number being 0.1 is the same as for it being 0.9. This is known as a uniform distribution where the chances of being above the upper limit or below the lower limit, here 1 and 0, are zero and the chances of having any specified value within the range of 0 and 1 are the same for all values.

Suppose that the price of a commodity, based on its history, can be modeled with a normal distribution with a mean of 100 and a standard deviation of 10. Such a normal distribution can be created by adding up 12 random numbers, subtracting 6, multiplying the result by the standard deviation, and adding this to the mean. Of course, this has to be done many times in order to collect a sufficient number of values to create a normal distribution.

Normal Distribution = Mean + Std Dev*(Sum of 12 random numbers − 6)

Given that random numbers fall within the range of 0 and 1 with equal probability, random numbers should average around 0.5. The sum of 12 random numbers is around 6. Subtracting 6 leaves a small number, which when multiplied by the standard deviation and then added to the mean results in individual values being reasonably close to the mean. In other words, there is a relatively high probability of values being close to the mean. However, it is possible to draw 12 random numbers that are all near 0 or all near 1. While highly unlikely, it is possible for the value of a normal distribution to be the mean less 3–6 standard deviations or the mean plus 3–6 standard deviations. Most of the time, values will be fairly close to the mean. Appendix 1.A contains the detailed instructions for creating a normal distribution on an Excel spreadsheet. The normal distribution in Figure 1.2 consisted of over 65,500 rows in an Excel spreadsheet where each row generated a single value of a normal distribution.

Looking closely at Figure 1.2, one can see slight aberrations from a perfect curve. A normal distribution made up of only 10, or 20, or 30 generated values, or rows, has an appearance that may be far from normal. A normal curve derived from 10 rows would have a different appearance from one derived from 20 rows. The fact that the appearance of the normal curve changes when the iterations are increased from 10 to 20 means that the simulation results are not stable. The number of iterations in a simulation should be large enough to achieve stable results; that is, the results essentially do not change if a larger number of iterations are run. For instance, the normal curve in Figure 1.2 would be essentially the same whether there were 66,500 iterations or 66,000 or 100,000 or 1 million iterations. For this reason, the simulation result depicted in Figure 1.2 is deemed stable.

Figure 1.2
A Random Number-Generated Normal Curve

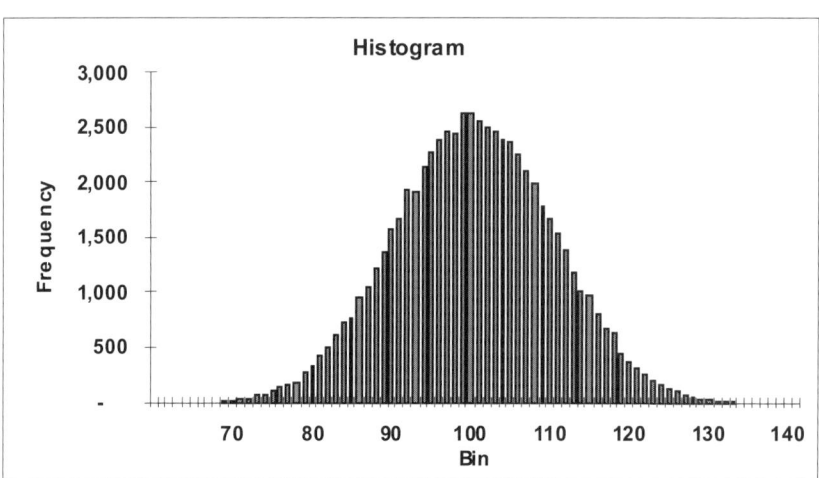

Once we have the normal curve for the price of a commodity whose mean is 100 and the standard deviation is 10, then we can evaluate risk in the form of a probability. Suppose a price below 80 is the threshold of financial pain. The probability in the tail in Figure 1.2 for prices less than 80 can be found by adding the contents of bins in Appendix 1.A below a value of 80. This is then compared to the contents of all bins to obtain a probability of the risk of a financially painful experience. If we know that Figure 1.2 is a normal curve, the chances of a value being less than 20 below the mean of 100, or more than two standard deviations (2 * 10) from the mean, is 2.28% (sometimes rounded to 2.5%).

THE LOGNORMAL CURVE AS A RANDOM MODEL OF PROBABILITIES

Another probability function that is used frequently in risk analysis is the lognormal distribution. Let's take a look at the sinking of the *Titanic*. The sinking is the result of a series of unlikely events. The probability of a sequence of events occurring is the multiplication of the respective probabilities of each event occurring independently. As already covered, the probability of fire occurring in one year is 50%; the probability of fire occurring in two consecutive years is 50% * 50% or 25%. The probability of the *Titanic* sinking is the probability of the vessel leaving the port when it did and following its track multiplied by the probability of the iceberg breaking off from a glacier when it did and following its intersecting track with the vessel multiplied by the probability of the lookouts not having binoculars to help see the iceberg multiplied by the probability of the ocean being as smooth as a millpond (an iceberg is harder to spot without waves splashing against it) multiplied by the probability of an absolutely pitch-black night (this makes spotting of white icebergs easy but not black icebergs that simply block out the stars in the background) multiplied by the probability of the iceberg being black (a rarity when an iceberg rolls over exposing its dark underside) multiplied by the probability of the design of the rudder being too small for the size of the vessel multiplied by the probability that the officer of the deck, ordering all back astern, further reduced the rudder's capacity to turn the vessel multiplied by the puncturing of the hull just beyond the point where the vessel was "unsinkable." The horrendous loss of life could have been averted if a merchant vessel only nine miles away knew what was happening. Hypothetically, this ship could have pulled alongside the *Titanic* and saved just about everybody. The ship was stopped for the night, a clear recognition of hubris of those in command of the *Titanic*. We can continue multiplying the probability obtained so far by the probability of this vessel's radioman not recognizing the SOS distress signal being transmitted by the *Titanic* (SOS had just been introduced as the international distress signal, and the *Titanic* was the first vessel to use it) multiplied by the probability of the crew mistaking the distress flares as fireworks for a party on deck multiplied by the probability of the crew not understanding why the lights on the ship were slanted rather than horizontal multiplied by the probability of the captain of this vessel, when informed of these matters, rolling over and going back to sleep.

The nuclear tragedy at Chernobyl was another case of a sequence of highly unlikely events lining up and happening against all odds. The happenings at Chernobyl read like another *Titanic*, only more steeped in technology and more difficult to appreciate except for such things as chaining and locking shut the emergency cooling values with no one on watch knowing who held the keys. It is in the tail of a probability distribution, that region of remote chances where all the action is in the world of risk.

The logarithm of probabilities multiplied together ($p1*p2*p3*p4$) is the sum of the logarithms ($\log p1 + \log p2 + \log p3$ and so forth). The log of the probability of an event happening can be modeled as the sum of the logs of random numbers. The curve created from the logarithms of probabilities becomes the lognormal curve. The lognormal curve is frequently used to describe the probability distribution of a casualty, the end point of a series of independent events each with a low probability of occurrence.

@RISK GENERATED PROBABILITY DISTRIBUTIONS

@Risk software provided by Palisade Corporation takes all the work out of what has just been accomplished.[1] Exactly what has been accomplished up to this point? Formulas were created to model a normal distribution. Random numbers were generated to determine values. The values were then assigned to bins to obtain their frequency distribution (the number of times values between 83 and 84 as an example were generated) in order to construct a histogram. @Risk automates this process. Figure 1.3 is the @Risk menu on a Microsoft Excel spreadsheet.

Figure 1.3
@Risk Menu

The *Define Distributions* function creates a number of different probability functions. Figure 1.4 sets up the normal probability distribution for a mean of 100 and a standard deviation of 10.

The formula for a normal distribution with a mean of 100 and a standard deviation of 10 is seen in the upper left. Selecting *Apply* would apply this formula to the indicated cell. *Tools/Options/Calculations/Manual* will generate a new value by pressing function key F9 repeatedly. If these were recorded separately, or if =RiskNormal (100,10) were replicated down as a substitute for adding 12 random numbers and subtracting 6 and so on, and if bin values were set up to record frequencies, and if an Excel histogram were selected to create a frequency distribution, then a normal curve would be generated. But as seen in Figure 1.2, it would

Figure 1.4
Defining a Normal Distribution

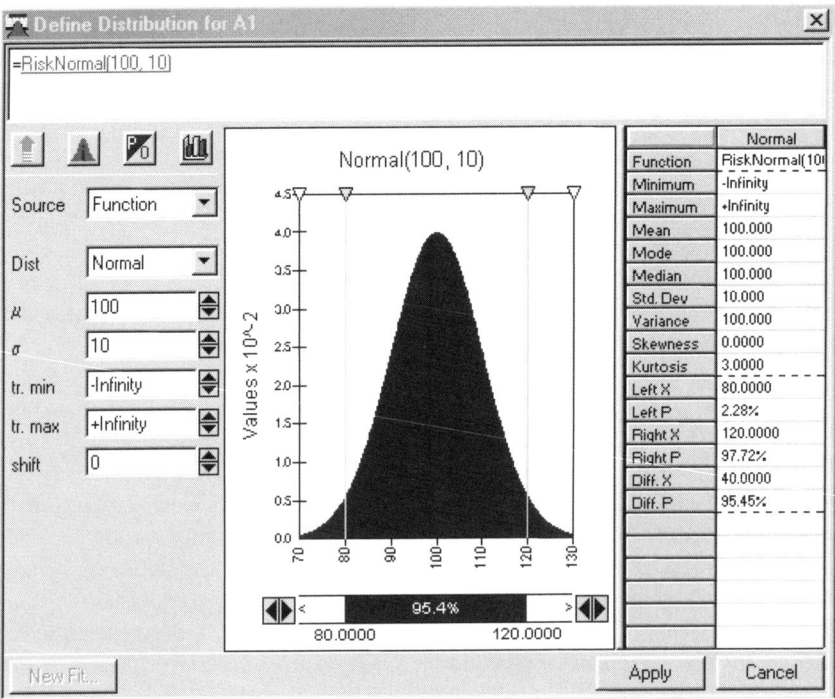

not be perfect, with little bumps here and there. In Figure 1.4, the normal curve is perfect, the hypothetical normal curve generated from an infinite number of random values and it is so much easier to attain. The integration of all these steps into one @Risk function is a major advantage of @Risk software.

The right-hand side of Figure 1.4 shows conventional statistical measures such as the mean, mode, and median. The mean, of course, is the average, the mode is the value that occurs most frequently, and the median marks the point where half of the values are greater and half are less. In a normal distribution, all three are the same. The standard deviation, which is the square root of the variance, is a measure of the scatter in the data. The variance is calculated by adding the squares of the differences between each individual value and the mean and dividing the result by the number of values. If all the values were 100, the variance would be zero. The greater the difference between the individual values and the mean, the greater will be the variance and its square root, the standard deviation. The greater the variance, the greater is the degree of scatter in the data.

A skewness of zero means that the curve is perfectly symmetrical about the mean, another characteristic of the normal curve. Kurtosis is a measure of the "peakiness" of the distribution. A distribution with wider tails would have a lower value for kurtosis. Finally, @Risk permits reading the cumulative probabilities to the left of "Left X" and "Right X." As shown in Figure 1.4, the cumulative or total probability of the price of a commodity whose mean is 100 and standard deviation is 10 being less than 80 is 2.28%. The price of the commodity being over 120 is 100% less the probability of being less than, or to the left of, 120 or 97.72%. The price of being higher than 120, or to the right of 120, is 2.28%. The probability of the price being higher than 80 and less than 120 is 95.45% (rounded).

USING @RISK TO EVALUATE RISK

Suppose that you are a fire insurance underwriting company and that you have a choice of underwriting 100 houses at $100,000 each or buying a 10% participation of a portfolio of 1,000 houses insured at $100,000 each. Further suppose that the expected loss rate based on past claims is between 0% and 10% with an average value of ½%. Which should be selected?

This is a stochastic problem. Stochastic simply means that we do not know what the exact loss will be; all we do know is that we have a probability distribution whose average is ½% with a minimum of 0% and a maximum of 10%. Obviously, the probability associated with a 10% loss must be extremely small for the average to be ½%. If we knew for sure that the loss would be ½% per year, then we would have a deterministic model that would remove the risk of having losses in excess of the expected loss. Figure 1.5 is the Microsoft Excel screen with @Risk activated in preparation for defining a probability function to be placed in cell B9.

Figure 1.6 shows the selected lognormal distribution with the indicated values that create a probability distribution with a minimum of 0, a maximum of 10, and an average of 0.5.

Figure 1.5
@RISK Screen

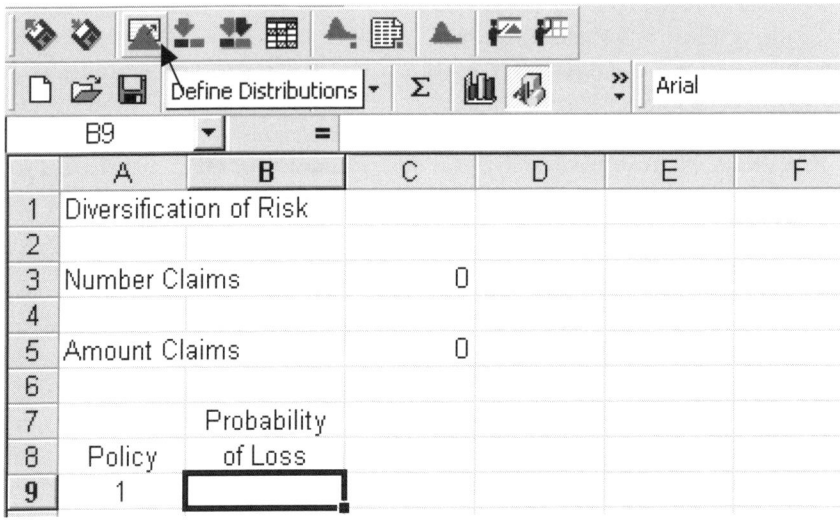

Figure 1.6
Define Distribution Function

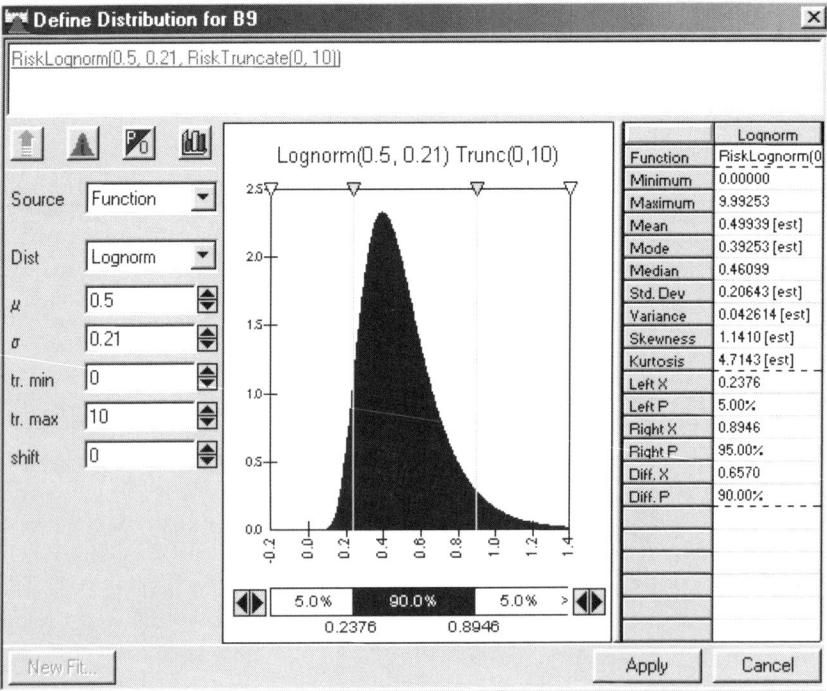

The distribution is truncated at 0 and 10 to ensure that the distribution does not draw values that will lead to a negative value or to the loss of more than 10 houses. The probability distribution has a positive value for skewness, meaning that the probability distribution is not symmetric about the mean but skewed to the right. A negative value means that the distribution is skewed to the left. The kurtosis is greater in value than the normal curve in Figure 1.4, indicating that the lognormal distribution has a higher peak and therefore narrower tails.

Appendix 1.B provides the details for obtaining the probability distribution or histogram of expected losses in Figure 1.7. The probability of losses being equal or greater than $150,000 is just under 9.1%.

The mean loss per year is $50,580, close to the expected loss of 0.5% or $50,000. But this never occurs. Losses are discrete values of $0, $100,000, $200,000, $300,000, $400,000, or $500,000. The possibility of higher losses is extremely remote. The probability of occurrence for each of these discrete possibilities is in Table 1.1.

There is a 60.2% chance of not having a claim in any given year, and there is a 30.7% chance of a single claim for $100,000. Suppose that $150,000 in losses is the threshold of pain for the underwriters. By underwriting 100 policies for $100,000 each, there is a 9.1% chance of feeling pain in any given year.

VIRTUE OF DIVERSIFICATION

Rather than underwriting 100 policies for $100,000, suppose that the insurance company underwrites 1,000 policies for $100,000 and then reinsures $90,000 of

Figure 1.7
Histogram of Expected Losses

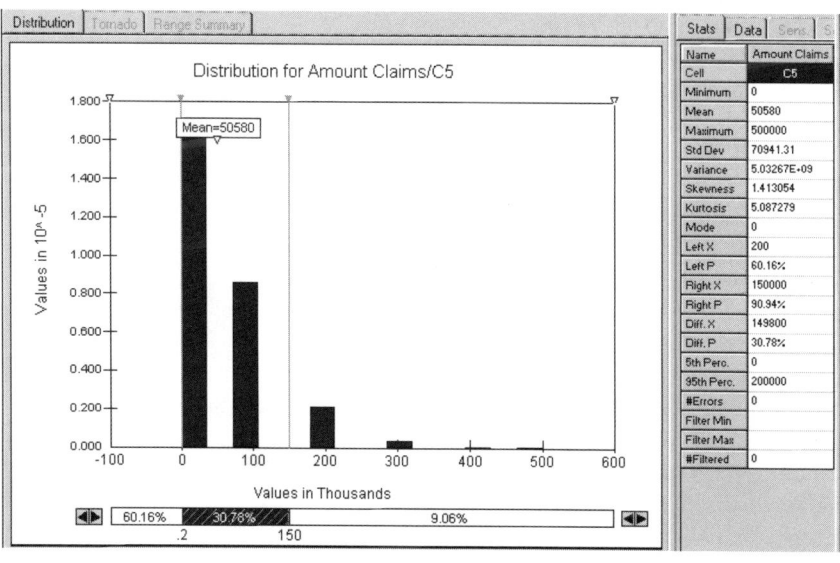

Table 1.1
Probability of Annual Loss

Annual Loss	Probability of Occurrence
$0	60.2%
$100,00	30.7
$200,00	7.6
$300,00	1.3
$400,00	0.1
$500,00	0.1

each policy. In effect, the company has underwritten 1,000 policies for $10,000. The modifications to accommodate a larger number of policies are described in Appendix 1.B, and the results of the simulation are in Figure 1.8.

This distribution has the property of being closer to being continuous, not discrete with only six outcomes as before. Although the number of outcomes is so large that the probability function takes on the aspect of being continuous, technically, it is still discrete. Figure 1.2 is discrete, made up of 80 separate bins summarizing the numeric results of 65,500 different iterations, but it can just as well and more easily be modeled as a continuous normal probability distribution as in Figure 1.4. In the next chapter the profile of risk in Figure 1.7 is modeled with a discrete probability distribution while the risk profile in Figure 1.8 is modeled with a continuous probability distribution.

The simulation run resulted in a mean loss of $49,277 versus a mean loss of $50,860 with fewer policies of higher insured amounts. Every simulation run will have slightly different results. While the average loss of both is close to what was expected ($50,000), this does not mean that the results were the same. Whereas having fewer policies of higher exposures carried a 9.1% risk of exceeding the threshold of pain of $150,000, more policies with less exposure results in a maximum loss of $130,000, not $500,000. Another simulation run ended up with a maximum loss of $140,000. Nevertheless, the maximum loss has been sharply reduced from a 9.1% chance of the loss exceeding the threshold of pain of $150,000 with a remote chance of being as high as $500,000 to essentially no chance of being above the threshold of pain.

Of course, for a more diversified portfolio of insurance policies, the chance of having no losses declines from the previous value of 60.2% to a minuscule 0.66%. The underwriters will be paying claims nearly every year with the same average amount of claims, but with an enormous reduction in the loss profile. This was achieved through diversification, that is, taking a smaller position in a larger number of policies.

Figure 1.8
Results of Diversification

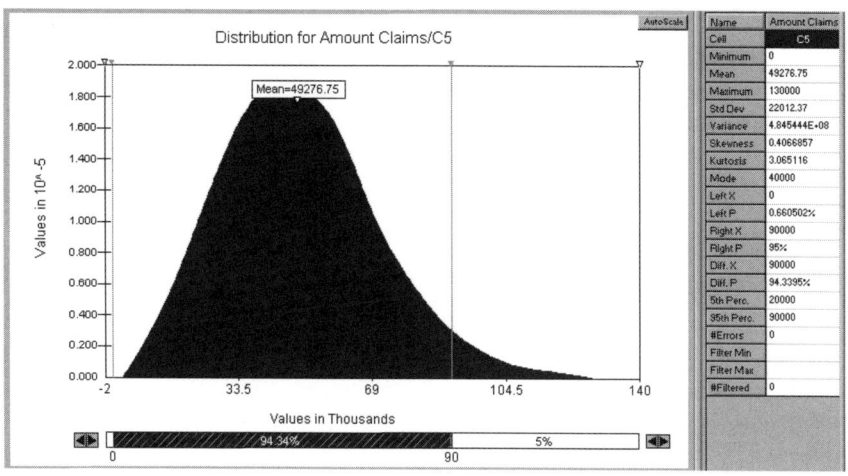

RISK: IT IS ALL IN THE TAIL

Insurance does not obviate the risk of loss, but insurance does affect who bears the risk. Passing the risk of loss to an insurer through the payment of premiums is a common practice in modern-day life. Now, an insurance company bears the risk of a house burning down. Whether an insurance company diversifies by taking a small part of many policies or doesn't, the average loss is still 0.5%. But if an insurance company takes a large part of a few policies, its profile of risk takes on a vastly different perspective. Risk is truly in the tail. Many holdings in a diversified portfolio of risk instruments assures the insurer that he or she will bear something close to the average loss rate and will have a smaller chance of experiencing the pain of severe losses. Fewer holdings in a nondiversified portfolio provide no advantage with regard to the average loss rate but open up the door to the possibility of severe losses.

NOTE

1. Company Web site is www.palisade.com.

APPENDIX 1.A
CREATING A NORMAL DISTRIBUTION ON A SPREADSHEET

On the Microsoft Excel spreadsheet, a random number generator can be created by =rand(). Enter this formula in cell A4 and select *Tools/Options/Calculation/Manual* to generate a new random number by pressing function key F9. Replicate cell A4 to the right 11 cells and total the 12 cells in cell N4. Notice that the values in column N in Figure 1.A.1 are near 6.

Figure 1.A.1
Creating a Normal Distribution

	J	K	L	M	N	O	P
1					Sum of 12		
2					Random		Normal
3					Numbers		Distribution
4	0.467279	0.359549	0.34325		6.236057		102.36057
5	0.632114	0.199835	0.790391		6.976156		90.238443
6	0.740352	0.205373	0.183217		5.900622		100.99378

Cell P4 in Figure 1.A.1 contains the formula:

$$=100+IF(RAND()<0.5,1,-1)*10*(N4-6)$$

This is "Excelese," the language of Excel. Believe it or not, Excelese can be easily translated into conversational English. The first part of Excelese is the mean of 100. This can be translated as "take the mean of 100 and add something to it." Add what? "First create –1 or +1 50% of the time. Then multiply this by 10, the standard deviation, and then again by the contents of cell N4, the sum of 12 random numbers less 6."

As formulated, a random number of exactly 0.5000 will generate +1. As the formula is constructed, this creates a slight bias for +1's to occur more frequently than –1's. Technically, a random number of exactly 0.5000 should cause another random number to be drawn to determine if the value should be +1 or –1. Suppose that cell A2 contains a random number generator. Then the formula in cell B2 would be:

$$=IF(A2<0.5,-1,IF(A2>0.5,1,IF(RAND()<0.5,-1,1)))$$

In Excelese the translation goes as follows. "Look at the value in cell A2, the random number generator. If the value is less than 0.5, the value in cell B2 will be –1. Oh, it's not? Then see if the random number in cell A2 is more than 0.5. Oh, it is? Then assign a value of +1 in cell B2. Oh, neither of these conditions has been fulfilled? Then the value in cell A2 must be exactly 0.5000. Now draw another random number. If it is less than 0.5 then assign a −1, and if greater than or equal to 0.5, then a +1, and enter the result in cell A2."

Even here, on the highly unlikely case where 0.5000 is drawn twice in a row, this procedure should be repeated to ensure an equal distribution of plus and minus 1's. But this is getting too detailed.

Cells A4 through P4 can be replicated to the bottom of the spreadsheet with over 65,500 rows. Each pressing of the F9 key creates over 65,500 values. These can be evaluated through the use of an Excel-generated histogram to generate a normal distribution. To do this, it is first necessary to create bin values that cover the entire spectrum of possible values. A frequency distribution is created by counting how many times values appear between the bin limits. For instance, suppose a bin is bounded by values between 83 and 84. Excel will go through all 65,500 plus values and count only those between 83 and 84.

The bin values are in column R of Figure 1.A.2 from 61 down to 140. Then invoke *Tools/Data Analysis/Histogram*. Figure 1.A.3 shows the menu entries. As seen in Figure 1.A.2, out of about 65,500 generated values, only 2 fell in the 63 to 64 bin. Selecting OK generates Figure 1.2.

Figure 1.A.2
Setting Up a Bin

	R	S	T
2		Bin	Frequency
3			
4	61	61	0
5	62	62	0
6	63	63	2
7	64	64	2
8	65	65	4
9	66	66	6
10	67	67	8
11	68	68	6
12	69	69	15
13	70	70	20
14	71	71	27
15	72	72	43
16	73	73	64
17	74	74	79

Figure 1.A.3
Histogram Menu

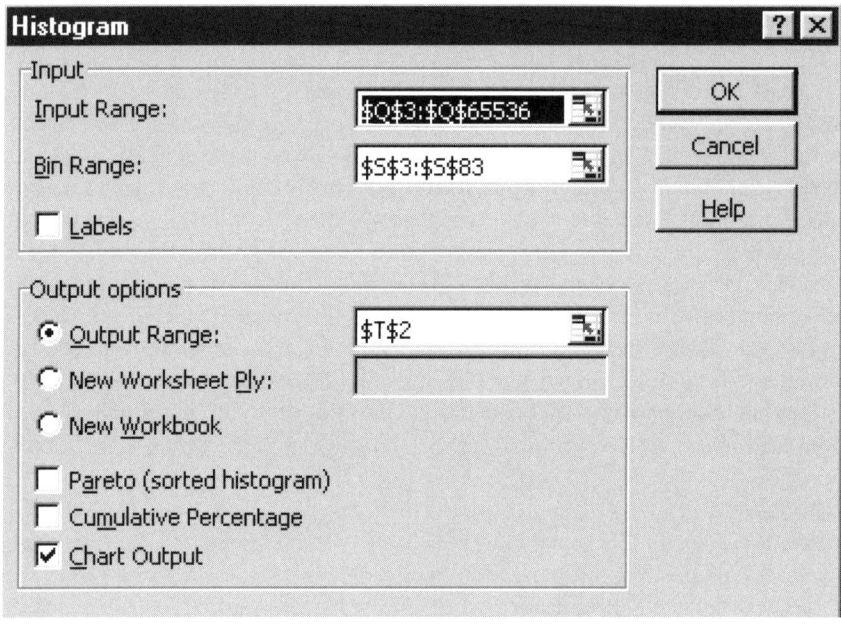

APPENDIX 1.B
CREATING A RISK PROFILE

This attachment describes the procedure to create Figure 1.7 and the changes necessary to create Figure 1.8. The distribution in Figure 1.6 is "applied" to cell B9 in Figure 1.B.1 and divided by 100 to obtain a percentage probability of loss:

$$=\text{RiskLognorm}(0.5, 0.21, \text{RiskTruncate}(0, 10))/100$$

Cell C9 draws a random number between 0 and 1. If the random number is less than the probability in cell B9, a "1" is generated denoting that the house has burned to the ground, otherwise a "0."

$$=\text{IF}(\text{RAND}()<\text{B9},1,0)$$

Cells B9 and C9 are replicated down 100 rows to simulate a portfolio of 100 insurance policies. These are totaled in cell C3 =SUM(C8:C108) to obtain the number of claims, and the contents of cell C3 is multiplied by \$100,000 in cell C5 to obtain the loss. Figure 1.B.1 defines cell C7 as an output cell.

Clicking on *Add Output* automatically changes the formula in cell C5 (see the formula bar in Figure 1.B.1) to designate it as an output cell. Figure 1.B.2 shows the icon for getting ready for a simulation run.

Figure 1.B.1
Output Cell

Figure 1.B.2
Simulation Settings

Figure 1.B.3 is the Iterations tab on the *Simulation Settings* menu with 5,000 iterations selected. *Update Display* shows all the iterated values in a simulation. It is not selected to speed up the simulation.

Figure 1.B.4 is the *Sampling* tab of the *Simulation Settings* menu. The *Monte Carlo* mode is selected under *Standard Recalculation* to permit the user to perform manual iterations on the spreadsheet by pressing function key F9.

In the *Monte Carlo* mode, each probability value is different as seen in column B of Figure 1.B.5. In the default condition *Expected Value*, probability functions are displayed with their expected values as seen in Figure 1.B.6. When setting up a spreadsheet program, *Expected Value* mode tends to hide programming bugs, whereas *Monte Carlo* mode makes it easier to detect them.

Figure 1.B.3
Simulation Settings Menu

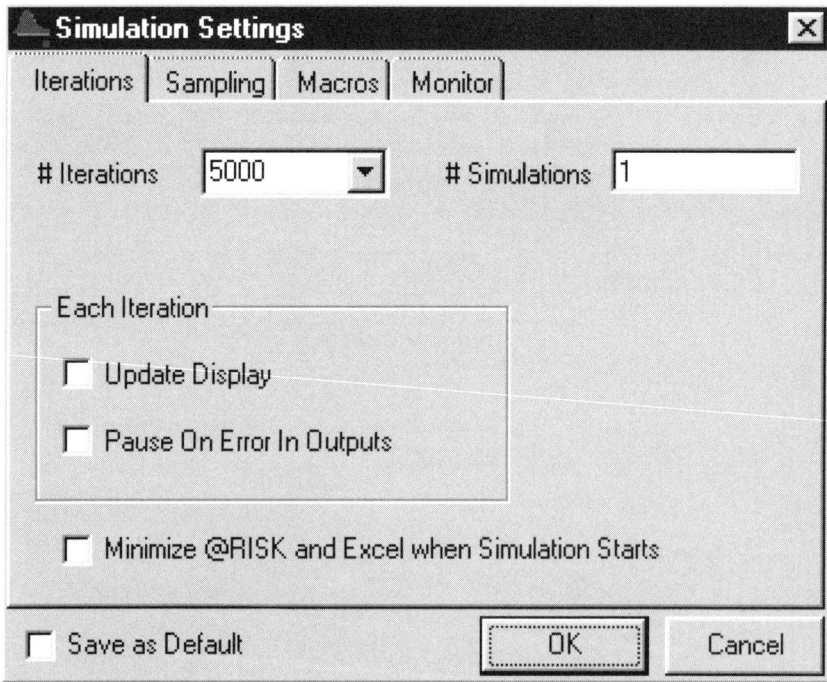

Figure 1.B.4
Simulation Settings Menu

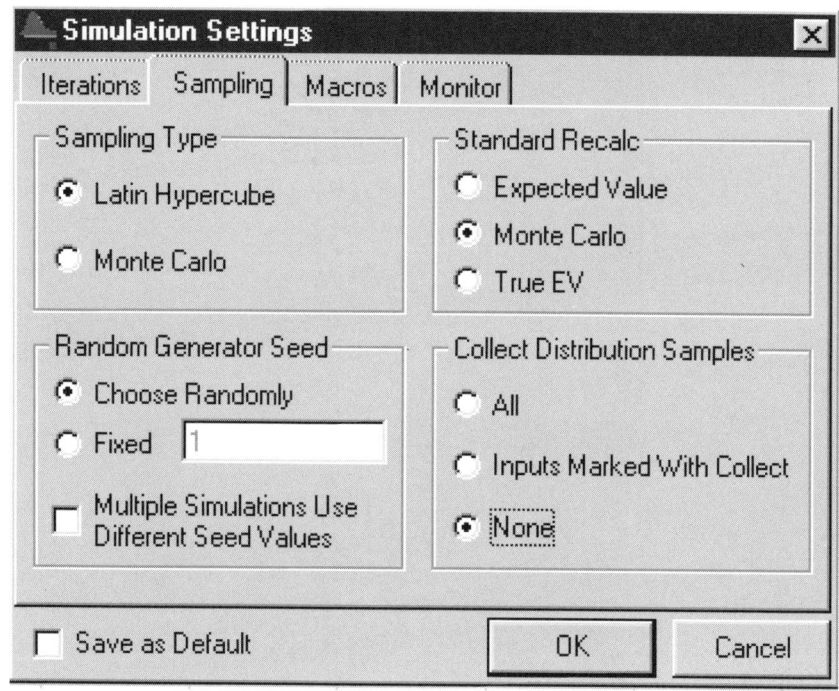

Figure 1.B.5
Monte Carlo Recalculation Mode

	A	B	C
1	Diversification of Risk		
2			
3	Number Claims		1
4			
5	Amount Claims		100000
6			
7		Probability	
8	Policy	of Loss	
9	1	0.461%	0
10	2	0.396%	0
11	3	0.270%	0
12	4	0.525%	0
13	5	0.276%	0
14	6	0.568%	1
15	7	0.467%	0

Figure 1.B.6
Simulation in Progress

	A	B	C
1	Diversification of Risk		
2			
3	Number Claims		6
4			
5	Amount Claims		60000
6			
7		Probability	
8	Policy	of Loss	
9	1	0.499%	0
10	2	0.499%	0
11	3	0.499%	0
12	4	0.499%	0
13	5	0.499%	0
14	6	0.499%	0

Simulating...
Sims: 1
Iters: 5000
Sim #: 1
Iter #: 1106
22%
Cancel

Monte Carlo under *Sampling Type* is not generally used. *Latin Hypercube* is a more efficient way of selecting random numbers that will more quickly generate a stable simulation result. The default condition is @Risk collecting data on all distribution functions unless otherwise directed. The user can select which inputs are to be collected or none (see Figure 1.B.4) whereby only output cell data are collected. This is a handy feature when there are a large number of @Risk input probability distributions for which sample data are not needed. In this application there is no reason to collect sample data on the 100 lognormal distributions for determining the probability of a fire. The only sample data of interest are the designated output cell C5.

Two icons to the right of the *Simulation Settings* is *Start Simulation*. Figure 1.B.6 shows the simulation in progress. Each simulation has unique results; that is, they are not exactly replicable. Simulations should be run sufficiently long to ensure stable results. Stability is achieved when there is little change in the results of a simulation with a greater number of iterations. The *Monitor* tab on the *Simulation Settings* menu permits one to monitor convergence. On more complex models run on slower-speed computers, computer run time has to be sufficient to ensure stability of results. This may not be onerous, as one can do other work while a simulation is running, eat lunch, or go home for the night.

The simulation results worksheet is generated automatically at the end of the simulation. Figure 1.B.7 results after right-clicking the output cell C5 at the left.

Selecting Histogram/Histogram yields Figure 1.7. Modeling diversification entails increasing the number of policies in the spreadsheet to 1,000, adjusting cell C3 to sum all the policies, and reducing the loss of each claim to $10,000 in cell C5. That's all there is to do to obtain Figure 1.8.

Figure 1.B.7
Simulation Results Output

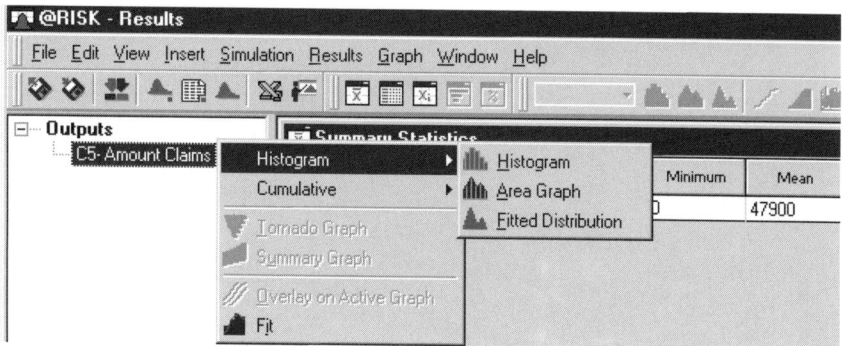

2
WHAT RATE TO COMPENSATE FOR RISK?

SYNOPSIS

This chapter expands on the previous chapter to devise a methodology to obtain an insurance rate and the necessary reserves to handle the risk of loss in providing insurance protection against losses. Obtaining the necessary reserves and insurance rate applies to two cases. One is insuring a relatively few houses for their total amount, and the other is insuring a small portion of a larger number of houses. The former utilizes a discrete probability function to describe the risk profile, and the latter a continuous probability function.

It is impossible for both cases to have a single insurance rate that applies for all times. Either the reserves are exhausted or they grow to excessively high levels. Three insurance rates are actually required for the system to function smoothly. The normal rate applies when reserves are kept within a certain range. A second and higher rate applies when reserves are drawn down by a larger than expected claims. To prevent reserves from becoming excessive, a third and lower rate applies to cover times of smaller than expected claims.

These same principles are then applied to generate an insurance premium in the form of an interest rate increment to insure against the higher losses expected from a lower-grade portfolio of bonds or loans using a higher-grade portfolio of bonds or loans as reserves against losses.

DEVISING AN INSURANCE PREMIUM

Suppose that you wanted to start a company to issue fire insurance policies on 100 houses for $100,000 each. The historical record of fires is the same as in the previous chapter—it can best be modeled with a lognormal distribution with an average of ½%, a minimum of 0%, and a maximum of 10%. Leaving administrative costs aside or treating them as an add-on to the quoted rate, the two key business decisions for going into the insurance underwriting business would be the appropriate rate to charge and the amount to be held in reserves.

The simple answer is that the quote should be ½% to cover the average loss. But there is a question of what would be the appropriate amount of reserves to cover those times when actual losses exceed expected losses. Table 2.1 is the risk profile derived in Chapter 1.

This can be modeled by the @Risk discrete probability function:

$$=100000*\text{RiskDiscrete}(\{0,1,2,3,4,5\},\{0.602,0.307,0.076,0.013,0.001,0.001\})$$

The distribution mirrors the values contained in Table 2.1. The chance of generating a 0 is 60.2%, the chance of generating a 1 is 30.7%, the chance of generating a 2 is 7.6%, and so on. This probability distribution for the annual number of houses expected to burn to the ground, when multiplied by $100,000, yields the monetary loss or claim.

Disregarding administrative costs or treating them as an add-on to the derived insurance rate, would you charge ½%? What if you had a succession of losses? Would not your appetite for underwriting sour unless you could sweeten the medicine by increasing the insurance rate? This would certainly help replenish reserves that have been drawn down by excessive losses. Reality more than suggests that insurance companies raise their rates to rebuild reserves after a string of losses. Thus, there are going to be at least two insurance rates—one for normal times and one for extraordinary times, the latter defined when reserves are close to being exhausted or not sufficient to cover another string of losses.

The objective at this point is to define a break-even insurance rate where there is no benefit in underwriting insurance, that is, an insurance rate where one would be no better off in underwriting insurance than in investing the reserves in, say, bonds. The whole point in underwriting insurance is to add an increment of return to reserves. If this cannot be done, then there is no point in taking on the additional risk of underwriting insurance.

Table 2.1
Risk Profile

Claims	Probability of Occurrence
$0	60.2%
$100,000	30.7
$200,000	7.6
$300,000	1.3
$400,000	0.1
$500,000	0.1

Therefore, one more insurance rate is necessary. With only the normal and extraordinary insurance rates, it is possible for reserves to become "excessive" during times when claims are low. While this is no sin for insurance underwriters, the objective here is to obtain the average break-even insurance rate with the optimal amount of reserves. For this reason, a third insurance rate is introduced that is less than the normal rate in order to liquidate excessive reserves. This, too, mirrors reality, for anyone in the underwriting business knows that during times when claims are low and profits high, insurance underwriters become more aggressive in adding policies to their portfolios even to the extent of cutting rates to attract new business. Once a break-even insurance rate is obtained, then an underwriter can compare it to the market rate for underwriting insurance. If the market rate is higher than the break-even or minimum acceptable rate, then there should be a benefit in underwriting insurance; if not, the underwriter would be better off putting his or her money somewhere else.

Figure 2.1 is a spreadsheet description of underwriting insurance. At first glance it may look daunting, but the spreadsheet simply reflects underlying commercial realities.

The normal insurance rate is 0.56% as long as reserves are within a stipulated range of the starting reserves of $500,000, which were arbitrarily selected. Reserves

Figure 2.1
Obtaining the Break-Even Rate

	A	B	C	D	E	F	G
1	Determining an Insurance Rate						
2							
3	Base Rate	0.560%	56				
4	High Rate	0.740%	18				
5	Low Rate	0.380%					
6							
7	Start reserves	$ 500,000					
8	Upper Trigger	$ 530,000	30				
9	Lower Trigger	$ 470,000					
10	Earnings Rate	6%					
11							
12	Total Policies	$ 10,000,000					
13							
14	Avg Ins Rate	0.584%					
15							
16	Objective:	$ 80,837					
17							
18				Annual		Reserves		Ending
19			Annual	Premium	Reserves	Income	Claims	Reserves
20	Year		Rate	($000)	($000)	($000)	($000)	($000)
21	1		0.56%	$ 56,000	$ 500,000	$ -	$ -	$ 556,000
22	2		0.38%	$ 38,000	$ 556,000	$ 3,360	$ 100,000	$ 497,360
23	3		0.56%	$ 56,000	$ 497,360	$ (211)	$ 100,000	$ 453,149
24	4		0.74%	$ 74,000	$ 453,149	$ (3,748)	$ -	$ 523,401
25	5		0.56%	$ 56,000	$ 523,401	$ 1,404	$ 200,000	$ 380,805
26	6		0.74%	$ 74,000	$ 380,805	$ (9,536)	$ 200,000	$ 245,269
27	7		0.74%	$ 74,000	$ 245,269	$ (20,378)	$ 100,000	$ 198,891
28	8		0.74%	$ 74,000	$ 198,891	$ (24,089)	$ -	$ 248,802

are examined later to determine the appropriate amount. The lower trigger point is $30,000 less than the starting reserves of $500,000, or $470,000. When reserves fall below $470,000, the insurance rate escalates by the increment of 0.18% on top of the normal rate of 0.56% or 0.74%. If, on the other hand, reserves rise above the starting reserves of $500,000 plus the increment of $30,000, or $530,000, then the insurance rate of 0.56% is reduced by the increment of 0.18% to 0.38%.

Reserves can be looked upon as a borrowed portfolio of bonds whose interest earnings are kept by the lender. The break-even insurance rate is calculated on the basis of preserving the principal of the bond portfolio at the end of 30 years. The reason for not including the interest earnings in the bond portfolio is that if the bond portfolio is permitted to grow at its inherent interest rate of, say, 6%, then the reserves are forever increasing. Since the step-ups and step-downs in insurance rates are based on increments measured from the starting reserves, the rules governing changes in the step-ups and step-downs would become somewhat moot as reserves continue to grow from the compounding of interest. This complicates the rules for changing the insurance rate. Treating starting reserves as principal only in a bond portfolio whose interest earnings are removed ensures the consistent application of the rules. Moreover, it is easier to see the benefit of underwriting when viewing principal only. The break-even insurance rate is determined on the basis of preserving the initial reserves, or principal amount of the bonds, after 30 years of underwriting.

Column B in Figure 2.1 is the insurance rate determined by the state of the reserves in column D. There are only three values permitted: the base rate of 0.56%, the base rate plus the increment of 0.18% or 0.74%, and the base rate less the increment of 0.18% or 0.38%. Column C is the premium income of multiplying the insurance rate against 100 policies of $100,000 each, or $10 million shown in cell B12. Any accumulation of premium income above the starting reserves of $500,000 earns a 6% return in column D. The interest rate could be varied reflecting changing interest rate environments, but in this example the interest rate remains fixed. Any drawdown on reserves will be charged a 2% punitive rate, or 8% interest, as bonds have to be liquidated to cover claims and the holder of the bonds would still want the interest income on the bonds. The 2% punitive charge is to compensate for the costs of selling and eventually replacing the bonds.

The starting reserves at the beginning of year 1 are $500,000 in cell B7. This is the principal amount of a portfolio of bonds "lent" to underwrite insurance. If underwriting is successful, then the ending reserves will be greater than $500,000; and if not, the ending reserves will be less than $500,000. Referring to Figure 2.1, business starts off on the right foot with no claims. The ending reserves of $556,000 for the first year are the starting reserves of $500,000 plus the $56,000 in insurance premiums with no interest income or expense on reserves. The ending reserves for year 1 become the starting reserves for year 2 in column D. Since year 2 starting reserves in cell D22 are higher than the upper trigger point of $530,000 ($500,000 plus the increment of $30,000), the insurance rate is lowered to 0.38%. Premium income is then $38,000. With reserves at $556,000, the interest earnings on the surplus over

$500,000, or $56,000 at 6%, are $3,360. However, there is a claim for $100,000 that reduces year 2 ending reserves to $497,360 ($556,000 plus premiums of $38,000 and reserve income of $3360 less $100,000).

The start of year 3 reserves of $497,360 is within the band where the base insurance rate of 0.56% applies, generating $56,000 in premiums. The deficit in reserves of $2,610 creates an interest charge of $211 at a rate of 8%. This charge keeps the interest income on the portfolio of bonds pledged to the insurance fund whole and compensates with any costs associated with liquidating and eventually replacing bonds held in the reserves. The end-of-year reserves of $453,149 consist of $56,000 in premium income added to the start-of-year reserves of $497,360 less the $211 in interest charges less the $100,000 in claims.

This logic pervades the entire spreadsheet formulation. Perhaps the most instructive part of Figure 2.1 is the claims shown in column F. Claims are supposed to average 0.50% or $50,000, or a claim every other year. This is clearly not happening with this iteration of a simulation. We are far above the average amount of claims one would expect. Performing manual iterations of a simulation by pressing the F9 function key can create very distressing scenarios for a budding underwriter. Obviously, there will be offsetting iterations of extended periods with very few claims. This, of course, is what underwriters have in mind when they issue insurance policies. But we are focusing not on the potential for making money but on the risk of losing money. Manual iterations on an Excel spreadsheet vividly reveal what is hidden in an average—the tail of a probability distribution. This is where risk resides, and a @Risk simulation makes this risk apparent. Sometimes it is scary to behold the true nature of risk, but it is better to appreciate its nature rather than to hide smugly behind an average only to be shocked at an outcome that was not, but perhaps should have been, anticipated. Appendix 2.A contains the detailed formulation of Figure 2.1.

RISKOPTIMIZER

Referring to Figure 2.1, what are the break-even insurance rate and its associated increment and the upper and lower reserve trigger points for increasing and decreasing the insurance rate? @Risk runs can be done over and over using trial and error for different values in three cells (cells B3, B4, and B8) to come up with the three specific values whereby the average ending reserves after 30 years of underwriting would be the same as the starting reserves. But we don't have a lifetime to spend on this. Palisade Corporation has another software package, called RiskOptimizer, that does just that—run many simulations to come up with an optimal choice for the desired adjustable cells to satisfy a stated objective.[1]

GETTING READY FOR A RISKOPTIMIZER RUN

A few items in Figure 2.1 have already been formulated in preparation for a RiskOptimizer run contained in Figure 2.2.

Figure 2.2
Getting Ready for a RiskOptimizer Run

	A	B	C
3	Base Rate	=C3/10000	56
4	High Rate	=B3+C4/10000	18
5	Low Rate	=B3-C4/10000	
6			
7	Start reserves	500000	
8	Upper Trigger	=B7+1000*C8	30
9	Lower Trigger	=B7-1000*C8	
10	Earnings Rate	0.06	
11			
12	Total Policies	10000000	
13			
14	Avg Ins Rate	=AVERAGE(B21:B50)	
15			
16	Objective:	=D50-B7	

The formulation limits the insurance rate and increments to four decimal places and the reserve increments to the nearest thousand dollars. The adjustable cells C3, C4, and C8 will be constrained to integer values for a RiskOptimizer run where the solution values are in column C, not column B. Integer values reduce solution time by restricting the number of combinations of possible values to be investigated. Moreover, it is desired that the trigger-point increment be in thousands of dollars such as $30,000, not $29,712.78.

Care has to be exercised to ensure that the lower insurance premium is not negative. This can happen when the permissible incremental rate is greater than the base rate. One way to do this is to ensure that the permissible range for the incremental rate is smaller than one would expect for the base rate. If the incremental rate is too large, it is possible for the lower insurance rate to be negative. Now a constraint would have to be incorporated ensuring that the lower rate is not negative. RiskOptimizer operates better with a minimal number of constraints, and avoiding constraints if possible should be a consideration in spreadsheet formulation.

The objective is for the mean of the ending reserves to be the same as the starting reserves. This provides a benchmark for determining the minimum acceptable rate for underwriting fire insurance policies. The objective in cell B16 is for the difference between the starting and ending reserves in cells D50 and B7 to be as close to zero as possible. Figure 2.3 is the RiskOptimizer menu.

The objective cell B16, the difference between the starting and ending reserves, is to be set as close to zero as possible. This is to be achieved by adjusting or varying cells C3, C4, and C8 with integer values within the indicated range. This selection of permissible values guarantees against a negative insurance rate because the min-

Figure 2.3
RiskOptimizer Menu

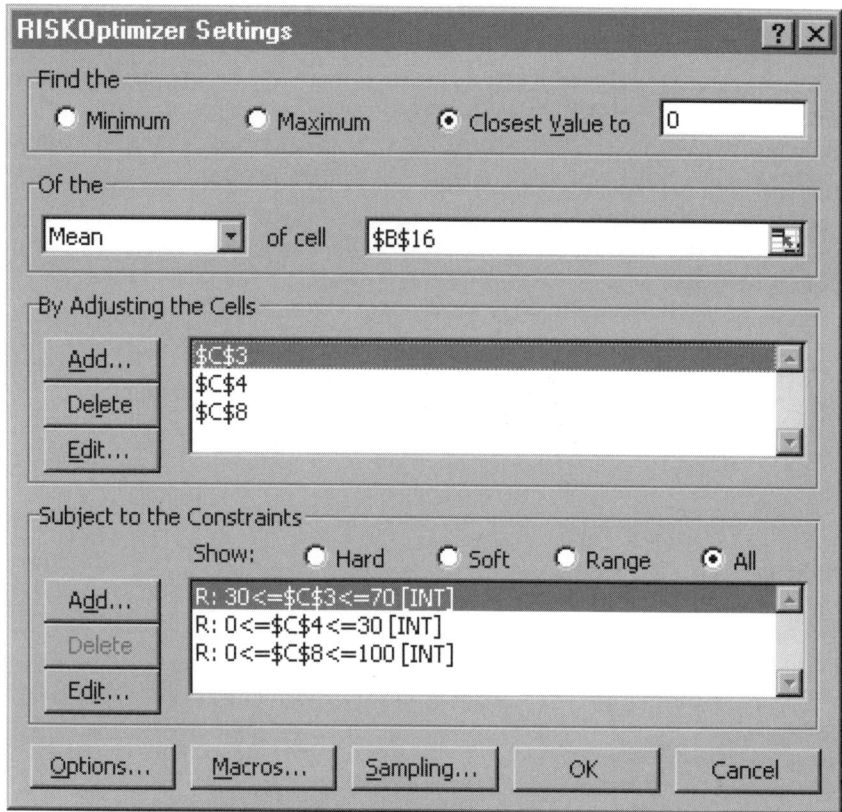

imum for the base rate is set at 30 and the maximum increment to be subtracted from the base rate is also 30.

Restricting the permissible range of adjustable cells has to be handled with care. Settings that are too restrictive may preclude RiskOptimizer from finding an optimal solution if the solution resides outside the range boundaries. If a solution is at or near the range boundaries of any adjustable cell, then the range limits on the pertinent adjustable cells should be expanded for another RiskOptimizer run. It is best not to be too restrictive on setting range limits on adjustable cells and to consider solution values close to range limits as suspect. In this case, a rerun should be made with adjusted range limits to obtain solution values that do not hug a range limit.

RiskOptimizer is basically a search engine using algorithms that seek an optimal solution. A solution environment can be likened to a range of mountains. In maximizing the objective cell, RiskOptimizer is looking for the peak of the highest mountain. The algorithms use the results from previous runs to identify the next set of values for the adjustable cells in order to continue climbing the mountain. The problem is that as RiskOptimizer makes its way up a mountain, there may be another mountain in the realm with a higher peak. From time to time RiskOptimizer tries out an entirely different set of values for the adjustable cells to see if it can spot a mountain higher than the one it is on. If this trial-and-error search is successful, RiskOptimizer shifts mountains and continues climbing up the new mountain, sending out spotters, so to speak, from time to time to search for an even higher peak.

The run started with the adjustable cells initially set to zero, as RiskOptimizer seems to work better with a starting point for the adjustable cells that is far from the solution values. Progress during a RiskOptimizer run can be monitored several ways. One is the Detailed Log shown in Figure 2.4.

Solution times can vary greatly from five minutes to an hour. RiskOptimizer has to run long enough to convince the user that sufficient time has passed from the previous best solution to consider it the final solution. It is always possible that another and better solution would have been attained if the run had continued just a few seconds more. Generally speaking, when time between one optimal solution and the next becomes rather long and the difference in the results between the two becomes quite small, then there is reason to stop the run.

Select *Monte Carlo* under *Standard Recalc* on the *Sampling* tab of the RiskOptimizer menu and press function key F9 to generate single iterations of a simulation. A great deal of variation can be seen in the objective cell B16. @Risk provides a good picture of the risks inherent in underwriting fire insurance on 100 houses. Invoke @Risk and designate cell B16, the difference between the starting and ending reserves after a 30-year period, and cell B14, the average insurance rate, as output cells along with ending reserves in cell D50. Under *Simulation Settings*, select 10,000 iterations and *None* for collecting distribution samples. This limits

Figure 2.4
Detailed Log of RiskOptimizer Watcher

	Time	Iters	Result	Output Mean	Output Std Dev	Output Min	O
64	00:03:32	300	847467.3383	847467.3383	923516.6254	193067.2721	8726
66	00:03:38	600	842056.6755	842056.6755	1051344.039	156466.9751	1.17
67	00:03:40	300	810151.714	810151.714	711175.4296	193067.2721	7133
125	00:11:29	1100	807224.5068	807224.5068	637461.9452	192930.3713	7947
153	00:16:06	800	799734.5295	799734.5295	555071.4269	191263.157	6136
154	00:16:14	1600	793107.8933	793107.8933	558567.5838	191263.157	7527
158	00:16:56	3700	771080.6465	771080.6465	884985.3355	141121.5568	2.30
159	00:17:04	1600	763067.1615	763067.1615	728372.2239	142140.0324	1.07

data collection to the two designated output cells. The histogram of the difference between starting and ending reserves in cell B16 is shown in Figure 2.5.

The optimal solution for the adjustable cells in Figure 2.1 generated a positive mean differential of $43,575, somewhat above zero. Compared to the amount of reserves that are required, this is not that far away from the objective of the starting and ending reserves being the same. Thirty years of underwriting results could end up being ahead as much as $2.4 million above the starting position of $500,000. This basically represents 30 years of extremely few claims. But for the average to be ½%, there must be an offsetting year where houses are burning down left, right, and center. This can be seen in the maximum loss of $5.6 million below the starting reserves of $500,000. Of course, the chance of this happening is extremely remote (1 in 10,000 iterations of a simulation). On a somewhat more realistic basis, the chances of a diminishment in initial reserves of $2 million from a starting point of $500,000 is 1.39% and 5.65% for $1 million. Extreme losses of this nature would force the insurance company to add another increment to the upper insurance rate or voluntarily defer from writing any more policies or face involuntary liquidation.

What spurs an underwriter? The answer is the remote possibility of houses hardly ever burning to the ground, with ending reserves becoming $2.4 million above the starting point of $500,000. This is a nice sweetener to a portfolio of bonds worth $500,000. That is one end of a probability tail. The other end is ending reserves being in deficit by $5 million after liquidating the initial reserves of $500,000. An insurance underwriter can focus on either the right-hand tail of potential opportunity for making money or the left-hand tail of the potential risk of losing money. It really doesn't matter what an underwriter focuses on because the ultimate outcome is based on the actual number of houses that burn down. That is one

Figure 2.5
Histogram of the Difference in Reserves

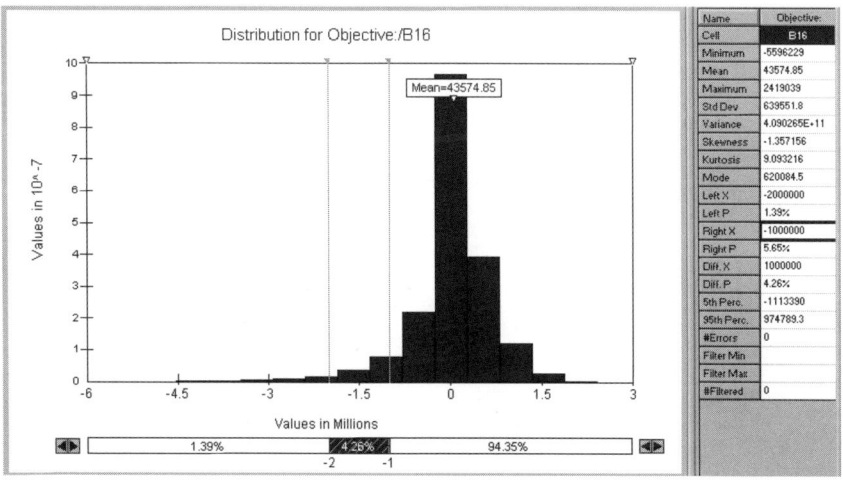

a priori value that an underwriter does not know when he or she hangs out his or her shingle. This is the risk of being in not only the underwriting business but any business. One simply does not know the future.

The ending reserves in Figure 2.6 provide another perspective on the amount of required reserves. Starting with initial reserves of $500,000, the average result is ending reserves of $543,575. The chance of reserves ending up worth less than a negative $1.5 million is 1.39% and 5.65% for a negative $0.5 million. These are the equivalent results in Figure 2.5. The difference is that it may be easier to assess the proper amount of reserves with Figure 2.6. Starting reserves of $1 million have a 1.39% chance of ending up with reserves being less than a negative $1 million and a 5.65% chance of exhausting reserves (ending reserves of zero or less). Starting reserves of $2 million have a 1.39% chance of being exhausted. The proper amount of reserves can be obtained by assessing the chances of exhausting initial reserves.

The average insurance rate, illustrated in Figure 2.7, of 0.525% is greater than the expected 0.500% loss rate. This can be partly ascribed to the 2% punitive charge ascribed to reserve balances below the starting point.

The maximum average insurance rate of 0.734% is very close to the maximum permissible of 0.74%, meaning that claims on two or more houses were occurring nearly every year. This is the only way to get a maximum negative differential of over $5 million between starting and ending reserves when premium income is sufficient to cover 1.5 houses burning to the ground per year. Talk about being in the wrong business at the wrong time! However, the spreadsheet could be reformulated to have another incremental rate increase when reserves depart too far from the initial reserves. While it may be difficult to believe that an outcome can be

Figure 2.6
Ending Reserves

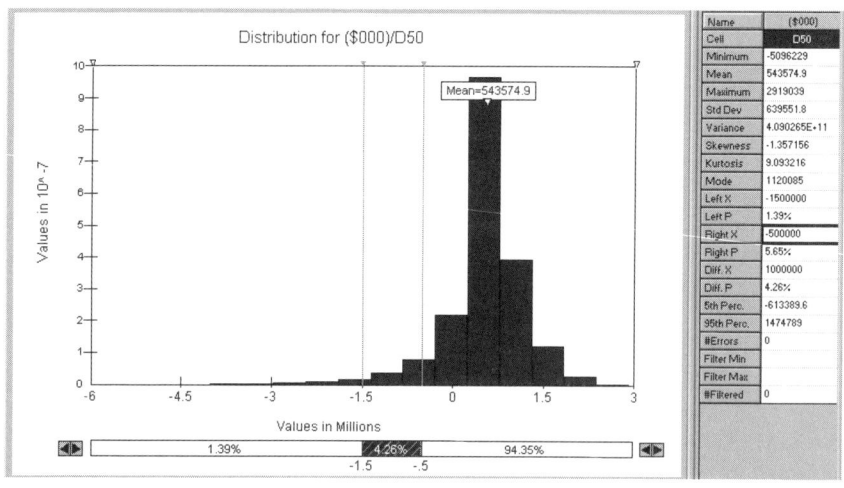

that bad given the probabilities of having 2 or more houses burning down consecutively year after year, the point is that it has happened. Risk is the roll of the dice, and sometimes weird sequences can arise, confounding the statisticians, enriching the gamblers, and making gambling houses a little less rich.

On the other hand, the minimum average insurance rate of 0.386% is also quite close to the lower insurance rate of 0.38%. This essentially translates into 30 years of virtually no claims, letting ending reserves climb to over $2.4 million. Talk about being in the right business at the right time! But how does one know a priori how many houses will burn down when one decides to be a fire insurance underwriter? This is the whole crux of the matter. All that is known a priori are the history of claims and the possible range of outcomes, but not the future outcome. Granted, the probability of extreme outcomes is highly remote, but the point is that extreme happenings can and do occur. We never know when we start a business or make an investment what the outcome will be no matter how diligently we do our homework.

DIVERSIFICATION

The previous chapter concluded that having a few policies of larger amounts was inherently more risky than having many policies for smaller amounts. The first item of business is rerunning the simulation from the previous chapter of 1,000 policies of $10,000 in order to obtain a continuous probability distribution function to model claims. Figure 2.8 is the output of a simulation of 10,000 iterations.

The mean is $49,800, quite close to the hypothetical ½% or $50,000. The maximum loss is $150,000, as noted previously. While it would be possible to model this

Figure 2.7
Insurance Rate

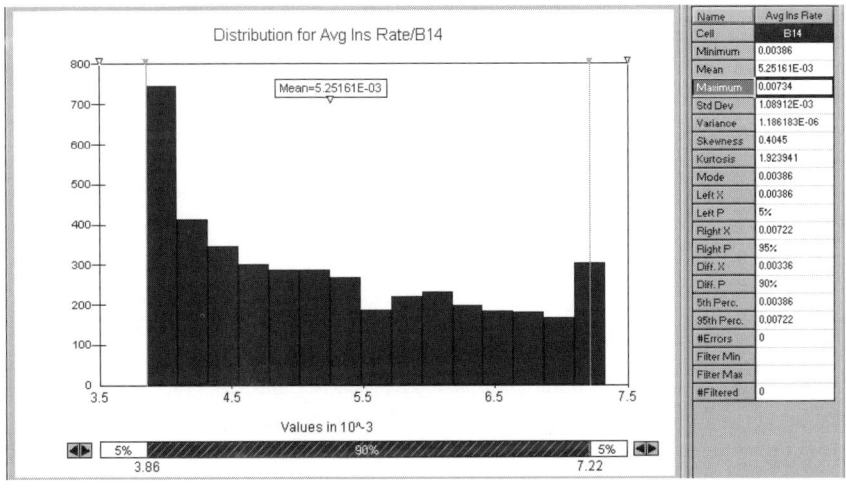

Figure 2.8
Histogram of Claims

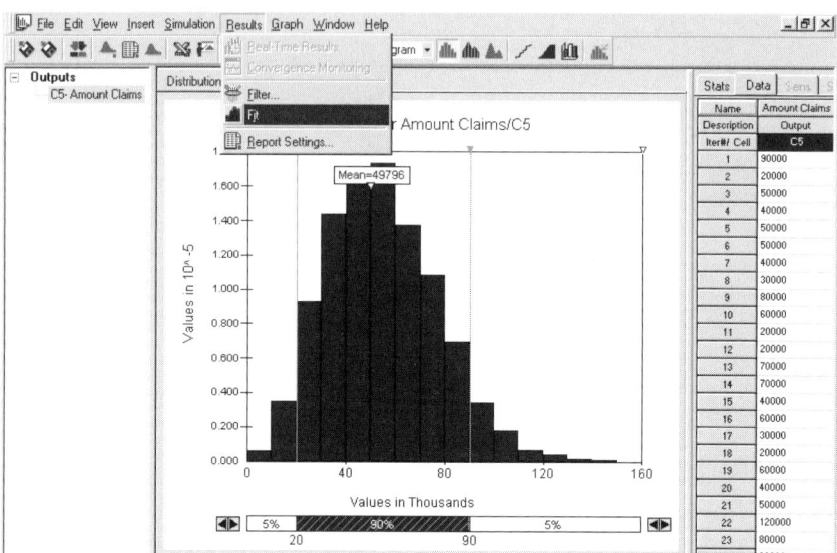

with a discrete probability distribution, the resulting formula would be inordinately long and cumbersome to use. It is far more convenient to use a continuous probability distribution. *Results/Fit* at the top of the screen generates the best-fitting probability distribution function, illustrated in Figure 2.9.

This simple operation is all that it takes to generate the best-fitting probability distribution for any set of data. This is an extremely handy feature of @Risk. While the data in this case are the simulation results, data could also be entered from another source, and the *Fit Distributions to Data* feature of @Risk can be used to identify the best-fitting probability distributions.

The best-fitting continuous probability distributions are listed next to the data from the simulation results on the left side of the screen with the lognormal distribution selected. The lognormal distribution is compared to the histogram both visually and in terms of statistics to the right of the screen that matches up the respective values of the probability distribution with the actual data. Some of the other listed probability distributions could have been substituted for the lognormal distribution with close to the same statistical justification.

The lognormal does have a small chance of having negative claims, but truncating the distribution at zero takes care of that. Also the lognormal distribution maximum is hypothetically infinity, but truncating the distribution at $200,000 takes care of this. The P-P (probability-probability) curve is a means of judging fit. The P-P curve compares the probability of occurrence of the derived distribution values to the corresponding probability of occurrence of the actual values to see if the two probabilities match up. A straight line (linear) P-P curve suggests a good

Figure 2.9
Best Fitting Probability Distribution

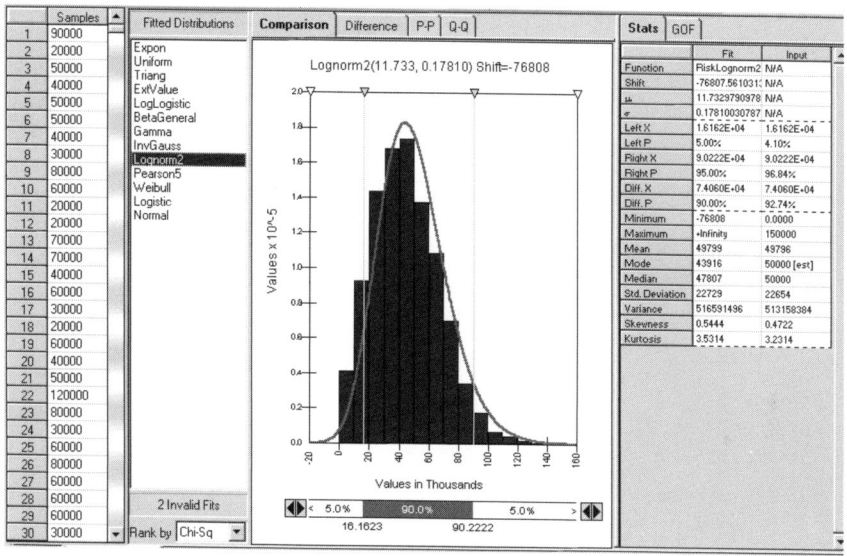

matching of the probabilities between the actual data and the derived curve. Figure 2.10 is the P-P curve for the lognormal distribution.

The bend at the lower left is caused by the lognormal probability curve generating negative values that do not actually occur in the simulation results. This is taken care of shortly by truncating the distribution. Nevertheless, there is a reasonably good matching of the corresponding probabilities between the hypothetical curve and the actual data, although a perfectly straight line would be preferable. The derived probability distribution for claims can be inserted in the same spreadsheet in Figure 2.1 using the *Define Distributions* function shown in Figure 2.11.

Selecting Apply automatically places the following formula in the claims column (cell F21), which eliminates the errors inherent in manually entering the probability distribution formula.

=RiskLognorm2(11.733, 0.1781, RiskShift(–76808), RiskTruncate(0, 200000))

This formula is replicated down the column, the adjustable cells reset to zero, and RiskOptimizer run with the solution shown in Figure 2.12.

The major difference between insuring 100 houses against fire with an individual claim of $100,000 and 1,000 homes with an individual claim of $10,000 is seen in the claims column. There are claims every year, but they're not catastrophic in nature. The normal insurance rate of 0.51% rises to 0.72% when reserves fall below $493,000 and falls to 0.30% when reserves rise above $507,000. The base insurance rate holds for a rather narrow range around the starting reserves. If this is deemed too narrow,

Figure 2.10
P-P Curve

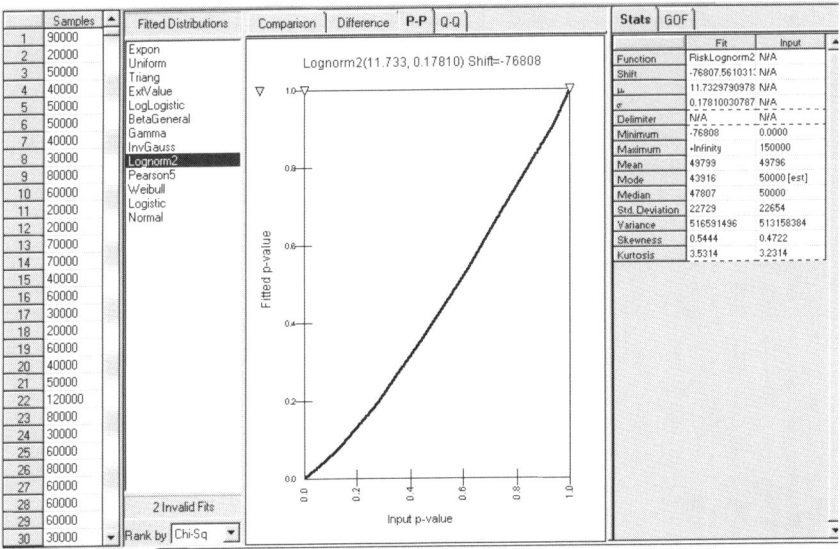

Figure 2.11
Define Distributions

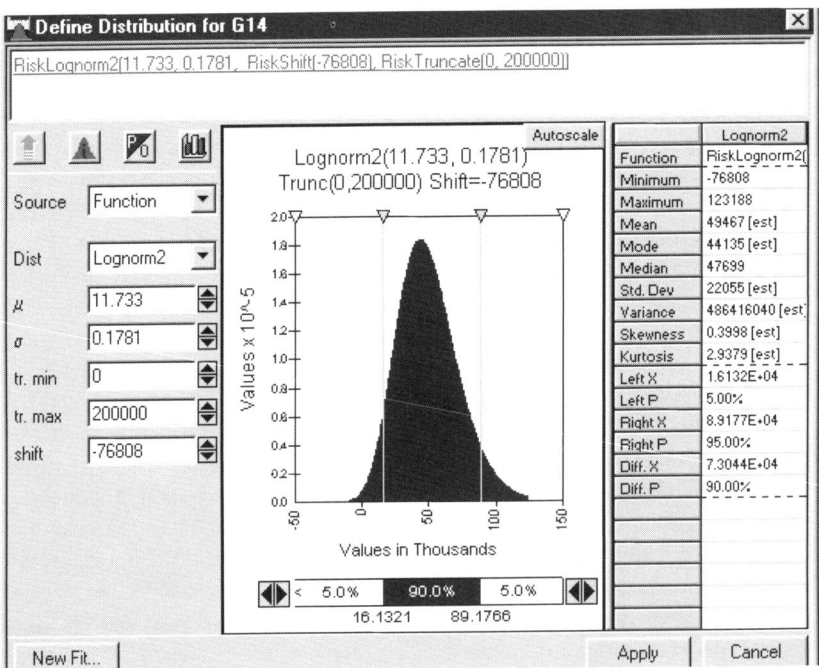

Figure 2.12
RiskOptimizer Solution

	A	B	C	D	E	F	G
1	Determining an Insurance Rate						
2							
3	Base Rate	0.510%	51				
4	High Rate	0.720%	21				
5	Low Rate	0.300%					
6							
7	Start reserves	$ 500,000					
8	Upper Trigger	$ 507,000	7				
9	Lower Trigger	$ 493,000					
10	Earnings Rate	6%					
11							
12	Total Policies	$ 10,000,000					
13							
14	Avg Ins Rate	0.489%					
15							
16	Objective:	$ (2,269)					
17							
18			Annual		Reserves		Ending
19		Annual	Premium	Reserves	Income	Claims	Reserves
20	Year	Rate	($000)	($000)	($000)	($000)	($000)
21	1	0.51%	$ 51,000	$ 500,000	$ -	$ 15,079	$ 535,921
22	2	0.30%	$ 30,000	$ 535,921	$ 2,155	$ 37,211	$ 530,866
23	3	0.30%	$ 30,000	$ 530,866	$ 1,852	$ 29,745	$ 532,972
24	4	0.30%	$ 30,000	$ 532,972	$ 1,978	$ 107,212	$ 457,739
25	5	0.72%	$ 72,000	$ 457,739	$ (3,381)	$ 36,366	$ 489,992
26	6	0.72%	$ 72,000	$ 489,992	$ (801)	$ 34,239	$ 526,953
27	7	0.30%	$ 30,000	$ 526,953	$ 1,617	$ 61,357	$ 497,213
28	8	0.51%	$ 51,000	$ 497,213	$ (223)	$ 49,122	$ 498,867
29	9	0.51%	$ 51,000	$ 498,867	$ (91)	$ 30,791	$ 518,986
30	10	0.30%	$ 30,000	$ 518,986	$ 1,139	$ 55,646	$ 494,478
31	11	0.51%	$ 51,000	$ 494,478	$ (442)	$ 106,058	$ 438,978

then it is advisable to rerun RiskOptimizer to obtain the corresponding rates for a fixed trigger point. The histogram of the ending reserves is in Figure 2.13.

Figure 2.13 shows that a substantial reduction in reserves can be instituted for the same average risk. The chance of reserves falling below $350,000, or $150,000 below starting reserves of $500,000, is 0.03%. If starting reserves were reduced to $150,000, then the chances of exhausting reserves is 0.03%. Similarly, the chance of reserves falling below $400,000 is 0.24%. Reducing reserves from the initial $500,000 to $100,000 has a potential risk of 0.24% in exhausting reserves. Initial reserves are not part of the solution of a RiskOptimizer run but can be determined by examining the probability distribution for ending reserves.

In Figure 2.14, the average interest rate is 0.496% with a nearly normal distribution versus a far from normal 0.525% for a less diversified portfolio in Figure 2.7.

COMPARATIVE ANALYSIS

Table 2.2 shows the comparison of the two alternatives to underwriting insurance on houses.

Figure 2.13
Histogram of Ending Reserves

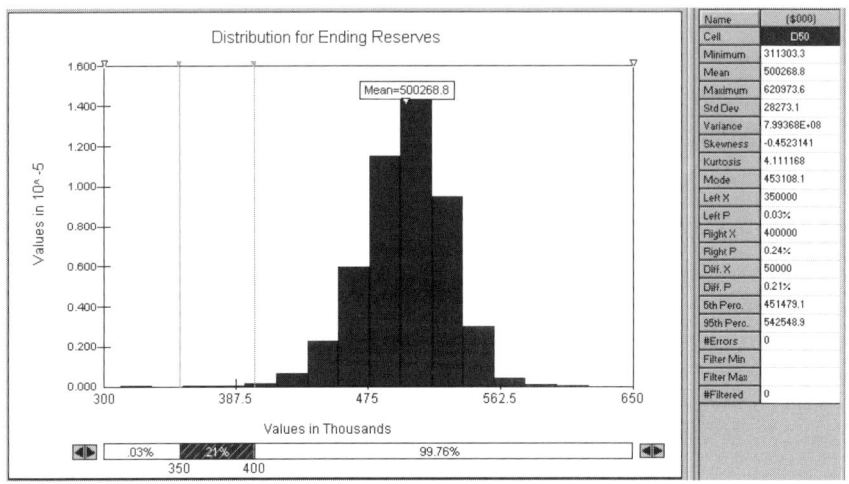

Figure 2.14
Insurance Rate

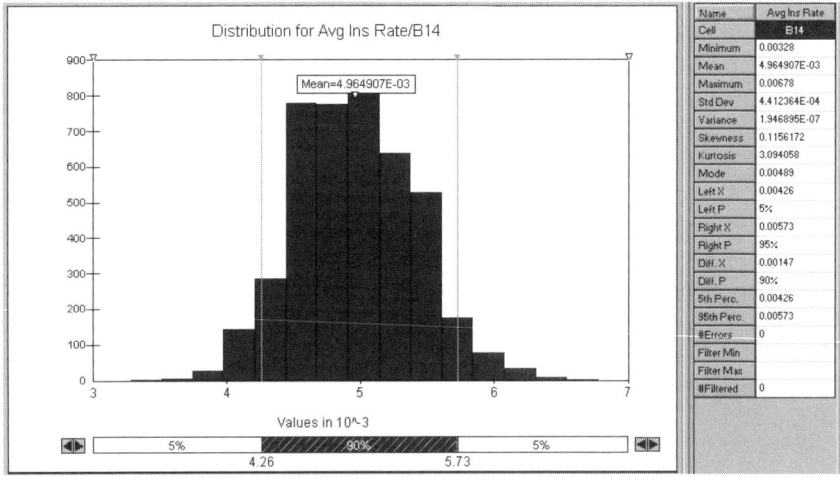

Table 2.2
Comparison of Results

Outcomes at End of 30 Years	100 Houses at $100,000 Each	1,000 Houses at $10,000 Each
Average Insurance Rate	5.25%	4.96%
Reserves	$2,000,000	$100,000
Maximum Ending Reserves	$4,400,000	$221,000
Minimum Ending Reserves	-$3,600,000	-$89,000
Range	$8,000,000	$310,000
Standard deviation	$640,000	$28,000

While incorporating different rules for changing the insurance rate with different levels of reserves affects the outcomes, the conclusion is nevertheless clear. There is much less risk of loss for the underwriter to insure a larger number of houses for a smaller amount for a great deal less in reserves.

An investment is deemed less risky if outcomes are more narrowly defined. For the most part, the outcome of a creditworthy portfolio of bonds is known within fairly prescribed limits. A portfolio of stocks, however, can have a wide spread in possible outcomes, some better, some worse than the bond portfolio. A stock portfolio is considered to have a greater degree of risk because there is a greater potential spread in outcomes. The spread in outcomes can be measured by the range (maximum less minimum outcomes) or by the standard deviation. The greater the spread in outcomes, the greater is the perceived risk. As seen in Table 2.2, the safer course of action is to insure more homes for a smaller insured value because the spread in outcomes expressed as the range or standard deviation of possible outcomes is much less.

HOW MUCH OF A PREMIUM TO COMPENSATE FOR RISK?

Risk is in the eye of the beholder. Concentrating on insuring 1,000 houses for $10,000 each, an underwriter with an average insurance rate of 0.496% will have the same average ending reserves as the starting reserves. On average, an underwriter might be indifferent whether he or she is involved in insurance. However, in underwriting insurance, there is a remote possibility that at the end of 30 years, an initial portfolio of bonds would not be worth $100,000, but $121,000 more or $221,000. This is good, but there is also the other side of the coin of an equally remote possibility that it would be worth $289,000 less or a deficit of $189,000. This is bad. Which of these two figures catches the underwriter's eyes? This has a great deal to do with an individual's perception of risk.

Risk is in the eye of the beholder. The underwriter could focus on the potential gain of $121,000 on top of the starting portfolio of $100,000. If this is the case, then the underwriter could be a risk seeker. Many individuals are risk seekers. Day traders in hot stocks spend their days with their eyes glued to the computer screen reading meaning into each twitch of a stock price. Dentists who call their brokers to see how much they made or lost trading crude oil futures between cavities are risk seekers. They like the thrill of being on the edge to compensate for carrying on a one-sided conversation with a patient whose mouth is immobilized with fluid-sucking probes and Novocain. Entrepreneurs who start new companies are by nature risk seekers, as are oil drillers and prospectors. Anyone who likes to sky-dive rather than read a book or buy a little sports car instead of a big old Cadillac with a ton of steel plate protection surrounding the driver is a risk seeker. A risk seeker may even accept an insurance rate less than the break-even rate because he or she is mesmerized by the prospects of high returns if houses do not burn to the ground at the expected rate. In fact, a risk seeker may prefer to insure fewer houses for a larger amount in order to capture a higher potential gain.

For a risk-averse individual, the left tail of a probability distribution depicting losses outweighs the prospects for profit embodied in the right tail. While the risk-neutral individual would presumably accept an average insurance rate of 0.496%, a risk-averse individual would not. The individual would want some sort of premium to compensate for the fact that he or she can lose a substantial amount of money.

What should that premium be? Again, risk is in the eye of the beholder. Suppose we ask the individual what the real loss of the entire bond principal would be in terms of a psychological loss, some other figure that reflects his or her fear of losing the initial investment of $100,000. Suppose that the individual said that losing $100,000 is equivalent in terms of nausea and disgust to losing $1 million. First, this makes the individual risk-averse; second, we can use this as a marker. What would be the break-even insurance rate if an ending reserves of a loss of $100,000 would be equivalent in pain and suffering to losing $1 million?

For the case where cell D50 is equal to –$100,000, which is the loss of the entire bond portfolio of $100,000, then the value of cell D51 should be –$1,000,000. To do this, the formula in cell D51 would be:

=IF(D50>B7,D50,D50–10*(B7–D50))

In Excelese: "If the ending reserves in cell D50 for year 30 are greater than those in cell B7 ($100,000), then let the contents of the cell D51 be the same as in cell D50. If not, subtract the quantity of 10*$100,000 less the contents of cell D50 from the value in cell D50."

Any result for ending reserves below the value in cell B7 is "punished" by an increment that reflects the degree of risk aversion of the underwriter. The greater the difference between the ending and starting reserves, the greater is the punishment. Suppose that reserves are wiped out. Cell D50 has a value of zero. The expression

D50–10*(B7–D50) has a value of $0–10*($100,000–$0) or –$1 million. While the spreadsheet is still in dollars, cell D51 is in "utils," or perhaps "util-dollars," an expression from utility theory that incorporates the degree of risk aversion for an individual investor. The last details are for the objective cell B16 to be =D51–B7 rather than =D50–B7.

Table 2.3 compares the various parameters with an individual being neutral and averse to risk. The major change is in the higher step-up rate of 0.93% versus 0.67% and a higher base rate for the risk-averse individual of 0.59% versus 0.50% for the risk-neutral individual. Most importantly, risk aversion did not change the average insurance rate. Changes to the rate increment along with the trigger points as to when the insurance rates apply impacted ending reserves. The decision rules for the risk-averse individual allowed for a greater accumulation of reserves to handle times when claims were high. Figure 2.15 shows the probability distribution of ending reserves for the risk-neutral individual.

Risk aversion was handled by changing the parameters associated with step-ups and step-downs in insurance rates and by raising the base insurance rate shown in Figure 2.16. It would be presumed that these changes would affect the average insurance rate, but they don't. This is an interesting finding in that one would have presumed that risk aversion would necessarily entail a higher average insurance rate. What is primarily affected is the nature of the step-up when reserves decline from a higher rate of claims and the increase in average reserves.

Table 2.3
Comparing Parameters of Risk-Neutral and Risk-Averse Individuals

1,000 Houses at $10,000 Each	Risk-Neutral	Risk-Averse
Initial reserves	$100,000	$100,000
Base insurance rate	0.50%	0.59%
Step up to:	0.67%	0.93%
When reserves fall below:	$64,000	$55,000
Step down to:	0.33%	0.25%
When reserves rise above:	$136,000	$145,000
Average insurance rate	0.497%	0.489%
Probability of ending reserves <$50,000	11.8%	1.3%
Probability of ending reserves < $100,000	48.3%	16.7%

Figure 2.15
Ending Reserves Risk-Neutral

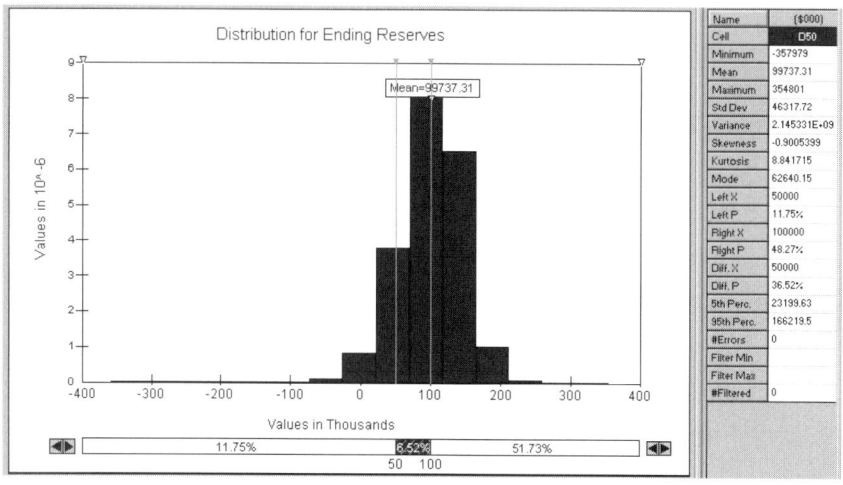

Figure 2.16
Ending Reserves Risk-Averse

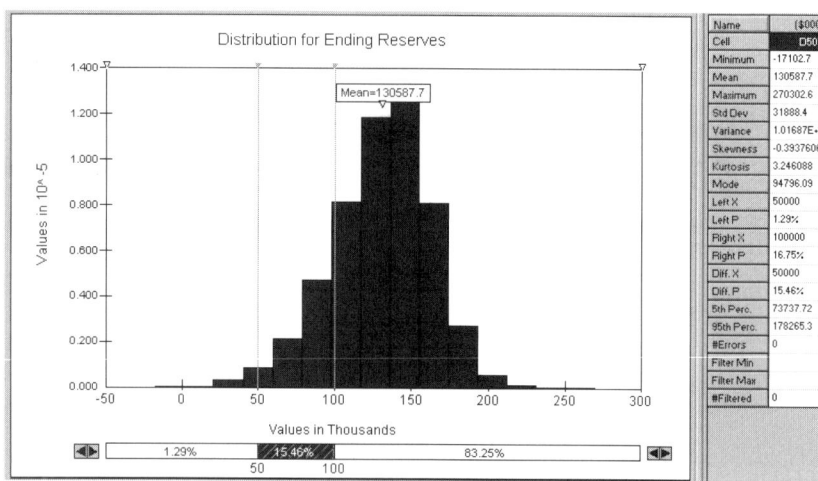

SELF-INSURING A PORTFOLIO OF LOANS

The same spreadsheet for insuring houses against fire can be used to self-insure a portfolio of bank loans. Suppose that you are running a bank and you desire to add a portfolio of lower-grade credits. The reason for doing so is obvious: lower-grade credits have a higher yield, and higher interest income enhances profits. However, the higher interest rates associated with lower-grade credits should include an increment to cover the additional risk of a loan default. An internal reserve is to be set up by segregating an existing portfolio of high-grade loans and government securities to act as reserves for insuring a lower-grade portfolio. The objective is to obtain the minimum acceptable interest rate to preserve ending reserves with regard to starting reserves and to identify the proper amount of reserves. This is the incremental interest associated with the lower-grade loans to cover the higher risk of loan defaults. If the actual interest rate increment associated with the lower-grade loans is higher than the minimum acceptable interest rate increment, then it is in the bank's interest to have a portfolio of lower-grade loans along with its more creditworthy loans to enhance earnings. If not, then the bank should not invest in lower-grade loans.

The first step in this process is to derive a probability distribution curve for loan losses. This could be the historical loss record experienced by the bank or statistics collected by credit rating services for equivalent grade loans. Suppose for the sake of illustration that it is the same lognormal probability distribution of loan losses varying between 0 and 10% with an average loss rate of ½% used previously:

=RiskLognorm(0.5, 0.21, RiskTruncate(0, 10))/100

This loss rate may be too modest, but the point is in establishing a methodology. Suppose the portfolio will consist of 1,000 loans whose maximum loan amount is $50 million. The number of loans going bad in any one year will vary between 0 and 100 with an average of 5. Suppose that the amount outstanding of each loan follows a triangular distribution with a minimum of 0, a mode of $35 million, and a maximum of $50 million as illustrated in Figure 2.17. The triangular probability distribution is handy when the general shape of the probability distribution is not known. Presumably, the outstanding amount of every loan in the portfolio is known. These could be listed on an Excel spreadsheet, and the best-fitting probability distribution can be obtained by using the *Fit Distributions to Data* function of @Risk.

The average size of the loan in this probability distribution is $28.3 million. A portfolio of 1,000 loans would be a rather imposing $28.3 billion.

Bad loans don't necessary mean a 100% write-off. Banks have workout divisions whose task is to recoup as much as possible for loans associated with companies in trouble, which, by the way, need not necessarily mean bankruptcy. Loan workouts can occur without the legal necessity of companies declaring bankruptcy. Banks may force a company into bankruptcy if it is in their interest to do so, or loans can be recast without a formal hearing in a bankruptcy court. The one disadvantage of bank-

Figure 2.17
Loan Amount Probability Distribution

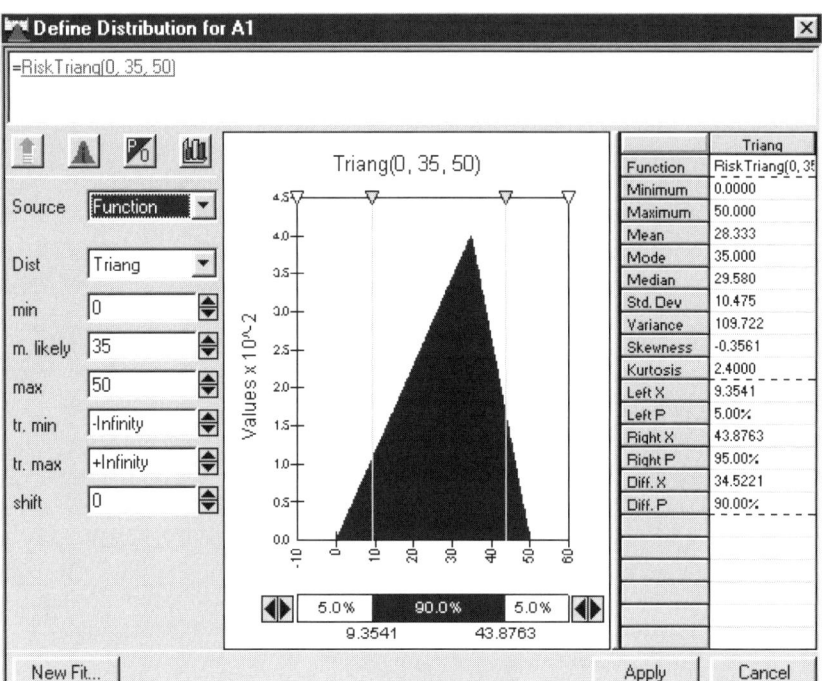

ruptcy proceedings from the bankers' perspective is that the loan workout is under the control not of bankers but of a bankruptcy judge who decides what's best for all creditors. So if all parties associated with the transaction are in agreement, then a loan workout can be conducted without the borrower declaring bankruptcy.

Suppose that it has been the bank's experience for loan losses to be a minimum of 20% with a mode of 60% and a maximum of 100%. The triangular probability distribution formula would be:

$$=RiskTriang(0.2, 0.6, 1.0)$$

Appendix 2.B is the spreadsheet formulation for deriving a probability distribution for loan losses.

In Figure 1.18, the premium is applied to the mean of the triangular distribution for the average loan of $28.333 million or $28,333 thousand multiplied by 1,000 loans. An initial run was made without incorporating risk aversion with results shown in Figure 2.18.

The probability of any diminution of reserves was 43%, and the chance of reserves falling below $400,000 was 4%. Another run was made with the same aversion to risk in cell E51 as in the previous example:

$$=\text{IF}(D50>B7,D50,D50-10*(B7-D50))$$

The optimal solution for risk aversion is in Figure 2.19 with starting reserves arbitrarily selected at $500 million. The interest rate increment is 0.47%, which is hiked to 0.74% when reserves fall below $480,000 and cut to 0.20% when reserves climb above $520,000.

The ending reserves are shown in Figure 2.20. Without incorporating risk aversion, the simulation results showed a relatively high probability of exhausting reserves. By incorporating risk aversion, the mean of ending reserves in cell D50 is $554,000 in actual dollars, not the presumably $500,000 "util-dollars" in cell D51. The strong bias against ending reserves being less than starting reserves reduced the chances of ending reserves being less than the initial reserves from 43% without risk aversion to 15% and the chances of ending reserves being less than $400,000 from 4% to 0.7%. This means that reserves of $100,000 would have a 0.7% chance of being exhausted.

If initial reserves are $100,000, then Figure 2.18 can be interpreted as follows. As long as reserves are between $80,000 and $120,000, the interest increment to compensate for the additional risk is 0.47%. If reserves rise above $120,000, then the interest increment is cut to 0.20%. If reserves fall below $80,000, then the interest increment is hiked to $0.74%. The settings are such that reserves grow over time adding about 54% to reserves over 30 years. The higher ending reserves are necessary to compensate for the risk aversion associated with ending reserves being less than the starting reserves.

Figure 2.18
RiskOptimizer Solution

	A	B	C
1	Determining an Insurance Rate		
2			
3	Base Rate	0.320%	32
4	High Rate	0.490%	17
5	Low Rate	0.150%	
6			
7	Start reserves	$ 500,000	
8	Upper Trigger	$ 516,000	16
9	Lower Trigger	$ 484,000	
10	Earnings Rate	6%	
11			
12	Total Policies	$ 28,333,333	
13			
14	Avg Ins Rate	0.292%	
15			
16	Objective:	$ 19,334	

Figure 2.19
Solution with Risk Aversion

	A	B	C
1	Determining an Insurance Rate		
2			
3	Base Rate	0.470%	47
4	High Rate	0.740%	27
5	Low Rate	0.200%	
6			
7	Start reserves	$ 500,000	
8	Upper Trigger	$ 520,000	20
9	Lower Trigger	$ 480,000	
10	Earnings Rate	6%	
11			
12	Total Policies	$ 28,333,333	
13			
14	Avg Ins Rate	0.290%	
15			
16	Objective:	$ 87,967	

Figure 2.20
Histogram of Ending Reserves

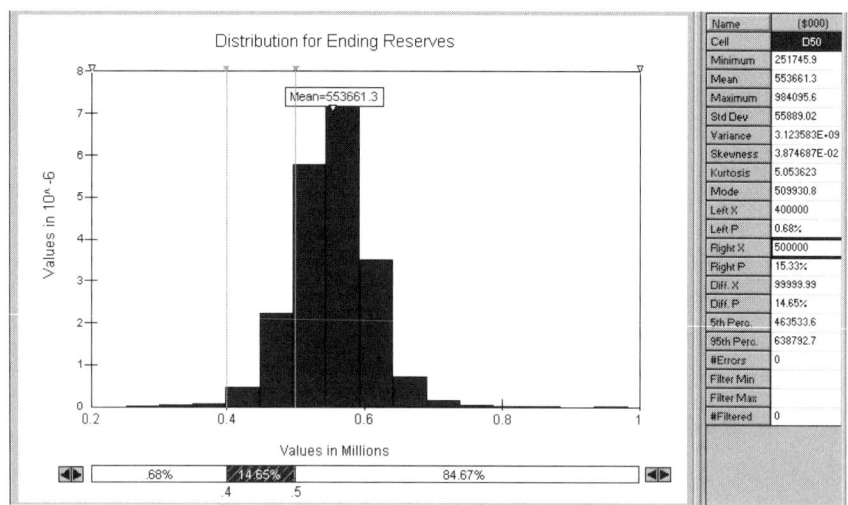

The average incremental interest rate to compensate for the additional risk of 0.296% illustrated in Figure 2.21 is essentially the same as running the program without risk aversion, which was 0.302%. The slight reduction in the interest rate reflects the smaller chance of the reserves being less than their starting point, which reduces the amount that is exposed to the punitive 2% charge for liquidating and eventually replacing reserves. The major difference between the two was in the rules affecting changes to size of the interest rate increments and the reserve trigger points. The change in these settings has little impact on the average interest rate but a major impact on the outcome for ending reserves.

The reason the interest rate increment, which can be likened to an internal insurance rate for accepting a lower-grade portfolio of loans, is lower than the expected loss rate of 0.5% is that there is only a small chance of a total loss in case of a loan default. A fairly healthy portion of a potential loan loss can be recouped through the efforts of the workout group.

CONCLUSION

The findings for accepting the risks of a lower-grade portfolio of loans are in line with accepting the risks of underwriting fire insurance policies. Risk is in the tail of the probability distribution, whereas most individuals focus on the average loss of houses burning down or loans going bad. In basing an insurance rate or an incremental interest rate to cover the average loss rate, a great deal of risk can be assumed without the underwriter or the banker being fully aware of its potential magnitude. Software packages like @Risk provide a better understanding of the nature of the risks that lie in the left tail and the opportunities that lie in the right. This

Figure 2.21
Insurance Rate

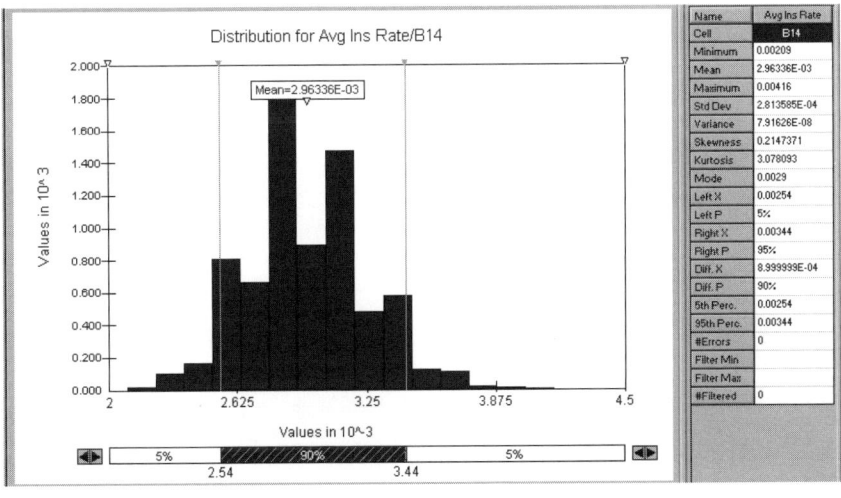

added knowledge should lead to a better appreciation of risk for those managing risk in underwriting insurance policies or in selecting a bank loan portfolio. Moreover, incorporating different rules for changing the insurance rate either directly or by incorporating risk averseness makes it possible to maintain the same average insurance rate while substantially reducing the risk of ending reserves being less than initial reserves.

NOTE

1. See company web site www.palisade.com.

APPENDIX 2.A
SPREADSHEET FORMULATION FOR DETERMINING AN INSURANCE RATE

Figure 2.A.1 is the same as Figure 2.1. The verbal equivalent of the formulas is quite straightforward. The formula in Cell B16 is:

=IF(D21<$B$9,$B$4,IF(D21>$B$8,$B$5,$B$3))

The translation of the formula from Excelese to conversational English follows. "If reserves in cell D21 are smaller than the lower trigger point for reserves in cell B9, then the insurance rate in cell B4 applies. If this condition is not true and if the reserves in cell D21 are greater than the upper trigger point in cell B8, then the insurance rate in cell B5 applies. If neither of these two conditions is true, then the insurance rate is the base rate in cell B3."

The annual premium income in column C is the insurance rate in column B multiplied by 100 policies at $100,000 each or $10 million in cell B12. The formula in cell C21 is =B21*$B$12. The initial reserves in column D are =B7. After that, column D is the start of year reserves that refer to the previous year's end of year re-

Figure 2.A.1
Spreadsheet Formulation

	A	B	C	D	E	F	G
1	Determining an Insurance Rate						
2							
3	Base Rate	0.560%	56				
4	High Rate	0.740%	18				
5	Low Rate	0.380%					
6							
7	Start reserves	$ 500,000					
8	Upper Trigger	$ 530,000	30				
9	Lower Trigger	$ 470,000					
10	Earnings Rate	6%					
11							
12	Total Policies	$ 10,000,000					
13							
14	Avg Ins Rate	0.584%					
15							
16	Objective:	$ 80,837					
17							
18				Annual		Reserves		Ending
19			Annual	Premium	Reserves	Income	Claims	Reserves
20	Year	Rate	($000)	($000)	($000)	($000)	($000)
21	1	0.56%	$ 56,000	$ 500,000	$ -	$ -	$ 556,000
22	2	0.38%	$ 38,000	$ 556,000	$ 3,360	$ 100,000	$ 497,360
23	3	0.56%	$ 56,000	$ 497,360	$ (211)	$ 100,000	$ 453,149
24	4	0.74%	$ 74,000	$ 453,149	$ (3,748)	$ -	$ 523,401
25	5	0.56%	$ 56,000	$ 523,401	$ 1,404	$ 200,000	$ 380,805
26	6	0.74%	$ 74,000	$ 380,805	$ (9,536)	$ 200,000	$ 245,269
27	7	0.74%	$ 74,000	$ 245,269	$ (20,378)	$ 100,000	$ 198,891
28	8	0.74%	$ 74,000	$ 198,891	$ (24,089)	$ -	$ 248,802

serves (e.g., the formula in cell D22 is =G21). Reserve income in column E is determined by the formula:

$$=IF(D21>\$B\$7,\$B\$10*(D21-\$B\$7),(\$B\$10+0.02)*(D21-\$B\$7))$$

In Excelese: "If reserves in column D are above initial reserves in cell B7, then the excess reserves over the initial reserves earn the interest rate in cell B10. If the reserves are less than the starting reserves, then there is an interest charge with a 2% punitive increment."

Earnings on the reserves are not part of the calculation of the insurance rate. Reserves can be looked upon as bonds whose interest earnings are kept by a third party. The bonds are there to ensure that claims can be satisfied. The calculated insurance rate reflects the nature of the claims stemming from the assumed risks. The 2% punitive charge is for costs associated with liquidating bonds to cover claims and replacing them when reserves begin to increase. Moreover, the insurance premium has to be sufficient over time to continue paying the interest on the bonds that have been sold to cover claims. This preserves the interest income of the party that provided the bond portfolio to cover claims.

Column F contains the loss function that varies with each example. Column G contains the formula =C21+D21+E21–F21, which simply states that ending reserves are starting reserves plus premium income plus interest earned or charged depending on how reserves relate to initial reserves less claims. The indicated cells are replicated down to cover a 30-year period. The formula for incorporating risk averseness is in the main text.

It is essential to be in the *Monte Carlo* mode (*Simulation Settings/Sampling/Standard Recalc/Monte Carl*) when setting up the program to ensure, for instance, that interest is positive or negative as reserves depart from the initial starting point. In the *Expected* mode, it is relatively easy to incorporate a bug in the program without knowing its existence. Spreadsheet values have to be checked one by one in the *Monte Carlo* mode to identify and eliminate programming bugs. Like those in charge of the *Titanic*, hubris or overconfidence can take over a spreadsheet programmer, leading to erroneous results.

APPENDIX 2.B
DERIVING THE LOAN LOSS PROBABILITY DISTRIBUTION

The spreadsheet for deriving the loan loss probability distribution is shown in Figure 2.B.1. The probability of bad loans in cell A6 is multiplied by 1000 and transformed into an integer in cell B6 (the 0.5 is for rounding up):

$$=INT(A6*1000+0.5)$$

Bad loans number up to 100 in column A, the maximum permissible number in a portfolio of 1,000 loans. Column B assigns a "1" up to the number of bad loans in cell B6, then a "0" for the remaining loans:

$$=IF(A11<=\$B\$6,1,0)$$

The amount of the loan and the percent loss are determined by the aforementioned triangular probability distributions. The loss amount in column E is obtained by multiplying column B by column C by column D. Column E is totaled in cell E6 and multiplied by 1,000 to obtain loan losses in thousands. Figure 2.B.2 contains the best-fitting probability distribution for a simulation of 10,000 iterations.

The sample data are seen at the left. The chart shows that there is a small chance of some rather large loan losses. The best-fitting curve is a lognormal probability distribution. The P-P curve (not shown) is a straight line indicating an excellent fit.

Figure 2.B.1
Loan Losses

	A	B	C	D	E
1	Loan Loss Probability Distribution Generator				
2					
3		Number			Annual
4	Loss	Bad			Loss
5	Rate	Loans			$thousands
6	0.005184	5			$ 109,994
7					
8	Bad		Loan	Loan	Amount
9	Loan		Amount	Loss	Loss
10	Number	Yes/No	$mm	Percent	$mm
11	1	1	40.6	59%	$ 24.0
12	2	1	6.9	69%	$ 4.8
13	3	1	36.0	84%	$ 30.3
14	4	1	27.3	79%	$ 21.5
15	5	1	43.7	67%	$ 29.4
16	6	0	33.7	62%	$ -
17	7	0	17.2	52%	$ -

This probability distribution curve can be substituted into the same spreadsheet used for determining the minimum insurance rate using the *Define Distributions* function truncated at 0:

=RiskLognorm2(11.515, 0.36514, RiskShift(−22017), RiskTruncate(0))

Figure 2.B.2
Loan Loss Probability Distribution

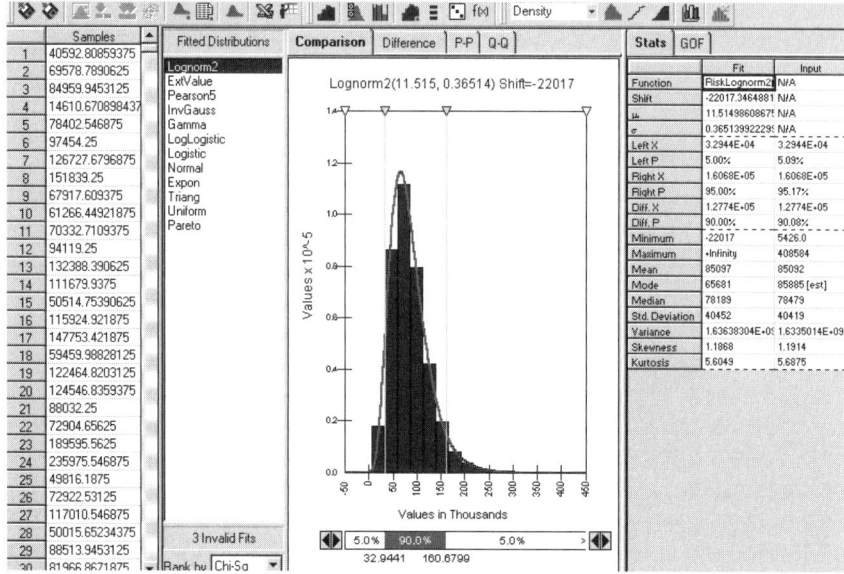

3
MANAGING RISK IN A PROJECT FINANCING

SYNOPSIS

This chapter examines the means available to manage risk in a project financing. The inherent risk of a project financing is usually hidden from view when a loan is under review. A traditional cash flow spreadsheet presented to the bankers has certain characteristics that are guaranteed to be present: positive cash flows, adequate coverage of cash flow to debt servicing charges, a reasonable profit. Yet loans go bad. Thus, there has to be a disconnect between the projection of future cash flow offered to the bankers and its realization.

One reason for this divergence is that there is no variation in price, volume, and costs. In this chapter the traditional cash flow spreadsheet is reconstructed incorporating good and bad times in the business cycle and the uncertainties that surround price, volume, cost, and interest assessments. While in the *Expected* mode the project financing appears doable, in *Monte Carlo*, risk abounds.

Risk, of course, takes the form of negative cash flows. Any project can survive minor negative cash flows, but perhaps not if negative cash flows are of a magnitude to exhaust working capital funds. This makes the project technically insolvent unless there is outside support to maintain a positive working capital. The outside support takes the form of an infinite line of credit that assures that the project always remains solvent. This line of credit is called, for obvious reasons, the solvency loan. The frequency of use and the outstanding balance of the solvency loan become the measure of risk in a project financing. Managing risk in a project financing is done by adjusting the minimum working capital requirement and the amount of the loan to reduce the risk to an acceptable level for a lending institution.

THE NATURE OF PROJECT FINANCING

Project financing is stand-alone financing. No wealthy parent is around to bale out an errant son. The project either succeeds on its merits or fails. A mortgage on an office building may be viewed as a project financing. An owner may guarantee the mortgage, but if the mortgage far exceeds the net worth of an owner, the guarantee may not be worth much more than the paper it's written on. The risk inherent in financing a building depends on the nature of the leases. The risk profiles of an office building built on speculation and one filled with creditworthy tenants with long-term leases are profoundly different.

Electricity-generating plants in developing nations have been financed on a project basis. The lenders look only to the cash flow generated by the power plant as a source of repayment. The degree of risk is embedded in the selling price of the electricity less the capital and operating costs of the plant and the cost of the fuel. Investors may take solace in the inferred reluctance on the part of government authorities to let a power plant go bankrupt because of adverse repercussions on the local economy. Having said that, there may also be reluctance on the part of government authorities to have consumers pay the full cost of electricity. Perhaps the primary customer is a government-owned distribution company. While this may sound comforting to lenders, the owners of the electricity-generating plant may have little recourse if the distribution company turns out to be grossly delinquent in paying for the purchased electricity. While the economic factors are relatively easy to model, the political aspects of government involvement are not.

Ships may be viewed as a project financing when lenders do not have meaningful recourse beyond the revenue-generating potential of the vessel itself. But a vessel under a long-term charter to a major oil company has a materially different risk profile from that of a vessel continually having to seek out cargoes in a volatile market environment. A cruise vessel can look only to its current fare-paying customers to keep itself going. A cruise vessel financed with the primary support being other cruise vessels may not provide much solace to the lender because a single cruise vessel that is not able to attract sufficient passengers probably means that the rest serving as collateral are suffering the same plight. This observation holds for financing airplanes, container vessels, and a slew of other service companies.

A gold, coal, or other type of mineral deposit or an oil field may be financed on a project basis where the lenders' primary means of repayment is the revenue generated by selling a natural resource. Risk lies in the price of the mineral or oil that is outside the control of the mine owner and the financing institution. Risk also resides in the estimates of reserves to obtain the financing remaining valid, in the mine not suffering from unexpected difficulties in extracting the mineral such as flooding, and in the market being able to absorb the output. A factory is a project financing when the lenders depend on the revenue generation of the factory's output as the primary means of repayment. Both volume and price are subject to the whims of the marketplace, over which the factory owner has little control. While the attributes, quality, and price of a product are under the control of the manufacturer, this does not mean that the public will buy sufficient quantities to keep a firm in business no matter how attractively a quality product is priced.

An example of this is cell phones. Cell phones are high-quality items selling for a reasonable price. But cell phone manufacturing companies suffered in 2001, when cell phones made the transition from the growth to the maturity stage of the product life cycle. In the growth stage, cell phone sales were extremely robust as consumers bought their first phones. Cell phones entered the maturity stage when most consumers already owned a cell phone and sales become primarily replacements. This structural change in the sales profile wrought havoc on the manufacturers. Their making an attractively priced, high-quality product was not sufficient to sustain their volume and therefore their profits.

PERSONAL CASH FLOW

There is a great similarity from a financial perspective between running a household and running a company. We as individuals have revenue, presumably a paycheck. The money is deposited in a checking account, and we spend the rest of our lives as disbursement clerks. The checks we write represent our living expenses or operating costs. However, our net cash flow also has to take into account income taxes. Income taxes are a side calculation of revenue less certain expenses such as property taxes, interest on the mortgage, medical expenses above certain limits, charity and personal deductions, and the like. Then we take what is left, multiply it by the tax rate, and write a check to Uncle Sam, something we didn't have to do for the first 150 years of our nation's history.

Our net cash flow is revenue less living expenses less taxes where taxes are a side calculation involving revenue and certain deductible items. If the net cash flow is positive, we sleep comfortably at night; if not, worry and stress keep us awake except for a precious few tens of millions who sink forever into debt without seemingly a care or worry. As we approach retirement, we can do a calculation on our early years of negative cash outflows for our education followed by years of hopefully positive cash inflows in order to obtain the rate of return on an investment in tuition, room, and board plus income foregone while getting an education. We could do this, but few actually do. If the return turns out meager, what do you do—give less at the next annual alumni drive?

RISK IN A PROJECT FINANCING

The evaluation of risk in a project financing is the probability of the project not generating sufficient funds to pay off the underlying debt. As will be shown, a project financing based on average expected estimates of price, volume, and costs can portray a comfortable projection of cash flows to support the requested level of debt. But when average expectations are replaced by low, high, and most likely estimates, an entirely different picture emerges. Average expectations encourage somnolence on the part of the lender because superficially everything looks fine. A calm sea becomes a tossing sea when variability is introduced. The risks inherent in changing prices, volume, and costs may represent a degree of risk for the lending institution that cannot be justified by the spread in interest rates between borrowing money from depositors and lending it to borrowers.

A number of steps have to be taken to get to this point of evaluating risk in a project financing. For the most part, these steps are the same as the traditional approach in evaluating a loan proposal by determining the coverage of cash flow to support debt servicing charges. The discussion on cash flow as an arithmetic exercise of revenue, fixed and variable costs, depreciation, taxes, and debt amortization serves as a backdrop to the introduction of risk.

Risk enters the picture when revenue, as a product of sales volume and price, is no longer a single value for the next 20 years of the project's life. Not only do price and volume change, but they are also affected by the business cycle. The business cycle may correlate price and volume positively whereby high prices and high volume go together during the good times. Here the borrower is the sole beneficiary as excess cash flow lines his or her pockets. But the converse is bad for the lender when the bad times bring together low prices and low volume. Now it becomes the lender's problem when the project does not throw off enough cash to pay debt servicing charges.

The evaluation of risk takes the form of a solvency loan. A solvency loan is a nonexistent, infinitely large line of credit to ensure the solvency of the project. In theory the solvency loan should never be drawn down, and in practice it does not exist. As will be seen, there is no need for a solvency loan when the loan proposal is made on the basis of expected values. The need for a solvency loan becomes apparent when there is not enough cash being generated to pay debt servicing charges. Drawdowns on the solvency loan and the state of the solvency loan when the loan is presumably paid off will be the chief indicators of risk.

Risk in the form of the inability of the project to adequately fund debt servicing charges can be handled by two means. One is the traditional lender's response of reducing the amount of the loan and the other is increasing working capital requirements in the form of minimum cash holdings. Both are effective in providing protection against the bad times.

CORPORATE CASH FLOW

A corporate cash flow is quite like a personal cash flow. The major difference is that what is termed living expenses can be assigned to categories, most of which are tax-deductible. In addition, the tax calculation for a corporation includes depreciation, the noncash write-off of assets. The first step in establishing a cash flow projection is determining revenue. Revenue is then netted of variable or cost of goods sold, fixed costs, interest expenses, taxes, and repayment of debt to obtain a corporate cash flow.

REVENUE AND ECONOMIC CONDITIONS

For a factory that makes a single product, revenue is price multiplied by volume. We tend to think of price and volume as independent entities. But volume may be a function of price, which complicates matters. An economics textbook teaches that if you want to increase sales volume, lower the price. This means that there is a negative relationship between price and volume: the higher the price, the lower the volume, and similarly, the lower the price, the higher the volume.

This observation is true on a transient basis. If business conditions are good and you want to increase volume, lower the price. But in the good times of the business cycle, both price and volume are high, and you may be selling more or less all that you make at the asking price. You may want to think twice about lowering your price under these conditions. On the other hand, in the bad times of the business cycle, both price and volume are low. Your factory is not busy, orders are anemic, and prices are low. Certainly you can lower your price even more to increase volume, but would it do any good?

Viewed as a micropicture of a moment in time, price and volume are negatively correlated. Viewed as a macropicture of the cyclical swings in business activity, price and volume are not negatively, but positively, correlated. When times are good in the business cycle, orders are flowing in, and prices are high. When times are bad, volume shrinks along with price. This is positive correlation. Positive correlation adds to the instability of the free market system not because things are extra good during a business boom, but because they are extra bad during a bust. While it is true that we can increase volume by lowering price at any point in the business cycle, the overriding factor is that good times are especially enjoyable and bad times are especially frustrating.

COSTS OF GOODS SOLD

In a personal cash flow, living expenses are lumped together. Few of us actually categorize outgoing checks as companies do. In a corporate cash flow, operating costs are broken down into two general cost categories. Variable cost or cost of goods sold includes all costs related to manufacturing a product. Two examples of cost of goods sold that are solely variable are material and shipping. Make nothing, and there is no material consumed, and there is no need to ship anything. Material and shipping costs vary directly with production. Direct factory labor is normally considered a variable cost. As production increases, more workers are hired to produce a greater volume of goods. If direct factory labor is to remain variable, then the workers have to be let go as production declines. To the degree that factory workers are retained rather than being laid off on the first dip in sales, their cost becomes partly fixed.

Many expense items in cost of goods sold are partly variable and partly fixed. Utility, maintenance, and repair costs exist even if nothing is being produced and vary as machines are turned on or off in response to changes in production volume.

FIXED COSTS

Cost of goods includes those costs generally attributable to manufacturing a product. Fixed costs are everything else with the exceptions of interest payments on debt, debt repayment or amortization, taxes on profits, dividends, and capital expenditures. Fixed costs or general and administrative (G&A) expenses consist of rental and leasing fees on buildings, salaries for the executive, marketing, accounting, financing, and product development staffs, property taxes, insurance, remodeling the corporate headquarters, gala annual meetings for shareholders, Christmas parties for the employees, and a slew of others. Though called fixed, they have a variable element. As sales increase, more people are added to accounting to handle the higher level of orders and to marketing to handle the higher volume of sales. As revenues expand, a bone may be thrown at research and development to hire another person to help dream up a new product or improve the existing product line. As profits expand, bigger bones may be thrown at the executives in the form of generous bonuses. But these may be cut as revenue and profits fall. So there we have it: variable costs are partly fixed, and fixed costs are partly variable.

GROSS PROFIT IS REVENUE LESS COST OF GOODS SOLD

DEPRECIATION

Depreciation is the write-down of assets. Straight line depreciation is the acquired cost of an asset less its expected residual value divided by the depreciation period. The depreciation period for an asset is often considered to be its physical life. For a building, the physical life may be 20 years; for a machine, 12 years. The problem here is that assets may be replaced before their physical lives are over. One prime example is the personal computer. How many personal computers are replaced because they are at the end of their physical lives (the computer is worn out and cannot be economically repaired) versus being at the end of their technological lives (memory too small and speed too slow for new application software)? Technological innovation often causes the early demise of machinery and equipment. Depreciation should reflect the economic, not the physical life, of the asset.

EARNINGS BEFORE TAXES ARE GROSS PROFIT LESS G&A AND DEPRECIATION

TAXES

Everyone wants to tax the corporations; "let the rich corporations pay, not the little people." But as in all things there is a counterargument. The corporations provide goods and services that form the basis for our standard of living. Oh, not true? What products do you purchase that are made by a government? The plethora of goods and services emanate from the collective efforts of those employed by corporations, not by governments.

Some people espouse that the economy is too vital to be in the hands of greedy, money-grubbing businesspeople and should be in the hands of fair-minded, benign government bureaucrats charged to protect our interests. However, privatization is the vindication of Adam Smith over the London School of Economics. Adam Smith said that the production of goods and services should be in the hands of greedy, money-grubbing businesspeople whose feet are firmly held to the hot coals of a profit-and-loss statement. The only way to make profits is to provide goods and services that people are willing to buy. The free enterprise system opens up the production of goods and services to anyone with the capital to start a new business. The free market gives buyers a choice of sellers. To remain successful, a seller must do a superior job in comparison to his or her competitors. This is what keeps the greedy, money-grubbing businesspeople honest.

The London School of Economics came to the conclusion that the workings of the economy are far too important to be left in the hands of money-grubbers. All would benefit if the workings of the economy were replaced by all-knowing government bureaucrats who would labor day and night under benign administrative guidelines to ensure that the people are well served for the common good of all, whatever that means. After World War II, graduates from the London School of Economics were successful in getting governments to nationalize a host of different industries in Europe and South America. Then 50 years went by.

Let's take one example of a nationalized company—the government-owned oil company in a Latin American nation. Fifty years after nationalization, the company was ringing up huge operating deficits as wave upon wave of citizens managed to get their names on the company payrolls without having to show up for work. In fact, they didn't know where to go if they had to report to work. To be hired, they just had to have a mother-in-law whose cousin knew the uncle of someone who worked in the payroll department. A little money here, a little money there, and now you are a paid employee whose check is mailed to you every other Thursday.

Meanwhile, the management of the company became so indolent in running the oil business that production declined and the nation had to import oil. There is absolutely no reason to exert oneself such as looking for oil when the government is picking up the tab, and everyone knows what happens to a bureaucrat who spends government money looking for oil and doesn't find any. This says a lot about human nature that Adam Smith apparently understood and the graduates of the London School of Economics didn't. The company owned and controlled by the government created two deficits—an operating deficit that sucked the government coffers dry and a negative trade deficit in oil that weakened the currency.

Eventually, the government became fed up with the situation and privatized the company. This was essentially an admission that matters couldn't get worse. Now management had a choice. Either they function as managers and try to restore profitability or remain as bureaucrats and lose their jobs with the liquidation of the company. That's what happens in privatization: the umbilical cord to the government coffers is cut.

The first act to restore profitability was to cut costs by getting rid of thousands of workers who received a check in the mail every other Thursday. The second act was for the government bureaucrats to start acting like oil company executives and look for oil rather than shuffle paper. They did and, lo and behold, they found oil. In about five years' time, the company was profitable, and nation became an oil exporter. The government now had two benefits from privatization. It received money in the form of taxes on profits rather than funding the operating deficit and earned foreign exchange through oil exports rather than funding a trade deficit.

This turnaround has been the general consequence of privatization. The mere talk about eventually privatizing can have profound effects on management. Not all privatizations are so successful, but by and large, privatization has reduced government outlays by transforming bureaucrats into managers. Privatization is clear proof that Adam Smith was right all along and that the economists at the London School of Economics were not.

This does not have a totally happy ending. The downside of putting business decisions in the hands of businesspeople is that businesspeople have a penchant of building too much productive capacity during the good times of a business cycle that lead to the bad times. Just a small example: the good times of the telecommunication companies and the benefits accruing to the telecommunication manufacturers in the late 1990s and 2000 versus the bankruptcies, layoffs, and general distress in this industry in 2001 and 2002. The telecommunication companies bought too much equipment and overexpanded productive capacity far in excess of demand in the late 1990s. They did not realize that they had made a mistake until the equipment was in place in 2000 and utilization was far below breakeven. They attempted to increase volume by introducing all sorts of money-losing gimmicks to siphon customers away from their competitors. All this did was make a bad situation worse by reducing aggregate revenue for the industry. Burdened with debt that could not possibly be serviced, the telecommunication industry went through a financial bloodbath with firms going bankrupt and thousands losing their jobs. Meanwhile, the telecommunication manufacturers saw orders evaporate. This led to massive layoffs and also financial distress as the value of their receivables evaporated with the disappearance of their customers.

A worker at Lucent lost her job and about 95% of the value of her savings and pension account that was all in Lucent stock. She was not alone. Thousands had the same thing happen in scores of other companies. This is why the London School of Economics promoted government ownership of vital areas of the national economy. The ups and downs of the business cycle are brutal in wiping out the livelihood and investments of countless thousands of innocent people. Sometimes it isn't even the business cycle that wipes out the employees, but gross mismanagement by individuals at the top whose first priority is to line their pockets before the doors are forever shut. In 2001, an energy company with an excellent credit rating collapsed almost overnight, wiping out $80 billion in stockholder value and thousands of jobs. The downward spiral started with a crisis in management when it was learned that top executives had cooked the books and organized all sorts of side deals to line their pockets at the company's expense. Adam Smith may be right and the London School of Economics wrong, but that is of little solace to those who lose their livelihood in a business contraction. In accepting the upside that private enterprise is the best way to improve living standards, we have accepted the downside of the instability inherent in the business cycle.

Nevertheless, corporations, whether we like it or not, are the primary engine behind our standard of living. Now let us return to the question of corporations paying taxes. By making corporations pay taxes, they are being robbed (word too strong?) of funds that could otherwise be reinvested in the production of goods and services to improve productivity or quality or variety of offerings. But corporations do not let taxes adversely affect their capital expenditures. To make up for the loss of funds from taxation, corporations simply borrow from the banks or issue debt. They are encouraged to do so, as interest is tax-deductible. The more you borrow, the less you pay in taxes.

Debt, as we all know, has its downside. Too much debt when the ill-wind blows from an economic contraction can cause a company to fold. Were its capital structure more heavily weighted with equity rather than debt, a company would better withstand the normal business, financial, and economic shocks that it must face. But not taxing a corporation does not make a businessperson rich per se. What a company pays out in salaries, bonuses, and dividends is taxed.

All this is ranting and raving. It is not to be. We live in a world where a substantial portion of a company's profits must be diverted to government coffers for all sorts of good reasons whose goodness may not be immediately apparent. But one last word: taxes are an expense. For a company to exist, all expenses must be passed on to the customer in the price of its goods and services. So just who ends up paying for corporate taxes?

TAXES ARE GROSS PROFITS LESS G&A AND INTEREST AND DEPRECIATION MULTIPLIED BY THE TAX RATE

Once taxes are paid, then we have after-tax earnings.

AFTER TAXES EARNINGS ARE BEFORE TAX EARNINGS NET OF TAXES

CASH FLOW

Nothing is more important to a company's well-being than cash flow. A corporation can bleed to death without sufficient cash flow. Cash flow is not a bookkeeping entry but the stuff in your checking account. It backs up the checks you write. Cash flow should not be confused with profitability, although they are linked.

Cash flow is after-tax earnings plus depreciation less debt repayment or amortization. Depreciation is part of before-tax earnings for calculating taxes. Now it has to be removed because it is a noncash expense. Interest has already been taken into account, so there is one other cash outflow yet to be taken accounted for—repayment of debt.

CASH FLOW IS AFTER TAX EARNINGS PLUS DEPRECIATION
LESS DEBT AMORTIZATION

There are three general ways to dispose of cash flow. It can remain in the company checking account and become part of working capital. Working capital is cash, accounts receivable (what you have produced and sold but not yet paid for), and inventory (what you have produced but not yet sold) less accounts payable (bills not yet paid) and short-term debt obligations (what you owe banks over the next 12 months). Cash flow generated from operations can be spent in expanding accounts receivable, in inventory, and in paying bills more quickly. On the other hand, cash can be generated by liquidating inventory and accounts receivable and by delaying payment of accounts payable, that is, not paying your bills. Working capital is a subject unto itself, and the project financing being set up does not include fluctuations in accounts receivable, inventory, and accounts payable. It is assumed that these remain constant. Other ways to dispose of cash flow are paying dividends to shareholders, funding capital expenditures, and retiring corporate debt ahead of schedule.

SOLVENCY LOAN

The risk of financing a project will be evaluated through the use of a solvency loan. A solvency loan is basically a fictitious and infinite line of credit. A drawdown of the solvency loan means that the company is not generating sufficient funds to make interest and debt amortization payments in a timely manner and has exhausted the cash portion of working capital. Risk can be evaluated in terms of the frequency and the amount of drawdowns of the solvency loan. In theory the solvency loan should not be used, but as will be seen, when times are bad in the business cycle, there may not be sufficient funds generated from operations to sustain the timely payment of interest and debt amortization. Thus, the company must draw down on the solvency loan to prevent insolvency, which, of course, is equivalent to running out of cash in your checking account.

MODELING THE BUSINESS CYCLE

Business never stands still. Talk to any businessperson—either business is better this year than last year, or it's not. What does that mean? It means that business never stands still. It is *highly* unlikely, with emphasis on highly, that a factory's sales volume and price are repetitive year after year.

It is the same with our national economy. Either it is up a little or a lot from last year or it is down a little or a lot from last year. An economy is a living and breathing animal whose lungs expand and contract to stay alive. There is no way to continually breathe in—economic expansions cannot last forever. There is no way to continually breath out—economic contractions cannot last forever.

Lending officers generally fail to take this into consideration. Normally, loans are made with the assumption that business conditions, as they exist when the loan is booked, will not change. There is absolutely no historical justification for this. There is some justification for presuming that averages or perhaps long-term trends may persist into the future. However, cell phones moving from the growth to the maturity stage of the product life cycle should dispel faith that trends persist forever. Sales and prices based on averages or an average trend are an understandable and convenient course of action made necessary in that there is no way to precisely forecast future business conditions. All that can be said is that tomorrow's business conditions will not be the same as today's. The default condition is to say that the average, or an average trend, will continue to persist ignoring the oscillations about the average or the trend.

A simulation does not forecast future business conditions. Simulation takes into account the oscillations about an average or trend. Future business conditions will be different without being specific as to what they will be next year and the year following. A simulation incorporates a range about a most likely assessment on price and volume. This generates an output with two tails. The right-hand tail is the potential for profit for the borrower when the good times in a simulation are more prevalent than the bad. The left-hand tail is the potential for loss when the bad times in a simulation are more prevalent than the good. The borrower salivates over the right-hand tail, but the lender worries over the left-hand tail. The borrower keeps all the profits in the right-hand tail; this is not for the lender's account. But the risk of nonpayment of a loan resides in the left-hand tail and that may end up in the lender's account.

Good and bad times are multiyear phenomena. Flipping a coin year after year does not mean that good and bad times alternate every year. It is not unusual to see five to seven years of consistently good or bad times as depicted in Figure 3.1 simply by having a 50–50 chance of good times following bad, and vice versa (row 3 is years and row 5 is business conditions, where 1 means good times and 0 means bad).

A formula to provide a 60% chance that one good year will follow another and a 60% chance that one bad year will follow another is set up in Appendix 3.A to show that control can be exerted over the duration of good and bad times. The 60% rather than 50% chance that either good or bad times will persist in the following year generates longer periods of good and bad times and a greater probability of a loan going bad. However, in so doing, it is possible to have truly extended periods of time, perhaps 18 or 19 years out of 20, that are either good or bad times. This extends the tails of the right (profit) and left (loss) tails of the probability distribution. A 60% or higher chance of continuance of good or bad times may result in an overstatement of the potential for extreme profits or losses.

It might be advisable to filter out these grossly unlikely results before analyzing the risk profile. Filtering out undesirable results may seem a bit dishonest (I don't like this result, so let's get rid of it). But a 20-year streak of bad times is going to bankrupt not the borrower but every borrower in the bank's loan portfolio. More-

Figure 3.1
Extended Periods of the Same Business Condition

	Q	R	S	T	U	V
3	15	16	17	18	19	20
4						
5	1	0	0	0	0	0

over, the longest period of bad times, the Great Depression, lasted for about a decade. Perhaps under these circumstances it may be appropriate to filter out truly extreme outcomes.

MODELING REVENUE

Price and volume assessments for the good and bad times of a business cycle should be the result of collaboration between the lender and borrower. Collaboration is necessary because price and volume figures provided by the borrower tend to be optimistic. This optimism is not intended to mislead the lender. Businesspeople have a penchant for being optimists; otherwise they would not be businesspeople (has any investor ever bought a share of stock thinking that the price would go down?). For this collaboration to be successful, the lender should be familiar with the industry. Familiarization can be gained by making loans in the same industry. Experience in lending to the industry is indispensable when reviewing a loan application. Lending officers who specialize in an industry are in a better position to evaluate risks than those who lack such experience.

Suppose that the lender and borrower have agreed to the assessments on price and volume in Table 3.1. These values were developed from historical data, adjusted to current dollars, incorporating a fair assessment of the outlook for the industry. There is an overlap between the worst of the good times and the best of the bad times, reflecting the difficulty in differentiating between two. Moreover, the maximum and minimum points may not have been actually experienced. They represent the feeling that price and volume will most probably (never say "never" in the realm of risk) not be above the high or below the low estimates.

Table 3.1
Price and Volume Assessments

Business Conditions	Minimum	Most Likely	Maximum
Good Times			
Price	$65	$70	$90
Volume (000)	900	1,000	1,200
Bad Times			
Price	$55	$60	$70
Volume (000)	500	800	1,000

It is possible to eliminate the business cycle and have a spread in price and volume that incorporates both good and bad times. This simplifies model building. As described in Appendix 3.A, the resulting revenue probability distribution was bimodal in nature, and the best-fitting probability distribution was not a good substitute. In this case it is better to have good and bad times and associated price and volume figures explicitly set forth in the spreadsheet rather than integrating these into a single probability distribution for revenue.

Price and volume have to be correlated. If not correlated, it is possible to have the highest price matched with the lowest volume and the lowest price matched with the highest volume. Experience suggests otherwise. When times are good, high prices and high volume tend to go together, as do low prices and low volume when times are bad. Figure 3.2 shows no correlation between price and volume. This means for any price, volume can be on the low or high side.

When price and volume are correlated, there is a tendency for high prices to be matched with high volume, and vice versa, as in Figure 3.3.

Appendix 3.A provides details for the formulation of price, volume, and revenue generation.

MOVING ON

Suppose that the lender and borrower agreed to the variable and fixed costs in Table 3.2. Higher unit costs during good times are a consequence of labor overtime to support a greater sales volume and more aggressive pricing by suppliers. Moreover, management becomes a little lax in controlling costs when the money is rolling in. During the bad times, management feels the pinch of falling revenues. Management becomes more diligent in controlling labor costs and more aggressive in negotiating price concessions from suppliers whose factories are also crying for work.

Fixed or G&A costs are also affected by the general business climate. Again management becomes a little lax during the good times in monitoring fixed costs. Moreover, there may be a need to hire extra accountants and marketing personnel to handle the higher volume of sales. Research and product development tends to be funded more generously when business is robust, as are executive bonuses. During the bad times, costs come under closer scrutiny.

The capital cost of the project is $150 million with a 70% chance that a cost overrun will occur with a minimum of 0%, most likely of 10%, and a maximum of 30%. The expected cost overrun as seen in Appendix 3.B is $20 million. The loan request for $140 million has no provision for cost overruns, which are to be funded by the equity owner. The equity owner, as a prospective borrower, estimates that $2 million will be necessary for initial working capital requirements. The total capital cost of the project including working capital and an anticipated cost overrun is $172 million, of which $140 million is the requested amount for the loan, leaving the remaining $32 million to be funded by the borrower. If there is no cost overrun, the equity will be only $12 million.

Figure 3.2
Price and Volume as Independent Variables

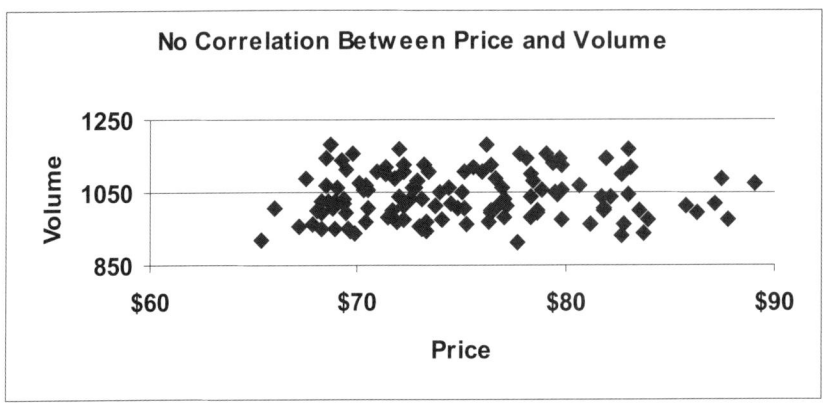

Figure 3.3
Price and Volume as Dependent Variables

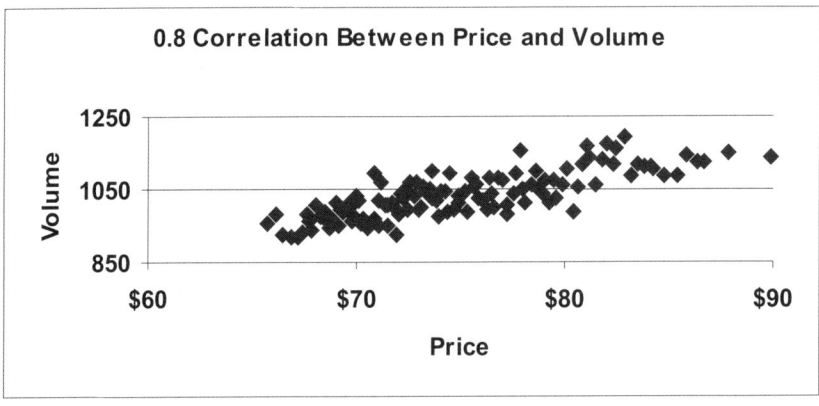

Table 3.2
Fixed and Variable Cost Assessments

Business Conditions	Minimum	Most Likely	Maximum
Good Times			
Variable Cost	$29	$31	$33
Fixed Cost $(000)	$10,000	$11,000	$12,000
Bad Times			
Variable Cost	$28	$30	$32
Fixed Cost ($000)	$9,000	$10,000	$11,000

Depreciation is a 20-year write-off of the capital cost plus any cost overrun with no residual value. Interest varies between 8% and 12% with a most likely rate of 10% during the good times of the business cycle and between 6% and 10% with a most likely rate of 8% during the bad. Debt repayment is over 15 years with equal semiannual repayments. Before-tax earnings are gross profit less G&A, depreciation, and interest. Details concerning the formulation of these cost factors are in Appendix 3.B.

The tax rate is 35%. The spreadsheet is set up to carry tax losses forward to shield future income. Table 3.3 illustrates tax payables and tax loss carryforwards.

In year 2 (column D) there is a before-tax profit of $10,946 of which 35% or $3,831 is paid in taxes, leaving an after-tax profit of $7,115. In year 3 there is a loss of $6,816, no taxes are due, and this becomes a tax loss carryforward. After-tax profits are also a loss of $6,816. Year 4 has another loss of $2,931, which when added to the previous tax loss carryforward of $6,816 becomes a new tax loss carryforward of $9,748. Year 5 has a profit of $9,401, which is completely shielded from taxes, reducing the tax loss carryforward to $347, resulting in after-tax profits of $9,401. Year 5 has a before-tax loss of $2,571, which increases the tax loss carryforward to $2,918. Year 6 has a before-tax profit of $8,745, which is partly offset by the tax loss of $2,918. The remaining before-tax profit of $5,827 is taxed at 35% for a tax payable of $2,039, leaving an after-tax profit of $6,705.

After-tax earnings are before-tax earnings net of taxes, and the all-important cash flow is after-tax earnings plus depreciation less amortization of debt. The formulation of these is in Appendix 3.B.

MEASURING FINANCIAL RETURNS

Having arrived at the annual cash flow, the financial performance of the project can be measured by net present value (NPV) and the internal rate of return (IRR). NPV requires a discount rate, which is related to a company's cost of capital. Suppose that the capital structure of a company is 60% equity and 40% debt, and its long-term average interest rate on debt is 10%. The minimum return on equity is something that management must decide, bearing in mind one observation: the return on equity must be higher than the return on debt. Equity holders have a

Table 3.3
Taxes

	D	E	F	G	H	I
61	$ 10,946	$ (6,816)	$ (2,931)	$ 9,401	$ (2,571)	$ 8,745
62						
63	$ 10,946	$ (6,816)	$ (9,748)	$ (347)	$ (2,918)	$ 5,827
64	$ 3,831	$ -	$ -	$ -	$ -	$ 2,039
65						
66	$ 7,115	$ (6,816)	$ (2,931)	$ 9,401	$ (2,571)	$ 6,705

riskier position, as seen in bankruptcy proceedings where bondholders have a first claim on all assets. Once the bondholders are satisfied, equity holders get what's left, which may be little or nothing. A higher rate of return is warranted for equity to compensate for its greater risk of loss.

If management decides that the appropriate rate of return for equity holders is 15%, then the resulting cost of capital is 60% equity multiplied by a 15% return (9%) plus 40% debt multiplied by a 10% return (4%) for a weighted average of 13%. This does not include the risk of making a bad investment. To compensate for this, a company's hurdle rate, or minimum rate to make a new investment, should be higher, such as 14%.

The three-year cash flow streams in Table 3.4 are for an initial investment outflow of $10. The cash flow for the second year is the same for each, but the third year's cash flow is different. The discount factor for calculating the NPV is 14%.

Table 3.5 shows the middle column of Table 3.4 with a first year's outflow of $10 followed by an inflow of $5 and $7.30. The cash flow stream is discounted by 14%, and the net present value is the sum of the discounted values. The discounting method presumes that the investment is made at the end of the first year.

The internal rate of return (IRR) is the discount rate that reduces the NPV of a cash flow stream to zero. In Table 3.5, the net present value of the discounted cash flow stream is zero for a discount rate of 14%; hence, by definition, the IRR is 14%.

The left-hand column on the Table 3.4 has a NPV of $1.83, which means that the return on the investment stream is higher than 14% and should, in strict financial returns, be approved. The corresponding IRR of 28% indicates not only that the return is above the company's hurdle rate of 14% but how much higher. It may be difficult to rank dissimilar projects by profitability with NPV, but not with IRR.

Table 3.4
Illustrating NPV and IRR

Year 1	($10.00)	($10.00)	($10.00)	($10.00)	($10.00)
Year 2	$5.00	$5.00	$5.00	$5.00	$5.00
Year 3	$10.00	$8.00	$7.30	$7.00	$3.00
NPV	$1.83	$0.48	$0.00	$(0.20)	$(2.90)
IRR	28%	18%	14%	12%	-15%

Table 3.5
Calculating the NPV

	Cash Flow	Time Value of Money	Discount Factor	Discounted Cash Flow
Year 1	$(10.00)	1/1.14^1 =	0.87719	$(8.77)
Year 2	$5.00	1/1.14^2 =	0.76947	$3.85
Year 3	$7.30	1/1.14^3 =	0.67497	$4.93
Net Present Value or total of the discounted cash flows (rounded)				$0.00

The two right-hand columns of Table 3.4 have a negative NPV. This means that the investment earns less than the hurdle rate and should not be approved. The positive IRR indicates that the project has returned its initial investment in the form of subsequent cash flows, but not at the desired rate of return of 14%. The negative IRR indicates that the project isn't even generating enough cash to pay back the initial investment.

In the author's opinion, IRR is a more descriptive means of evaluating investment results because the return can be directly related to the company's hurdle rate and different projects can be more easily compared by ranking in order of profitability. This is not true for NPV. A positive NPV means that the company's hurdle rate has been satisfied, and that's all. It may be difficult to select which of a dissimilar set of investments should be made based on NPV, but no such problem exists when investment returns are measured with IRR.

Relying on IRR to evaluate an investment cash flow stream is not always possible. There may be no discount rate that reduces the cash flow stream to zero. An IRR requires an initial negative cash flow in the form of an investment outflow followed by positive cash flows in subsequent years from operations in order for a discount rate to reduce the NPV to zero. It may not be possible to calculate an IRR for very low (negative) values of NPV. The @Risk simulation results overstate the IRR, as those iterations for which no IRR can be calculated are excluded in the statistical results. Moreover, it is possible for a project to have two different IRRs. This may occur if there are large negative cash flows sometime in the future. (Future negative cash flows such as decommissioning expenses of a nuclear power plant should be handled by setting up a sinking fund to meet these expenses rather than leaving them in the cash flow stream.) The NPV does not have these drawbacks; it generates a single value for any cash flow stream. Caution has to be exercised when relying on IRR as a measure of profitability.

One final word of warning: the NPVs and IRRs are being measured on the cash flow stream of the project that includes debt. As such, they are measuring the return on equity, not the return on capital. The economic NPV and IRR of a project should be evaluated without debt in order to fairly compare one project with another.

WORKING CAPITAL AND THE SOLVENCY LOAN

The net cash flow becomes part of working capital and replenishes working capital if it is below the required minimum. Working capital in excess of the minimum working capital requirement is the actual cash under control of the equity owner. It can be maintained in the company as cash or be used to fund further capital expenditures or retire debt faster than scheduled or be passed on to the equity owner in the form of a dividend. The spreadsheet is set up for all excess cash above the minimum working capital to be passed on to the equity owner as a dividend. This models the fact that the lender has no legal recourse to force the borrower to keep funds in the company in excess of the minimum working capital requirement. From the viewpoint of evaluating risk, it is better to siphon off all excess funds, which the borrower has the legal right to do.

The passing of excess funds to the equity owner in the form of a dividend provides a better measure of the NPV and IRR than the conventional measure of basing NPV and IRR on the cash flow. Calculating NPV and IRR on a company's cash flow that may have negative values at times in the future is dubious at best. However, discounting future dividends that can be paid only when funds are in excess of minimum working capital requirements eliminates negative cash flows in the calculation of NPV and IRR.

Figure 3.4 shows the disposition of the company's cash flow (row 68). Cell B68 is the equity outflow for calculating the NPV and IRR of the cash flow stream in cells B69 and B70. Rows 73 and 74 keep track of the amount and the number of occurrences of negative cash flows, respectively, during the period when debt is still outstanding. The maximum negative cash flow is in cell B73, and the total count in cell B74.

Row 77 permits step-downs of the minimum working capital requirement in row 78 as the loan is paid off (here it is kept at 100% throughout the project life). In year 1 (column C), the starting working capital is $2,000, and the cash flow in row 68 is $12,312. The balance at the end of the year is $14,312, of which $12,312 is siphoned off as a dividend to have a year-end balance of $2,000 in the working capital account. This becomes the starting balance for year 2, where the positive cash flow of $6,581 is also paid out as a dividend.

Troubles abound in year 3. The cash flow is a negative $8,424. The working capital account of $2,000 is wiped out, leaving a deficit of $6,424. Nothing is paid out as

Figure 3.4
Working Capital

	A	B	C	D	E	F	G
68	Cash Flow	$ (42,958)	$ 12,312	$ 6,581	$ (8,424)	$ 18,198	$ 7,663
69	Cash Flow NPV at 14%	$13,796					
70	Cash Flow IRR	18.8%					
71							
72	Negative Cash Flow						
73	Maximum Amount	$ 8,424	$ -	$ -	$ 8,424	$ -	$ -
74	Count	2	0	0	1	0	0
75							
76	Working Capital Account						
77	Allowable Step-Downs		100%	100%	100%	100%	100%
78	Minimum Required	$ 2,000	$ 2,000	$ 2,000	$ 2,000	$ 2,000	$ 2,000
79	(Before Paying Dividends)						
80							
81	Starting Working Capital		$ 2,000	$ 2,000	$ 2,000	$ (6,424)	$ 2,000
82	W.C. Plus Cash Flow		$ 14,312	$ 8,581	$ (6,424)	$ 11,774	$ 9,663
83	Equity/Dividend Flow	$ (42,958)	$ 12,312	$ 6,581	$ -	$ 9,774	$ 7,663
84	Ending Working Capital		$ 2,000	$ 2,000	$ (6,424)	$ 2,000	$ 2,000
85							
86	Dividend NPV at 14%	$14,551					
87	Dividend IRR	19.2%					

a dividend, and the ending balance in the working capital account is a negative $6,424. Luckily, there is a positive cash flow of $18,198 in year 4. The deficit of $6,424 is covered, leaving an end of year balance of $11,744, of which $9,744 is paid out as a dividend, leaving $2,000 in the working capital account. Year 5's positive cash flow of $7,663 is passed on to the equity owner as a dividend. The NPV and IRR on the dividend flow in cells B86 and B87 are superior to those in cells B69 and B70, which measure the return on the cash flow that may contain negative values. The NPV and IRR for dividend cash flow contain no negative cash flows other than the initial investment.

What funded the deficit of $6,424 in year 3? The firm is technically insolvent because it cannot pay its obligations. If there is no other source of funds, the firm may no longer be in business. Another source of funding is seen in Figure 3.5, where the working capital account is supplemented by drawing down on an infinite line of credit called the solvency loan.

Row 92 keeps track of negative balances in the working capital account. A negative working capital balance has to be funded or the company is insolvent, which can lead to its bankruptcy if the lender so desires. Cells B92 and B93 keep track of the maximum drawdown of the solvency loan and the number of occurrences that a drawdown is necessary. The solvency loan balance reflects the accumulation of working capital deficits from a succession of negative cash flows. Row 89 accrues interest income for positive balances in working capital, and row 94 accrues an interest expense on outstanding balances of the solvency loan.

FINANCIAL RATIOS

Financial ratios are used to judge creditworthiness of companies. Ratios remove the size of a company as a consideration. For instance, gross margin is a financial ratio of gross profit divided by revenue. A gross margin of 40% has the same meaning whether a company's revenue is $1 million or $1 billion. Both are placed on the same scale for evaluating creditworthiness. Table 3.6 contains the indicated financial measures incorporated in the project financing spreadsheet. These ratios are not uniformly defined among financial institutions. Some financial institutions have uniquely defined ratios for in-house analysis.

Figure 3.5
Solvency Loan

	A	B	C	D	E	F	G
89	Int Income on Positive W.C.		$ 142	$ 125	$ -	$ -	$ 132
90							
91	Solvency Loan						
92	Maximum Amount	$ 6,424	$ -	$ -	$ 6,424	$ -	$ -
93	Count	2	0	0	1	0	0
94	Solvency Loan Interest		$ -	$ -	$ 501	$ -	$ -

Table 3.6
Financial Ratios

Financial Ratio	Definition
Gross margin	Gross profit divided by revenue
EBIT (earnings before interest and taxes)	Gross profit net of G&A and depreciation divided by interest
Return on investment	Dividend flow divided by initial investment
Return on assets	Dividend flow divided by initial investment less accumulated depreciation

THE PRESENTATION

The prospective borrower would present the forecast of the cash flow on an expected value basis. The business cycle would presume to remain robust. This, by the way, is the time loans are booked. A company must arrange for financing when the lender hears nothing bad about the industry or the company. Walking into a bank when times are bad would more than likely end up as a waste of time for both the lender and borrower. Yet in a way this is the time loans should be booked. If a loan can sustain itself in the bad times, it certainly should sustain itself in the good. The problem is that loans are booked in the good times when inherent risks are masked by higher than normal sales and profits.

Figure 3.6 would be the first part of a spreadsheet presentation to the lender. Naturally, there would be no reference to the good and bad times of the business cycle.

The figures are comforting and unchanging, both rash assumptions. Figure 3.7 shows the desire of borrowers to have lenders fund projects to the maximum possible extent. This is in line with modern financial thinking that debt is a cheap form of financing compared to equity. Equity not only must have a higher return than debt, but the return on equity is based on after-tax dollars. Debt has a lower return than equity, with its return (interest) being tax-deductible. The more debt stuffed into a capital structure of a company, the cheaper the cost of capital. While individual businesspeople may be quite conservative, there are a sufficient number of exceptions such that businesspeople, taken collectively, are aggressive in building empires. The only damper on empire building is the periodic bad times brought on invariably from excessive expansion of productive capacity caused in part by the ease of obtaining debt. Then debt takes on a less attractive role of causing the liquidation of those who relied too much on debt and not enough on equity. One wonders if the attraction to debt exhibits the "intelligent design" of the Devil.

The allowance for a cost overrun, if any were shown, would probably be smaller than that in Figure 3.7. Taxes are paid because before-tax profits are positive. There are no tax loss carryforwards. The cash flow is healthy with an internal rate of return of 29.3% on the rather small equity base. Reducing debt to zero in cell B41

Figure 3.6
The Prospective Borrower's Presentation

	A	B	C	D	E
1	Project Financing				
2					
3	Year		1	2	3
4					
5	Good or Bad Times		1	1	1
6					
7	Good Times				
8	G-Price		$ 75.00	$ 75.00	$ 75.00
9	G-Volume		1,033	1,033	1,033
10					
11	Bad Times				
12	B-Price		$ 61.67	$ 61.67	$ 61.67
13	B-Volume		767	767	767
14					
15	Revenue		$ 77,500	$ 77,500	$ 77,500
16					
17	Cost of Goods Sold				
18	Good Times		$ 31.00	$ 31.00	$ 31.00
19	Bad Times		$ 30.00	$ 30.00	$ 30.00
20	Cost of Goods Sold		$ 32,033	$ 32,033	$ 32,033
21					
22	Gross Profit		$ 45,467	$ 45,467	$ 45,467
23					
24	General & Administrative (G&A)				
25	Good Times		$ 11,000	$ 11,000	$ 11,000
26	Bad Times		$ 10,000	$ 10,000	$ 10,000
27	General & Administrative (G&A)		$ 11,000	$ 11,000	$ 11,000
28					
29	Depreciation Period	20			
30	Residual Value	0			
31	Depreciation		$ 8,500	$ 8,500	$ 8,500
32					
33	Earnings Before				
34	Interest and Taxes (EBIT)		$ 25,967	$ 25,967	$ 25,967

yields an economic IRR of 13.7%. This is the return on the total project investment of $172 million ($150 million for the factory, $20 million for the cost overrun, and $2 million for initial working capital) that should be used by management in weighing the financial merits of this project with others. The higher return on a leveraged basis may mislead management as to the project's real profitability. As will be seen, the lower return on a nonleveraged basis is not all that attractive when the risks of low prices and poor sales volume are taken into consideration.

Figure 3.7
Continuation of the Prospective Borrower's Presentation

	A	B	C	D	E
36	Capital Cost	$ 150,000			
37	Overrun	$ 20,000			
38	Initial Working Capital	$ 2,000			
39	Equity	$ 32,000			
40					
41	Requested Debt	$ 140,000			
42					
43	Debt Repayment				
44	Years to Repay	15			
45	Annual Debt Payment		$ 9,333	$ 9,333	$ 9,333
46	Amount Debt Remaining	$ 140,000	$ 130,667	$ 121,333	$ 112,000
47					
48	Interest Rate				
49	Good Times		10%	10%	10%
50	Bad Times		8%	8%	8%
51					
52	Interest Expense				
53	Requested Loan		$ 13,533	$ 12,600	$ 11,667
54	Solvency Loan			$ -	$ -
55					
56	Interest Income				
57	Working Capital			$ 140	$ 140
58					
59	Total Interest Expense		$ 13,533	$ 12,460	$ 11,527
60					
61	Earnings Before Tax (EBT)		$ 12,433	$ 13,507	$ 14,440
62					
63	Tax Basis		$ 12,433	$ 13,507	$ 14,440
64	Tax Payable	35%	$ 4,352	$ 4,727	$ 5,054
65					
66	Earnings After Tax (EAT)		$ 8,082	$ 8,779	$ 9,386
67					
68	Cash Flow	$ (32,000)	$ 7,248	$ 7,946	$ 8,553
69	Cash Flow NPV at 14%	$37,508			
70	Cash Flow IRR	29.3%			

However, financial return is but one consideration that a company uses in evaluating new business prospects. The strategic objectives of the firm have to be included. It is not unusual for a company to accept a lower financial return of a particular project in relation to others in order to better position itself for the future. Management may not always take the short and easy route to maximizing near-term profits but prefer to take the longer and more arduous route of developing a niche market or dominating an industry as the primary driving force in its investment decisions.

Figure 3.8
The Portion of the Prospective Borrower's Presentation Never Shown

	A	B	C	D	E
72	Negative Cash Flow				
73	Maximum Amount	$ -	$ -	$ -	$ -
74	Count	0	0	0	0
75					
76	Working Capital Account				
77	Allowable Step-Downs		100%	100%	100%
78	Minimum Required	$ 2,000	$ 2,000	$ 2,000	$ 2,000
79	(Before Paying Dividends)				
80					
81	Starting Working Capital		$ 2,000	$ 2,000	$ 2,000
82	W.C. Plus Cash Flow		$ 9,248	$ 9,946	$ 10,553
83	Equity/Dividend Flow	$ (32,000)	$ 7,248	$ 7,946	$ 8,553
84	Ending Working Capital		$ 2,000	$ 2,000	$ 2,000
85					
86	Dividend NPV at 14%	$37,508			
87	Dividend IRR	29.3%			
88					
89	Int Income on Positive W.C.		$ 140	$ 140	$ 140
90					
91	Solvency Loan				
92	Maximum Amount	$ -	$ -	$ -	$ -
93	Count	0	0	0	0
94	Solvency Loan Interest		$ -	$ -	$ -
95					
96	Financial Analysis				
97	Gross Margin		59%	59%	59%
98	Interest Coverage		1.9	2.1	2.3
99	Accumulated Depreciation		$ 8,500	$ 17,000	$ 25,500
100	Return on Investment		4.2%	4.6%	5.0%
101	Return on Assets		4.4%	5.1%	5.8%

Company presentations stop at the annual cash flow. Figure 3.8 is the portion of the borrower's presentation that is never seen. The presentation has no negative cash flows other than the initial funding of the projects, no negative working capital balances, and certainly no need for a line of credit to keep the company solvent.

Figure 3.8 shows a hint of potential trouble in the financial ratios. The interest coverage, or EBIT divided by interest, with a value of 2 is a bit anemic. This does not provide much comfort for the lender if revenue does not materialize as anticipated. The low return on investment and assets is also of concern, but the cause of the low return is the relatively large amount of cash flow dedicated to servicing debt. On a nonleveraged basis where cash flow is not encumbered by debt servicing costs, the first year return on investment and assets are both near a more comfortable 15%. This is an indication of the drag of debt service on cash flow at the requested level of debt.

MEASURING RISK

The following outcomes have been selected with the *Select Output* icon for analysis using @Risk simulation.

Cell B87: Dividend IRR

Cell Q92: State of the solvency loan at the presumed end of the bank loan

Cell B91: Maximum balance of solvency loan

Cell B92: Number of years with an outstanding balance in the solvency loan

Cells C98-G98: Interest coverage for first five years

The result of a simulation of 10,000 iterations is shown in Table 3.7. The chance of the dividend IRR being below 0% was about 4% with a few occasions when IRRs were not calculated because of having even lower values than −33% (0.8% of all iterations). Thus, the IRR is slightly overstated. The high of 195% results from about 20 consecutive years of good times. These extreme, nearly 20-year runs of good and bad times may provide sufficient justification for filtering since good or bad times of this duration have not yet occurred in the economic history of the world.

The dividend IRR would not be of any particular interest to the bankers other than realizing that low values probably mean problems in funding debt. Management should not rely on this IRR, as it is a function of the amount of debt in the capital structure. Having said that, return on equity is sometimes used by management in preference to the economic NPV and IRR that is figured on the basis of no debt in the capital structure.

The average of the maximum balance of the solvency loan was $8.5 million, and the average number of years of an outstanding balance for the solvency loan was 3. The solvency loan had to be drawn down in 70% of the iterations. This means that there is a 70% chance that the solvency loan must be used at some point in the 15-year debt repayment period. There is a 5% chance of an outstanding balance for the solvency loan at the end of the debt repayment period with an average balance

Table 3.7
Simulation Results

	Dividend IRR	Maximum Solvency Loan (MM)	Solvency Loan at End 15th Year (MM)	Years Outstanding Balances on Solvency Loan
Minimum	-33%	0	0	0
Mean	31%	$8.5	$1.6	3
Maximum	195%	$281	$206	20

of $1.6 million. The maximum amount of the solvency loan is associated with 20 consecutive years of bad times, which, along with other excessively long streaks of bad times, should be filtered out.

With regard to interest coverage, suppose that a minimum value of 2 is preferred by a lending institution. The chances of interest coverage being below 2 are 55% in the first year, 65% in the second and third years, 60% in the fourth, and 50% in the fifth. The reason that the interest coverage is better in the first year is that business conditions are assumed to be robust when the loan is booked. Interest coverage improves as interest payments decrease with the repayment of loan principal.

It is clear that $140 million, although seemingly satisfactory using expected values, represents too great of a risk for the lender in the form of drawdowns on the solvency loan. This can also be seen in single iterations in the *Monte Carlo* mode. Individual outcomes without running a formal simulation can provide useful insights. Running the simulation provides the detailed statistical support seen in Table 3.7 along with a visual presentation in the form of charts.

Besides the loan request being too large, another aspect that is clear from running single iterations is that working capital is insufficient. It is not unusual for a lender to ask for a minimum working capital requirement equal to six months' or one year's debt servicing charges. This provides a cash buffer for times when revenue does not fully support the timely payment of interest and debt amortization. Once working capital has been drawn down, the borrower must retain future profits in the company until working capital has been restored to its minimum level.

MANAGING RISK

A simulation was run with debt reduced to $120,000 and the minimum working capital requirement expanded to $20 million. This increases owners' equity to $70 million to complete the financing of the $150 million project assuming a $20 million capital cost overrun and $20 million in working capital. The equity is $50 million if there is no cost overrun. The results of the simulation were a marked improvement from the perspective of the lender. The average maximum balance of the solvency loan declined from $8.5 million to $0.3 million, the solvency loan had a balance of zero in the 15th year more than 99% of the time, and the average number of years when the solvency loan was used dropped from 3.2 years to 0.1 years. The probability of interest coverage falling below 2 was reduced to 40% in the first year, 50% in the second, 45% in the third, 40% in the fourth, and 35% in the fifth. However, the IRR on equity fell for the borrower as a greater amount of equity is required to fund the project; but this is hardly of concern to the lender. Figure 3.9 shows the maximum amount drawn down on the solvency loan as per the borrower's request for $140 million loan with $2 million in working capital.

The indicated mean of $6.9 million is less than the $8.5 million in Table 3.9 because maximum solvency loan balances above $50 million have been filtered out on the basis that 15–20 consecutive years of bad times, while theoretically possible, might introduce an element of distortion in the analysis. Obviously, the use of fil-

Figure 3.9
Original Risk Profile of Maximum Drawdown of Solvency Loan

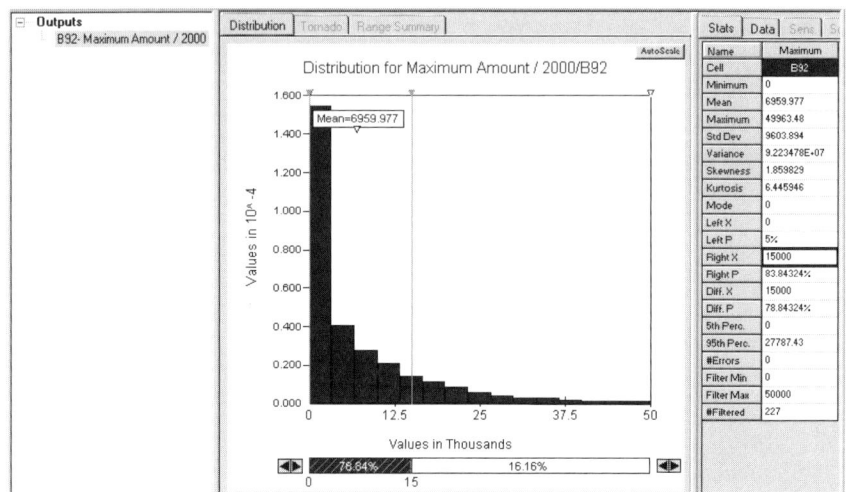

ters is discretionary and should be employed with caution. A line of credit of $15 million accompanying the loan would be sufficient to maintain solvency 83% of the time. However, there is a 17% chance that the maximum balance in the solvency loan will be above $15 million.

Figure 3.10 shows the maximum solvency loan balance for the counteroffer of financing $120 million of the project with a $20 million minimum working capital requirement. The average maximum balance in the solvency loan has been reduced to $0.3 million with virtually no chance of the balance being over $15 million.

These examples should make it clear that the lender has the tools to judge the risk profile for the requested amount of the loan. The lender is also in a position to respond on the basis of creating an acceptable risk profile by changing the amount of the loan and the minimum working capital requirement. This opens up a dialogue between the borrower and the lender that hopefully can lead to a mutually agreeable loan structure whereby the borrower receives the maximum support from the lender consistent with the lender sleeping well at night.

ECONOMIC NPV

Figure 3.11 shows the economic NPV with no debt. There is a substantial 83% chance that the project will not have a positive NPV at a discount rate of 14%, which means that the internal rate of return will also have a 83% chance of being less than 14%.

Rather than arguing with the bankers about the role of debt in financing this project, maybe the borrower ought to take a second look at the project itself.

Figure 3.10
Revised Risk Profile of Maximum Drawdown of Solvency Loan

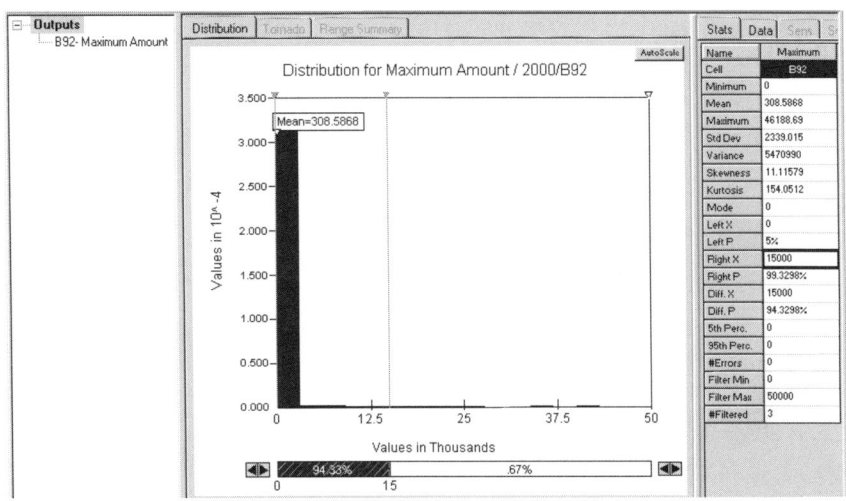

Figure 3.11
Economic NPV

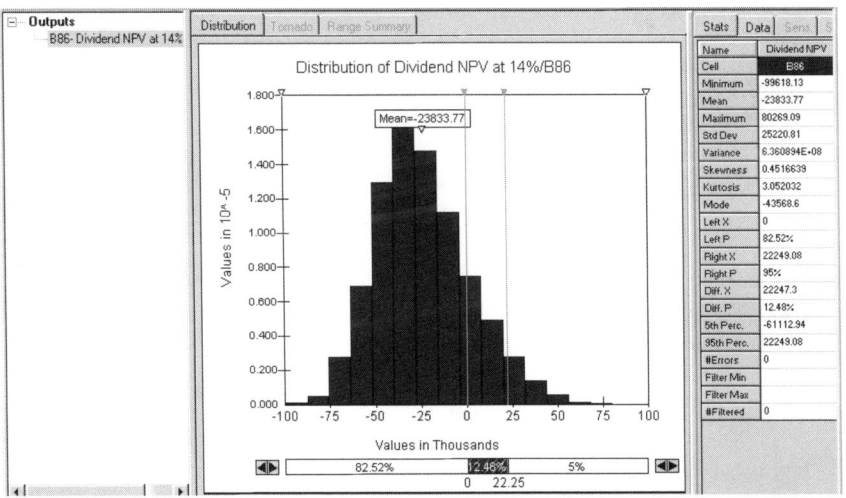

APPENDIX 3.A
PRICE, VOLUME, AND REVENUE GENERATION

DETERMINING GOOD AND BAD TIMES

Figure 3.A.1 shows the portion of the spreadsheet dedicated to establishing business conditions, price, and volume under either good or bad times, and revenue generation.

Figure 3.A.1
Revenue Generation

	A	B	C
1	Project Financing		
2			
3	Year		1
4			
5	Good or Bad Times		1
6			
7	Good Times		
8	G-Price		=RiskTriang(65, 70, 90,RiskCorrmat(GTimes,1))
9	G-Volume		=RiskTriang(900, 1000, 1200,RiskCorrmat(GTimes,2))
10			
11	Bad Times		
12	B-Price		=RiskTriang(55, 60, 70,RiskCorrmat(BTimes,1))
13	B-Volume		=RiskTriang(500, 800, 1000,RiskCorrmat(BTimes,2))
14			
15	Revenue		=IF(C5=1,C8*C9,C12*C13)

Row 3 contains the years, and row 5 the business conditions. It is assumed that the loan is booked while business is robust (when else will a bank finance a new factory?). The value of cell C5 is set at 1. Succeeding cells in row 5 could contain the formula where bad and good times are a flip of the coin:

$$=RiskDiscrete(\{1,0\},\{0.5,0.5\})$$

This @Risk discrete probability function generates a 1 for good times or a 0 for bad times on a 50-50 basis equivalent to the Excel formula:

$$=IF(RAND()<.5,1,0).$$

The actual formula used to generate business conditions is:

$$=IF(OR(C5+RiskDiscrete(\{1,0\},\{0.6,0.4\})=2,C5+RiskDiscrete(\{0,1\},\{0.6,0.4\})=0),1,0)$$

The only way for this function to create a year of good times is to generate a value of 2 in the first part of the formula. Since cell C5 is already equal to 1, there is a 60%

chance that the discrete probability function will generate a value of 1, which, when added to cell C5, generates another year of good times. Moreover with a value of 1 for cell C5, the second part of the formula cannot have a zero. If the value of the first part of the formula is not 2 and the second part is not 0, then the good times turn to bad.

Suppose that C5 has a value of zero for bad times. There is no way for the first part of the formula to generate a value of 2. For another year of bad times, the second part of the expression must generate a value of zero, and there is a 60% chance that it will do so. If the expression does not have a value of zero, then the bad times turn to good. The formula permits different probabilities for the continuance of good and bad times. However, setting the values too high will cause 20 years of bad and good times, which is not a realistic modeling of reality. A better model might be a provision to not simulate any year where there are, say, 7 or more consecutive years of good and bad times. As attractive as this sounds, the formulation in a spreadsheet environment is very difficult.

CORRELATING PRICE AND VOLUME

The good and bad times price and volume formulas in Figure 3.A.1 look formidable, but they started out simple. The formula in cell C8 was initially =RiskTriang(65,70,90) which could have been entered directly or by use of the *Define Distribution* function. Correlation is accomplished by first selecting *Display List of Outputs and Inputs* icon to the left of the *Simulation Settings* icon and then selecting the variables in the 8th and 9th rows as shown in Figure 3.A.2.

Not all of the variables are shown to the left, but for the record, cells A8 through V8 and cells A9 through V9 are selected. Then the *Define Correlation* icon is pressed to obtain Figure 3.A.3.

It is important that care be exercised in entering the correlation factors for correct matching such as cell C8 with cell C9, cell D8 with cell D9, and so on to avoid garbage in, garbage out (GIGO). Then *Apply*. This is then repeated with cells associated with the bad times.

There is a shortcut method possible when all the correlations are the same. This can be done by simply correlating cell C8 with cell C9 and then replicating these cells to the right and repeating this operation with cells C12 and C13. If this latter course of action is taken, then Figure 3.A.4 results.

As seen in Figure 3.A.1, revenue in row 15 is generated by multiplying price and volume either for the good times or for the bad times depending on the indicator value in row 3.

A SINGLE PROBABILITY DISTRIBUTION FOR REVENUE

A single probability distribution of revenue incorporating both good and bad times can be obtained by designating one of the revenue cells as output and running a simulation with 10,000 iterations. The minimum value attained in 10,000 it-

Figure 3.A.2
Getting Ready to Correlate Variables

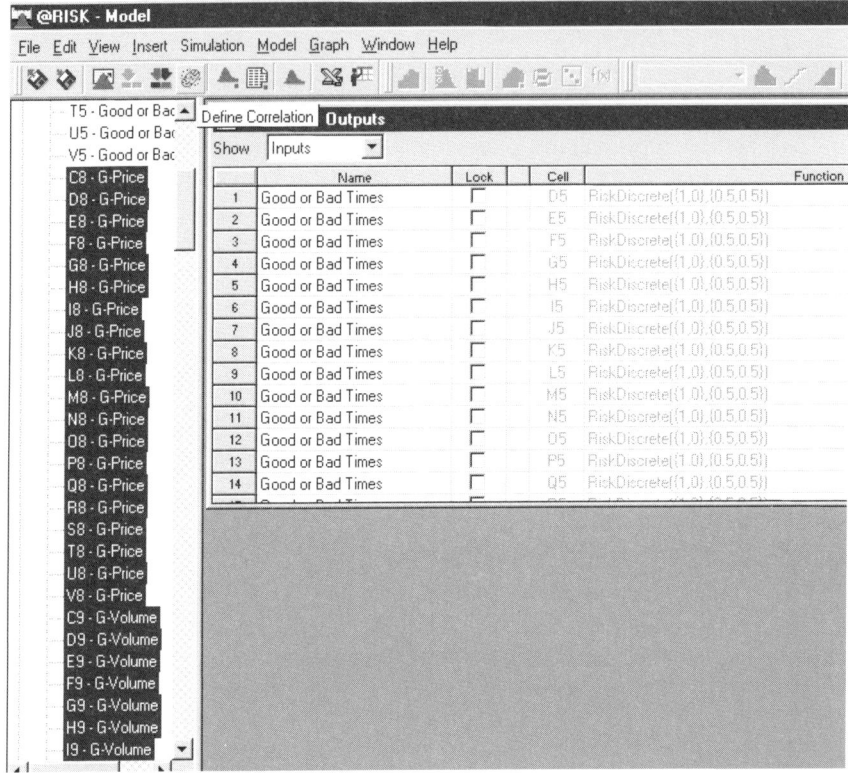

erations was $28,168. The absolute minimum that could possibly be attained is the lowest price ($55) and volume (500) during the bad times or $27,500. It would be an extremely low probability to have two remote possibilities of both the lowest price and the lowest volume occurring simultaneously, although it nearly did happen. The highest price ($90) and volume (1,200) during the good times yield an absolute maximum revenue of $108,000 compared to the actual maximum revenue attained in 10,000 iterations of $106,924, near but not at the absolute maximum. The positive correlation between price and volume is partially responsible for the minimum and maximum values being as close to the absolute limits as they are. Correlation increases the degree of risk in having large losses by matching low prices with low volumes.

The best-fitting probability distribution for modeling revenue is obtained by first selecting *Data Window* and right clicking on *Revenue* to the left of the screen and selecting *Fit* to obtain Figure 3.A.5.

While the indicated BetaGeneral may be the best-fitting distribution, it is masking the underlying bimodal nature of the probability distribution for revenue. The

Figure 3.A.3
Correlation Model

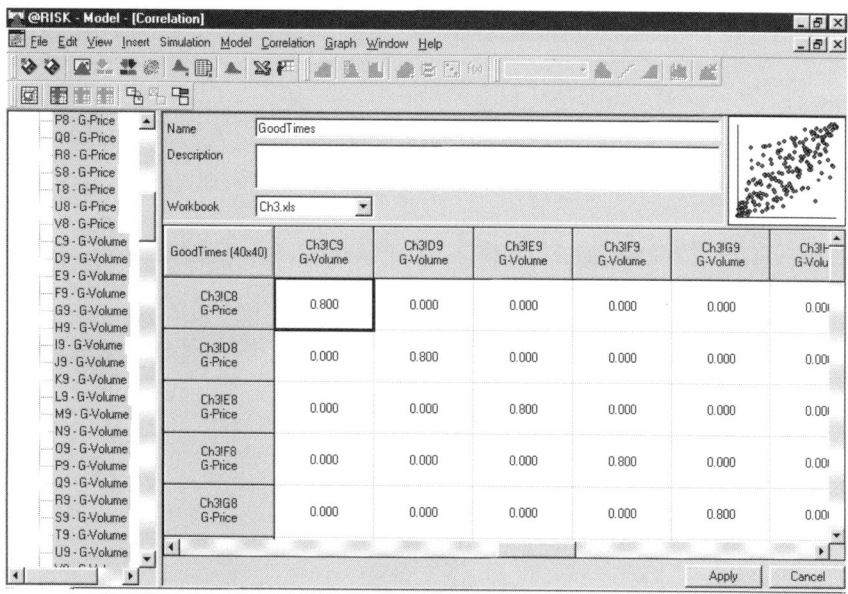

Figure 3.A.4
Correlation Shortcut

BTimes (2x2)	R4Sec2!C12 B-PRICE	R4Sec2!C13 B-VOLUME
R4Sec2!C12 B-PRICE	1	
R4Sec2!C13 B-VOLUME	0.8	1

GTimes (2x2)	R4Sec2!C8 G-PRICE	R4Sec2!C9 G-VOLUME
R4Sec2!C8 G-PRICE	1	
R4Sec2!C9 G-VOLUME	0.8	1

P-P (Probability-Probability) chart in Figure 3.A.6 compares the probabilities for values of the BetaGeneral formula to the probabilities associated with the corresponding values from the simulation.

A good fit results in a nearly linear plot, which is not occurring here because of the bimodal nature of the actual data. Hence, a probability distribution approximating the good and bad times for revenue should not be used.

Figure 3.A.5
Best Fitting Probability Distribution

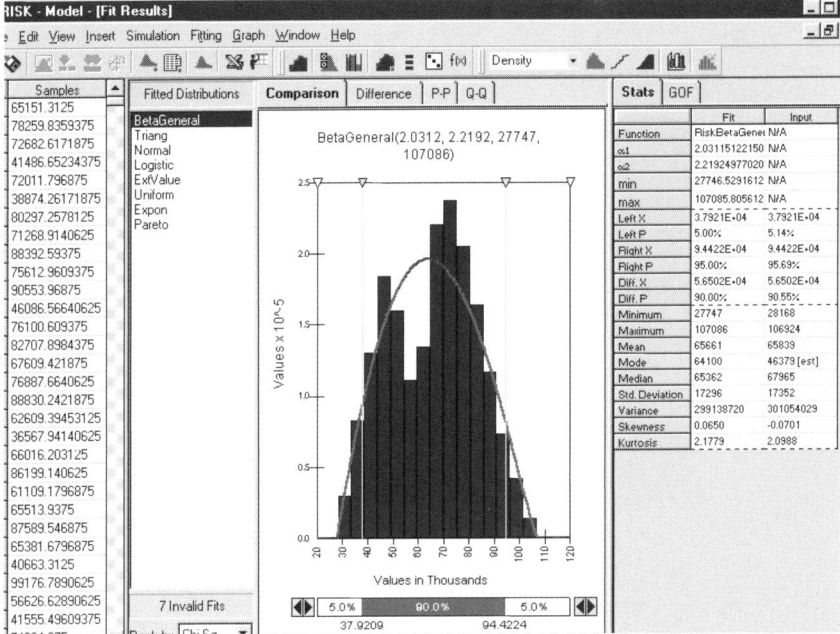

Figure 3.A.6
P-P Chart

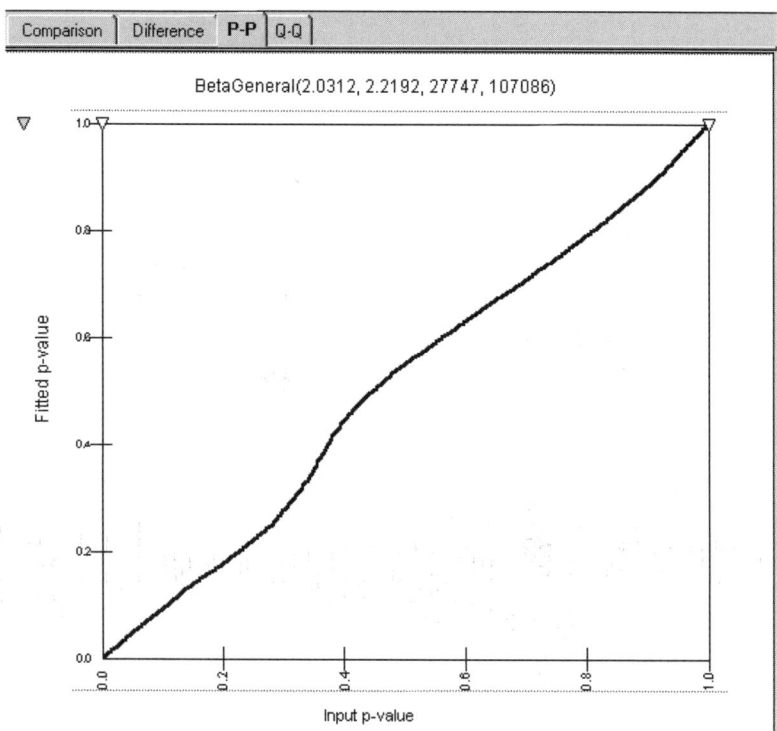

APPENDIX 3.B
FROM REVENUE TO CASH FLOW

Figure 3.B.1 shows the portion of the spreadsheet covering operating costs and depreciation.

Figure 3.B.1
Operating Costs and Depreciation

	A	B	C
17	Cost of Goods Sold		
18	Good Times		=RiskTriang(29,31,33)
19	Bad Times		=RiskTriang(28,30,32)
20	Cost of Goods Sold		=IF(C5=1,C9*C18,C13*C19)
21			
22	Gross Profit		=C15-C20
23			
24	General & Administrative (G&A)		
25	Good Times		=RiskTriang(10000,11000,12000)
26	Bad Times		=RiskTriang(9000,10000,11000)
27	General & Administrative (G&A)		=IF(C5=1,C25,C26)
28			
29	Depreciation Period	20	
30	Residual Value	0	
31	Depreciation		=IF(C3<=$B$29,1,0)*($B$36+$B$37-$B$30)/$B$29
32			
33	Earnings Before		
34	Interest and Taxes (EBIT)		=C22-C27-C31

The triangular probability distributions for variable and fixed costs are contained in rows 18, 19, 25, and 26. Rows 20 and 27 select either the good or bad time values in accordance with business conditions in row 5. Gross profit is revenue less cost of goods sold (variable costs). Depreciation in row 31 is a 20-year write-off of the cost of the project, plus any cost overrun, taking into account any residual value. The first part of the formula in cell C31 assures that depreciation does not extend beyond the depreciation period in cell B29. This would have more meaning if the depreciation period were 15 years rather than 20 years. The capital cost and cost overrun are shown in Figure 3.B.2.

Figure 3.B.2
Capital Cost Structure

	A	B
36	Capital Cost	150000
37	Overrun	=RiskDiscrete({0,1},{0.3,0.7})*RiskTriang(0,0.1,0.3)*B36
38	Initial Working Capital	2000
39	Equity	=B36+B37+B38-B41
40		
41	Requested Debt	140000

MANAGING RISK IN A PROJECT FINANCING 89

The capital cost is in cell B36. The cost overrun has a 70% chance of occurrence, and when it occurs, the degree of the cost overrun is a minimum of 0%, most likely of 10%, and a maximum of 30%. The initial working capital is in cell B38, and the requested debt is in cell B41. The owner's equity is the capital cost of the project including any cost overrun and the initial working capital less borrowed funds.

Figure 3.B.3 shows the formulation for debt repayment and interest. The first part of cell C45 stops amortization payments when the debt is retired, as indicated in cell B44. Row 46 keeps track of the year-end amount of outstanding debt in order to calculate interest payments.

Figure 3.B.3
Debt Repayment and Interest

	A	B	C
43	Debt Repayment		
44	Years to Repay	15	
45	Annual Debt Payment		=IF(C3<=$B$44,1,0)*$B$41/$B$44
46	Amount Debt Remaining	=B41	=IF(B46-C45>0,B46-C45,0)
47			
48	Interest Rate		
49	Good Times		=RiskTriang(0.08,0.1,0.12)
50	Bad Times		=RiskTriang(0.06,0.08,0.1)
51			
52	Interest Expense		
53	Desired Debt		=IF(C5=1,C49*(B46+C46)/2,C50*(B46+C46)/2)
54	Solvency Loan		
55			
56	Interest Income		
57	Working Capital		
58			
59	Total Interest Expense		=C53+C54-C57

Rows 49 and 50 are the interest rates for the good and bad times. Row 53 calculates the interest rate on the average amount of debt outstanding in the present and previous year. This approximates semiannual payments of interest and debt. The interest expense on the solvency loan and the interest income on working capital start in year 2 and will be covered shortly. The final step is the calculation of taxes in Figure 3.B.4 before arriving at the annual cash flow.

Before-tax earnings are in row 61, and the tax rate is in cell B64. Rows 63 and 64 work together to calculate taxes and tax loss carryforwards as shown in Table 3.3. Row 66 is after-tax earnings, and row 68 is the annual cash flow, which is after-tax earnings plus depreciation less debt repayment. Cell B68 is the equity outflow in year 0 for calculating the NPV and IRR.

Figure 3.B.5 shows the formulation of the NPV and IRR in cells B69 and B70 for the cash flow in row 68. Rows 73 and 74 keep track of the amount and the occurrences of negative cash flows while debt is outstanding as signified in the first part of the formulas. A banker is not interested in what happens after the debt is paid

Figure 3.B.4
Taxes and Annual Cash Flow

	A	B	C	D
61	Earnings Before Tax (EBT)		=C34-C59	=D34-D59
62				
63	Tax Basis		=C61	=C63+D61-C64/$B$64
64	Tax Payable	0.35	=MAX(C63*$B$64,0)	=MAX(D63*$B$64,0)
65				
66	Earnings After Tax (EAT)		=C61-C64	=D61-D64
67				
68	Cash Flow	=-B39	=C66+C31-C45	=D66+D31-D45

off. Cells B73 and B74 record the maximum amount of negative cash flow and the number of occurrences of negative cash flow, respectively. Row 77 permits step-downs of minimum working capital as debt is paid off. Minimum working capital provides a cushion of cash when business takes a downturn. It is treated here as equivalent to cash. In this application, minimum working capital remains the same throughout project life. After debt is paid off, the equity owner can liquidate the cash tied up in working capital if desired.

Row 78 contains the minimum working capital requirement in cell B38, incorporating any allowable step-downs in row 77. The working capital at the start of the project in cell C81 is that contained in cell B38. Cell C82 adds in the annual cash flow to obtain the year-end balance in the working capital account. If the balance is over the minimum in cell C82, the excess is passed on to the equity owner in the

Figure 3.B.5
Working Capital and Other Matters

	A	B	C
69	Cash Flow NPV at 14%	=NPV(0.14,B68:V68)	
70	Cash Flow IRR	=IRR(B68:V68)	
71			
72	Negative Cash Flow		
73	Maximum Amount	=MAX(C73:V73)	=IF(C45>0,1,0)*IF(C68<0,-C68,0)
74	Count	=SUM(C74:V74)	=IF(C45>0,1,0)*IF(C73>0,1,0)
75			
76	Working Capital Account		
77	Allowable Step-Downs		1
78	Minimum Required	=B38	=C77*$B$78
79	(Before Paying Dividends)		
80			
81	Starting Working Capital		=B38
82	W.C. Plus Cash Flow		=C81+C68
83	Equity/Dividend Flow	=-B39	=IF(C82>C78,C82-C78,0)
84	Ending Working Capital		=C82-C83
85			
86	Dividend NPV at 14%	=NPV(0.14,B83:V83)	
87	Dividend IRR	=IRR(B83:V83)	

form of a dividend. The starting working capital in year 2 references the ending working capital in year 1, which is replicated for the remaining years of the project. No cash is kept in the company in excess of the working capital, as it is paid out as a dividend whose NPV and IRR are calculated in cells B86 and B87.

Cell C89 calculates the interest earnings on the working capital account:

$$=IF((C81+C84)/2>0,(C81+C84)/2,0)*IF(C5=1,(C49-0.03),(C50-0.03))$$

If the average beginning and ending working capital balance is positive, then interest is three percentage points less than the applicable good or bad times interest rates (in a low interest rate environment, this spread has to be reduced). The three-point spread reflects the difference between what bankers pay for deposits and what they charge for loans. If the average balance is less than zero, then there is no interest income. Cell D57 is interest income on working capital calculated in cell C89. The reason that year 1 interest earnings are reflected in year 2 is to avoid a circular reference and also to acknowledge that interest is accrued after it is earned.

Figure 3.B.6 shows the formulation of the solvency loan.

Figure 3.B.6
Solvency Loan

	A	B	C
91	Solvency Loan		
92	Maximum Amount	=MAX(C92:V92)	=IF(C84<0,-C84,0)
93	Count	=SUM(C93:V93)	=IF(C84<0,1,0)
94	Solvency Loan Interest		=IF(C5=1,(C49+0.03)*C92,(C50+0.03)*C92)

Row 92 determines whether there is a negative balance in the end-of-year working capital account. If so, then this determines the positive balance of the solvency loan. The maximum balance in the solvency loan is recorded in cell B92. Row 93 keeps track of the years when the solvency loan is drawn down, which is totaled in cell B93. Interest is figured on balances in the solvency loan at three percentage points above that being charged on the debt, reflecting the added risk that bankers bear when extending a loan to keep a company solvent. Like working capital, interest charged for the solvency loan is shown a year later to avoid a circular reference. A circular reference results when a cell formula requires the value in another cell that has not yet been determined. In this case, a circular reference exists because interest is to be charged for a loan balance that has not yet been calculated. The circular reference can be avoided by posting the interest charge in the succeeding time period.

Figure 3.B.7 formulates the financial ratios. Gross margin is gross profit divided by revenue. Interest coverage is gross profit net of G&A expenses and depreciation divided by interest as long as the debt is outstanding. Return on investment is defined as dividend flow divided by the investment in the factory including any cost overrun and the minimum working capital requirement. Return on assets is de-

Figure 3.B.7
Financial Ratios

	A	B	C
96	Financial Analysis		
97	Gross Margin		=C22/C15
98	Interest Coverage		=IF(C3<=$B$44,1,0)*C34/C59
99	Accumulated Depreciation		=C31
100	Return on Investment		=C83/($B$36+$B$37+$B$38)
101	Return on Assets		=C83/($B$36+$B$37+IF(C84>0,C84,0)-C99)

fined as dividend flow divided by the investment in the factory including any cost overrun and the current balance in the working capital account, if positive, net of accumulated dividends. The formula in cell D99 to accumulate depreciation is =C99+D31.1

NOTE

1. All the spreadsheets in this book can be obtained from *@Risk Bank and Financial Credit Analysis*, available from www.nerses.com.

4
RISK IN FINANCING GENERAL CORPORATE CREDITS

SYNOPSIS

The difference between project financing and financing general corporate credits is that project financing is associated with a particular product or service. In the preceding chapter, project financing was built around price and volume of a single product. Moreover, funds generated beyond working capital requirements were spun off as a dividend for other uses.

This chapter looks at funds flow. Funds flow is defined as after-tax profits net of debt amortization, capital expenditures, and dividends. Capital expenditures under project financing occurred once when the factory was built. For ongoing concerns, capital expenditures are continually needed to update plant and equipment, to expand productive capacity, and to enter into new business activities. Excess cash flow is not automatically spun off but is retained by the company to satisfy debt repayment obligations, fund capital expenditures, and provide for regular dividend payments.

The chapter starts with the discussion that companies are collections of numbers that must add up positively. This insight was lost during the dot.com mania that caused much distress among employees and investors in dot.com companies and others that were swept up in the euphoria of the times. Then a model is set up based on an actual company for evaluating general corporate credits. The description provides a step-by-step process for developing the model along with an explanation of why certain actions were taken by the author. The chapter ends with an examination of funds flow, which is quite different from after-tax profits. Funds flow is the critical variable in determining the cash needs of a company, and after-tax profits are but one step in the process of determining funds flow.

NUMBERS THAT DON'T ADD UP POSITIVELY

A company is nothing more than a batch of numbers that add up positively or negatively. This may sound like a hard verdict for all the effort that people put into companies to ensure their survival and success. Yet it is so true. This may not be the total perspective of management, but investors as shareholders, bondholders, and lenders do hold this view. Shareholders want to see growing earnings per share fueling an increasing stock price. Bondholders and lenders want to see sufficient coverage of earnings to debt servicing costs to sleep comfortably. But others besides shareholders and bondholders are interested in the numbers adding up positively. Stakeholders such as employees want to feel secure about their paychecks, suppliers want to feel at ease about shipping goods to the company in return for a receivable, consumers want the company's products or services to satisfy their needs, and local government leaders want the company to continue contributing to the economic well-being of their communities. Numbers adding up positively do matter.

WHY THE NEW ECONOMY FAILED

The dot.com mania of the late 1990s was a radical departure from the truism that numbers are to add up positively. The so-called New Economy broke the shackles of the traditional way of viewing the ultimate value of companies as being somewhat loosely connected to the present value of its future stream of dividends. With shares of stock selling for over $100, $200, $300, no one seemed to care that revenue covered only half of operating costs. Just issue a few shares to get the money to pay the bills or pay the bills with shares of stock or get people to work for options—who cares? Whatever the shares are worth now, there is only one certainty: they will be worth more tomorrow. Some greater fool will always be there to buy the stock.

Amazon.com was to become the only way to buy books. Why go to a bookstore to view a selection of perhaps a few hundred books when Amazon listed nearly every book ever published? Amazon was responsible for the demise of untold thousands of mom-and-pop bookstores while Amazon itself wasn't generating a nickel of profit. Amazon is actually a success story; it's still around and began making a profit in the fourth quarter of 2001.

If you didn't know where to put your money in the late 1990s, the sage advice was to put it with the blue chip of dot.com companies, Exodus, a stock where "you couldn't go wrong." Exodus provided the hardware that made the Internet possible. The industry couldn't survive without Exodus and other Internet providers such as Excite@Home. Guess what? The Internet exists today without these providers. What happened? Their numbers didn't add up positively.

Take Lucent, a manufacturer of communications equipment. Orders were pouring in from newly organized communication companies that weren't making a dime because they had no equipment. How could Lucent sell to these companies? One way was not having the companies pay for the equipment. The equipment was sold not for cash but for a receivable or an equity position in the buyer's company. Could Lucent management be criticized for doing this when the shares in these companies are heading toward the stratosphere? Look at it from Lucent's position: orders galore generated by accepting receivables or equity positions instead of cash. Since the share values were continually going up, either the buyers could sell some of their stock to pay for the receivables, or Lucent could liquidate a part of their equity positions. Either way the receivables or the equity positions could be easily transformed to cash to pay for the equipment. This made Lucent management look smart. Lucent could sell $10 million in equipment for equity, and soon it was worth $20 million. Sell half of the equity and the equipment was paid for, and Lucent still had an equity position in a growing telecommunications company. Alternatively, the buyer could sell a few thousand newly minted stock certificates and liquidate the receivable.

Lucent management surely looked smart. The more the stock of their equipment purchasers went up, the greater the degree of coverage of Lucent's accounts receivable and the value of Lucent's equity investments, the greater the incentive to sell still more equipment to these companies, and the higher the reported profits.

Now here was the rub. Lucent was accounting for sales based on receivables and equity positions as though they were cash. Lucent reporting higher profits misled investors as to what was actually going on. After Lucent's customers installed far too much "free" equipment for them to operate profitably—well, we all know the outcome. The telecommunication companies struggled vainly with overcapacity without any possibility of earning the wherewithal to pay the overhanging debt and receivables. Their stock prices swivelled to nothing, and some went bankrupt, leaving Lucent with worthless equity investments and receivables. Employees of companies on both sides of the fence, whether as buyers or sellers of telecommunication equipment, lost their jobs and possibly a large part of their savings and retirement funds. The whole thing turned into a debacle.

What went wrong with the dot.coms and the telecommunication companies? Simple—the numbers didn't add up positively. It did not happen in one day. Gradually, the feeling began to spread that dot.com companies whose revenues did not cover half of their operating costs—never mind interest payments on debts, paying off receivables, bank loans, and a host of other incidentals—do not have eternal life. There came a time of reckoning. For most of the dot.coms, it was over in less than a year. Sometime after the Nasdaq peak of about 5,000 in March 2000 but long before its low of just under 1,400 in September 2001, it dawned on investors that the numbers did not and never would add up positively. In a way it was the eighteenth-century tulip bulb mania all over again, and those who went through the dot.com mania never realized they were dealing in overpriced tulip bulbs.

BACK TO EARTH

The previous chapter dealt with the risk associated with a project financing whereby too great of a reliance on debt creates a risk of insolvency when price and volume of a single product do not come up to expectations. The risk of revenue not being sufficient to cover debt servicing requirements can be managed by reducing the role of debt in the capital structure of the company or in establishing a more stringent minimum working capital requirement.

Cash flow in project financing included debt amortization, but not ongoing capital expenditures. Dividends were handled as spinning off all excess cash generation above the minimum working capital requirements. Here funds flow is defined as after-tax earnings net of debt amortization, capital expenditures, and dividend payments. After-tax earnings are only an intermediate step between revenue and funds flow, which determines the ending balance of a company's checking account. The risk under scrutiny is after-tax earnings, while positive, not being sufficient to cover debt repayment, capital expenditures, and dividends.

The principal difference between project financing and general corporate credits is that we cannot look at the price and volume of a single product to forecast revenue. Most companies have a slew of products and services with interests in many different activities. Lenders cannot deal with each product, service, and activity individually, unless, of course, they want to be as focused on a company's activities as management.

But not even top management of a diverse company in 100 different lines of businesses and activities has an intimate appreciation of all that is going on, although some come pretty close. That is why one of the prerequisites of being a successful top dog in a company is his or her ability to identify and recruit the right people. Success of a company as a whole depends on having the right person in the right place at the right time to manage each of the many diverse activities that make up a modern corporation. The right person must not just be competent but trustworthy because at the end of the day, the top dog in a company must trust his or her managers to carry out the overall objectives of a complex organization. In this respect, there is little difference between a general leading an army and a top executive leading a corporation. Both depend on competent and trustworthy subordinates to accomplish the twin missions of conquest (expanding market share for corporations) and survival (sometimes ignored by corporations such as the dot.coms).

One of the problems emerging during 2002 was the changing nature of the top dog. Jay Gould was a robber baron in the nineteenth century, but his legacy was the railroads that made him rich. The same could be said of the other robber barons. Rich and greedy, yes, but we have the railroads, steel and chemical plants, oil refineries, mines, and banks that made them rich. Robber barons nowadays actually live up to their name. They take established companies and through uncontrollable greed gut the corporations leaving themselves rich while impoverishing their employees, their shareholders, and, lest we forget, their nation. Their military counterpart might be Russian generals rumored to have sold the nuclear weapons entrusted to them to undisclosed parties.

It is not just outsiders such as shareholders and bondholders who are interested in whether numbers add up positively or negatively. Top executives and members of the board of directors normally rely on financial measures to gauge the success or failure of each product or service division within a company, augmented by direct communication with the appropriate manager. For lenders, time constraints and the incapacity of the human brain to grasp the entirety of every business aspect of a company effectively prohibit microanalysis for scores of borrowers. Another way is needed, a shortcut, if you will, to determine whether to lend and how much to lend without being as familiar about a company's operations as management. That way is to look at companies as a batch of numbers and see if they add up positively or negatively.

RISK IN FINANCING GENERAL CORPORATE CREDITS

General corporate credits focus on funds flow being adequate to repay debt, support capital expenditures to maintain and augment a company's productive capacity and enter into new lines of business, and make dividend payments. Risk takes the form of after-tax earnings from operations being inadequate to support funds flow. In other words, a corporation can pay taxes on profits, have a positive after-tax earnings, and still be starved of funds.

By examining an actual company, this chapter demonstrates a methodology of determining the risk of not generating sufficient funds. A spreadsheet is developed accompanied by commentary on the thought process involved in constructing a model for forecasting the funds flow for a particular company. Risk is then measured by the probability of a company not generating sufficient funds flow, that is, the chances of funds flow being negative. The model then provides a means to manage the risk of a negative funds flow through the raising of new capital in the form of debt and equity.

PICKING A BATCH OF NUMBERS

Standard & Poor's Stock Reports describes the financial performance of publicly traded companies in about 30 lines of figures. This reduces the complexity usually associated with modeling a company's annual report to a relatively simple format that can be used to see if a batch of numbers adds up positively or negatively. Such simplification of the financial figures may hide pertinent business facts. An annual report provides a deeper understanding of the financial figures; but figures may not tell the entire story. A common approach to assessing the creditworthiness of a company is to read the footnotes before examining the financial figures. The notes accompanying the financial figures often reveal vital insights hidden from view in the management's report and in the financial figures themselves.

But, as we all know, annual reports may not disclose everything such as the treatment of sales at Lucent or other companies hiding unrealized losses in derivative positions from the eagle eyes of external auditors. The financial debacle at Enron has put the entire accounting profession under scrutiny for Enron's accountant's failure to represent the interests of shareholders, bondholders, and lenders when certifying the company's reported earnings. Analysis of the creditworthiness or judging the investment desirability of a company by seeing whether the numbers add up positively or negatively begins with an accountant certifying that the numbers represent a true and fair view of a company's financial condition. In 2002 the accountants certified WorldCom's financial statements when billions in operating costs were classified as capital expenditures to enhance reported profits. The accountants certified Xerox statements when billions of discounted future revenues were included in current revenues to enhance reported profits. The supposedly independent auditors of WorldCom and Xerox did not provide a true and fair view of management's performance to the shareholders. Even with an external audit, risk is often difficult to detect and evaluate, and this observation is not limited to companies. Argentina defaulting on its debts in 2002 caught many bankers by surprise despite a developing deterioration of its internal and external financial condition reported by the International Monetary Fund (IMF) and others. This means that many banks did not sense the risk of the deteriorating financial condition as a prelude to a default.

A company was selected to serve as an example for evaluating the risk of an inadequate funds flow by a random pick of one of the two volumes of Standard & Poor's Stock Reports followed by a random pick of a page (not totally random as there was a penchant to select a company somewhere in the middle of the volume). About half of Standard & Poor's data will not be utilized such as per share values on cash flow, earnings, dividends, prices, price to earnings ratio and financial ratios on capitalization, gross margin, and return on assets and equity. The pertinent financial figures to evaluate the risk of not generating sufficient funds flow are in Figures 4.1 and 4.2.

A number of adjustments have to be made. The first is that 1991 dollars are not the same as 2000 dollars. In a way we are dealing with different currencies in terms of purchasing power. The same bag of groceries costs more in 2000 than it did in

Figure 4.1
Financial Figures Pertaining to Income

	B	C	D	E	F	G	H
5						Before	After
6		Operating	Operating		Interest	Tax	Tax
7		Revenues	Income	Depreciation	Expense	Income	Income
8	1991	$ 240.0	$ 35.3	$ 8.5	$ 5.2	$ 29.8	$ 27.1
9	1992	$ 286.0	$ 48.4	$ 14.4	$ 5.6	$ 35.5	$ 33.8
10	1993	$ 352.0	$ 50.1	$ 18.5	$ 8.0	$ 36.4	$ 34.3
11	1994	$ 423.0	$ 55.7	$ 19.6	$ 7.2	$ 4.2	$ 0.7
12	1995	$ 573.0	$ 89.6	$ 31.0	$ 7.6	$ 58.6	$ 51.1
13	1996	$ 720.0	$ 123.0	$ 46.1	$ 11.9	$ 81.6	$ 70.6
14	1997	$ 1,029.0	$ 223.0	$ 66.4	$ 16.5	$ 182.0	$ 115.0
15	1998	$ 968.0	$ 267.0	$ 84.9	$ 15.5	$ 200.0	$ 125.0
16	1999	$ 639.0	$ 155.0	$ 100.0	$ 30.4	$ 45.6	$ 27.7
17	2000	$ 1,327.0	$ 377.0	$ 152.0	$ 35.4	$ 227.0	$ 135.0

Figure 4.2
Financial Figures Pertaining to Balance Sheet Items

	I	J	K	L	M	N
5				Long		
6		Current	Current	Term		Capital
7		Assets	Liabilities	Debt		Expenditures
8	1991	$ 83.0	$ 67.8	$ 37.0		$ 80.0
9	1992	$ 102.0	$ 65.7	$ 47.0		$ 54.4
10	1993	$ 188.0	$ 80.3	$ 68.9		$ 62.3
11	1994	$ 160.0	$ 76.1	$ 57.5		$ 37.4
12	1995	$ 183.0	$ 151.0	$ 51.5		$ 109.0
13	1996	$ 329.0	$ 156.0	$ 230.0		$ 146.0
14	1997	$ 306.0	$ 235.0	$ 230.0		$ 268.0
15	1998	$ 266.0	$ 244.0	$ 217.0		$ 276.0
16	1999	$ 461.0	$ 265.0	$ 483.0		$ 82.1
17	2000	$ 1,018.0	$ 279.0	$ 855.0		$ 301.0

1991. Figure 4.3 shows the loss of purchasing power or the inflation rate during the 1990s, a period of relatively low inflation.[1]

The inflation data in Figure 4.3 can be used to construct an index to transform current dollars into constant 2000 dollars shown in Figures 4.4 and 4.5. Past dollar figures are larger when expressed in constant dollars for the same reason that it takes more 2000 dollars to buy the same bag of groceries in 1991 than 1991 dollars.

It is a matter of choice whether to restate financial figures in constant 2000 dollars or keep them as current dollars. But measuring growth in revenue in terms of current dollars leaves one in the predicament of a company's growth being partly

Figure 4.3
Changing Nature of Dollars

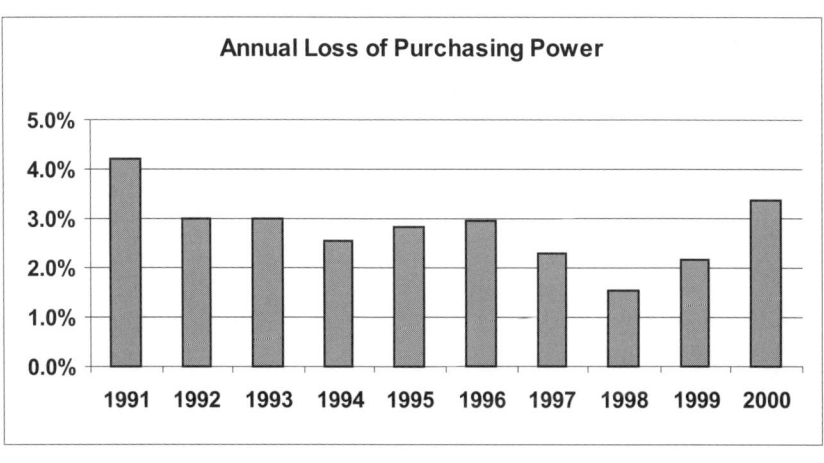

Figure 4.4
Income Items in Constant 2000 $

	B	C	D	E	F	G	H
20						Before	After
21		Operating	Operating		Interest	Tax	Tax
22		Revenues	Income	Depreciation	Expense	Income	Income
23	1991	$ 303.4	$ 44.6	$ 10.7	$ 6.6	$ 37.7	$ 34.3
24	1992	$ 351.0	$ 59.4	$ 17.7	$ 6.9	$ 43.6	$ 41.5
25	1993	$ 419.5	$ 59.7	$ 22.0	$ 9.5	$ 43.4	$ 40.9
26	1994	$ 491.5	$ 64.7	$ 22.8	$ 8.4	$ 4.9	$ 0.8
27	1995	$ 647.4	$ 101.2	$ 35.0	$ 8.6	$ 66.2	$ 57.7
28	1996	$ 790.2	$ 135.0	$ 50.6	$ 13.1	$ 89.6	$ 77.5
29	1997	$ 1,104.0	$ 239.3	$ 71.2	$ 17.7	$ 195.3	$ 123.4
30	1998	$ 1,022.6	$ 282.1	$ 89.7	$ 16.4	$ 211.3	$ 132.1
31	1999	$ 660.6	$ 160.2	$ 103.4	$ 31.4	$ 47.1	$ 28.6
32	2000	$ 1,327.0	$ 377.0	$ 152.0	$ 35.4	$ 227.0	$ 135.0

Figure 4.5
Balance Sheet Items in Constant 2000 $

	I	J	K	L	M	N
20				Long		
21		Current	Current	Term		Capital
22		Assets	Liabilities	Debt		Expenditures
23	1991	$ 104.9	$ 85.7	$ 46.8		$ 101.1
24	1992	$ 125.2	$ 80.6	$ 57.7		$ 66.8
25	1993	$ 224.0	$ 95.7	$ 82.1		$ 74.2
26	1994	$ 185.9	$ 88.4	$ 66.8		$ 43.5
27	1995	$ 206.8	$ 170.6	$ 58.2		$ 123.2
28	1996	$ 361.1	$ 171.2	$ 252.4		$ 160.2
29	1997	$ 328.3	$ 252.1	$ 246.8		$ 287.5
30	1998	$ 281.0	$ 257.8	$ 229.2		$ 291.6
31	1999	$ 476.6	$ 274.0	$ 499.4		$ 84.9
32	2000	$ 1,018.0	$ 279.0	$ 855.0		$ 301.0

physical and partly monetary. To say that a company sales growth is 6% per year when half of the increase is caused by inflation seems, as a minimum, misleading. When inflation is high, a company can have growing revenue despite a shrinking volume of sales.

EXACTLY WHAT IS THE OBJECTIVE?

The objective is to evaluate the risk of inadequate funds flow, even though after-tax income in Figure 4.4 is positive. After-tax income is not the end of the daisy chain in that debt amortization, capital expenditures, and dividends have yet to be taken into account. The risk of insufficient funds flow to maintain the solvency of a company can be managed by infusions of new debt and/or equity into the capital structure.

The attractiveness of a new issue of debt depends, among other things, on the degree of earnings coverage of debt servicing costs. The attractiveness of a new issue of equity depends on the price of a share of stock. This particular company does not pay a dividend, yet its share value varied between $4 and $60 per share between 1991 and 2000. An equity infusion when the stock price was at its low would cause far more shareholder dilution than if it had occurred when the stock price was at its high.

Hypothetically, an astute investor could have made 15 times on his or her money if the investor realized that $4 was the low and $60 was the high. That's the problem. At $4 per share there was every reason in the world not to buy the stock (why else would it be at $4?), and at $60 a share there was every reason in the world to buy the stock (why else would it be at $60?). If you did buy when there was every reason in the world to buy the stock, you would have lost only half of your investment by the end of 2001.

But at any price, what is the value of a company that does not pay a dividend? Think about it—there is no future stream of money to justify the investment. The investment must be justified that the company will continue to grow and that investors are always willing to buy the shares of stock based on earnings that they will never see in the form of a dividend—shades of dot.com?

One justification is that at some point another company may buy this company, giving a true cash value to the shares. Value perceived by the acquiring company is not the perception of the future stream of dividends but the future stream of profits and cash flow that now belongs to the acquiring company. A company whose share value is low with respect to its earnings becomes a target company for an acquisition. The possibility of an acquisition does create a basis of value for shares where management does not intend to pay dividends in preference to reinvesting corporate funds in the company's lines of business.

Ultimately, value is no more than what shareholders say it is through the continuous auction carried out on a stock exchange. The value of a dot.com company at $100 per share in 1999 is based on the willingness of someone to buy shares at $100. The value of the same company in 2002 at a few bucks per share is also based on the willingness of someone to buy shares at a few bucks. Many times stock market valuations seem to have little relationship with the underlying asset and earnings potential of a company except in bear markets when the balloon of unrealizable expectations is punctured. Yet even here the price may fall far below what it should be based on asset value and earnings potential. This tendency of stock markets to overvalue and undervalue companies gives credence to the well-worn, but sage, investment advice to buy low, sell high.

BACK TO THE CHORE AT HAND

To eliminate the underlying formulas that changed the financial figures from current dollars into constant 2000 dollars, the data contained in Figures 4.4 and 4.5 were *Copy* and *Paste Special Values Only* before making further alterations as shown in Figure 4.6.

Figure 4.6
Altering the Data Some More

	B	C	D	E	F	G	H	I	J
35				Other			Before	After	Effective
36		Operating	Operating	Income		Interest	Tax	Tax	Tax
37		Revenues	Income	(Expense)	Depreciation	Expense	Income	Income	Rate
38	1991	$ 303.4	$ 44.6	$ 10.4	$ 10.7	$ 6.6	$ 37.7	$ 34.3	9.1%
39	1992	$ 351.0	$ 59.4	$ 8.7	$ 17.7	$ 6.9	$ 43.6	$ 41.5	4.8%
40	1993	$ 419.5	$ 59.7	$ 15.3	$ 22.0	$ 9.5	$ 43.4	$ 40.9	5.8%
41	1994	$ 491.5	$ 64.7	$ (28.7)	$ 22.8	$ 8.4	$ 4.9	$ 0.8	83.3%
42	1995	$ 647.4	$ 101.2	$ 8.6	$ 35.0	$ 8.6	$ 66.2	$ 57.7	12.8%
43	1996	$ 790.2	$ 135.0	$ 18.2	$ 50.6	$ 13.1	$ 89.6	$ 77.5	13.5%
44	1997	$ 1,104.0	$ 239.3	$ 45.0	$ 71.2	$ 17.7	$ 195.3	$ 123.4	36.8%
45	1998	$ 1,022.6	$ 282.1	$ 35.3	$ 89.7	$ 16.4	$ 211.3	$ 132.1	37.5%
46	1999	$ 660.6	$ 160.2	$ 21.7	$ 103.4	$ 31.4	$ 47.1	$ 28.6	39.3%
47	2000	$ 1,327.0	$ 377.0	$ 37.4	$ 152.0	$ 35.4	$ 227.0	$ 135.0	40.5%

Column E is Other Income to ensure that operating income less depreciation and interest expense is equal to before-tax income. Column E contains a host of items not included in operating income and not described in Standard & Poor's condensation of financial data. In reality, discussions would be carried out with management to ensure the appropriateness of the entries in column E. As seen in Figure 4.6, all but one entry are positive, indicating other sources of income.

Another alteration is the effective tax rate in column J that is derived by comparing before- and after-tax earnings. It is not clear why the effective tax rates were so low in 1991–1993 and so high in 1994. There may have been tax loss carryforwards or write-offs taking place during 1991 through 1993. This would be another matter to be taken up with management. This variation in tax rates will have to be dealt with when forecasting future earnings. Figure 4.7 contains the final alterations to the financial data.

Working capital in column N of Figure 4.7 is current assets less current liabilities. Changes in working capital are either a source or a drain of cash. Changes in working capital have been very pronounced, but part of the variation can be explained. The major increases in working capital in 1996, 1999, and 2000 are partly due to the proceeds of new debt financings arranged during those years as seen in column P of Figure 4.7. The loan proceeds are temporarily parked in working capital as short-term cash until consumed by funding some combination of capital expenditures and debt retirement. Projecting working capital needs has to take the fluctuations caused by the acquisition of outside sources of capital into consideration.

Figure 4.7
Final Alterations

	K	L	M	N	O	P	Q	R	S
35					Changes	Long	Effective		
36		Current	Current	Working	in Working	Term	Interest	Interest	Capital
37		Assets	Liabilities	Capital	Capital	Debt	Rate	Coverage	Expenditures
38	1991	$ 104.9	$ 85.7	$ 19.2		$ 46.8	14.1%	6.7	$ 101.1
39	1992	$ 125.2	$ 80.6	$ 44.6	$ 25.3	$ 57.7	11.9%	7.3	$ 66.8
40	1993	$ 224.0	$ 95.7	$ 128.3	$ 83.8	$ 82.1	11.6%	5.6	$ 74.2
41	1994	$ 185.9	$ 88.4	$ 97.5	$ (30.9)	$ 66.8	12.5%	1.6	$ 43.5
42	1995	$ 206.8	$ 170.6	$ 36.2	$ (61.3)	$ 58.2	14.8%	8.7	$ 123.2
43	1996	$ 361.1	$ 171.2	$ 189.9	$ 153.7	$ 252.4	5.2%	7.9	$ 160.2
44	1997	$ 328.3	$ 252.1	$ 76.2	$ (113.7)	$ 246.8	7.2%	12.0	$ 287.5
45	1998	$ 281.0	$ 257.8	$ 23.2	$ (52.9)	$ 229.2	7.1%	13.9	$ 291.6
46	1999	$ 476.6	$ 274.0	$ 202.6	$ 179.4	$ 499.4	6.3%	2.5	$ 84.9
47	2000	$ 1,018.0	$ 279.0	$ 739.0	$ 536.4	$ 855.0	4.1%	7.4	$ 301.0

The effective interest rate in column Q is the interest expense in column G divided by the long-term debt in column P. This will be used to assess interest rates when taking a look at the future cash needs of the company. Apparently, a large portion of the borrowings in 1996, 1999, and 2000 was to refinance existing debt in order to lower the effective interest rate. Column R is interest coverage calculated by taking earnings before interest and taxes and dividing by interest expense (column H plus column G to obtain earnings before interest, then dividing by column G).

PROJECTING THE FUTURE

Ah, were it possible! Perhaps the most exposed profession for being judged for their proficiency to project the future is mutual fund portfolio managers. Every day their performance in judging the future is listed in the financial sections of the world's newspapers. Moreover, mutual fund investment services are available that rank funds by their performance over various periods of time.

The secret to success in being a portfolio fund manager is to be fully invested in a well-diversified portfolio of stocks just before the stock market heads north for an extended period of time and to be in cash just before it heads south for another extended period of time. Thus superior performance in managing a mutual fund compared to market performance can be achieved by simply forecasting whether the market will go up or down. If the outlook for the market is up, invest; if down, divest.

Portfolio managers are extremely intelligent individuals. Yet the majority of them can barely keep up with the broad market indices. In other words, portfolios managed by very astute individuals may not be able to keep up with an unmanaged average. This is why there are index-related portfolios modeled after unmanaged averages as investment vehicles. Even these don't keep up with the unmanaged averages because of management fees.

One way to judge whether the market is going up or down is to flip a coin. Heads the market is moving up, and tails it's moving down; if coin flipping is correct, then superior performance is your reward. The chance of being correct at first is 50%, the chance of being correct twice in a row is 25%, thrice 12.5%—get the picture? Sooner or later a bet is going to be made on the wrong side of the coin. But that doesn't preclude an individual being right 20 times over. All we have to do is identify him or her before the winning streak begins. Another way to superior performance is for the portfolio manager to have a vision of the future and invest in a portfolio of stocks that best fits that vision. Now the bet whether the market will go up or down is not a flip of a coin but selecting a portfolio manager whose vision is reasonably correct.

In a way, we are not much different from a portfolio manager. Rather than projecting the future price of a company's stock, we must project its future revenue to assess the risk of inadequate funds flow. One way is to extrapolate the trend line based on past revenue into the future. Figures 4.8 and 4.9 are two such extrapolations.

An R Square value of 100% means that all the data points fall on the regression line. An R Square value of 82% is a reasonable, but not an overly exciting, fit. Both trend lines have about the same R Square value, meaning that both regression lines fit the past revenue data points equally well. But as seen in Table 4.1, the extrapolation of these two trend lines ends up with radically different outlooks for sales in 2005.

Maybe companies are not a collection of numbers that add up positively or negatively. Maybe we better start paying attention to some fundamental issues such as what the company does for a living and the effectiveness of management. The choice of whether to select the exponential or the power trend line depends not on the fit of the trend line to actual revenue but on the perception of future revenue. This means that one better know the company's principal lines of businesses and their prospects in order to assess which of two widely divergent outlooks for revenue is more realistic. Maybe dealing only in numbers is a dangerous practice.

PROJECTING OPERATING INCOME

Of course, a trend line need not be used. A projection can be discrete values not linked to any mathematical formula. A revenue projection should not be assumed without some discussion with management to get a better sense of what lies ahead. Suppose that our understanding of the prospects of the principal businesses and activities of this company is embodied in the power trend line. The next step is to project operating income. One way to do this is to see whether there is a relationship between revenue and operating income through the use of a scatter diagram as in Figure 4.10.

There appears to be a statistical linkage between revenue as an independent variable (what we know) and operating income as the dependent variable (what we

Figure 4.8
One Projection of the Future

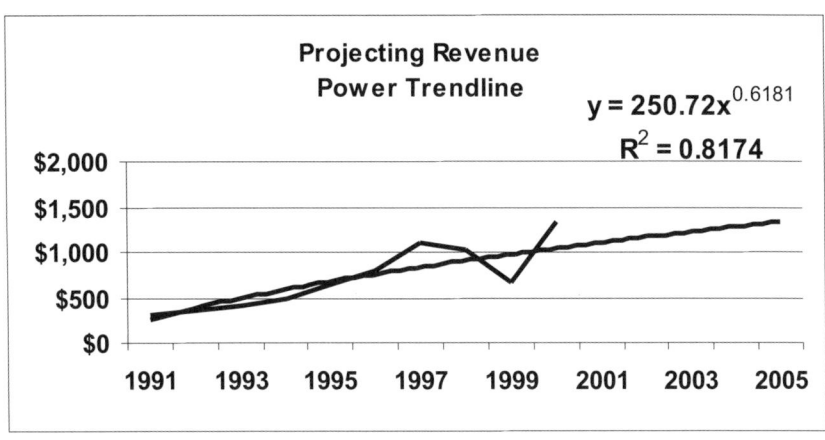

Figure 4.9
Another Projection of the Future

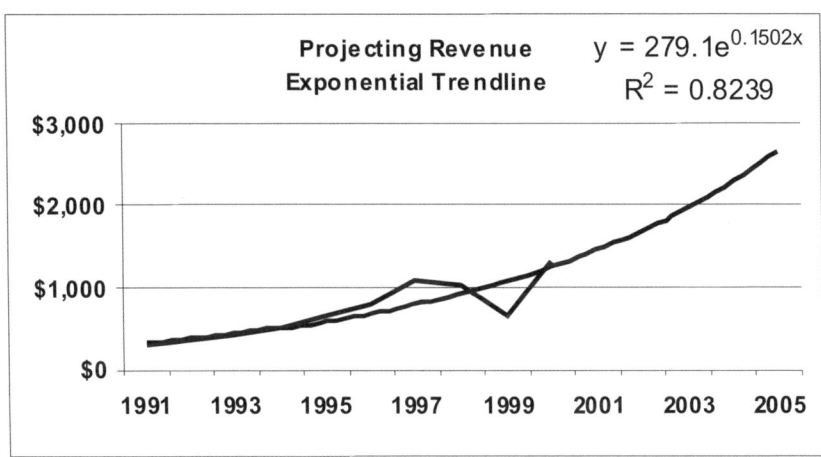

Table 4.1
Comparing Outlook of Two Trend Lines

	Exponential	Power	Difference
2001	$1,456	$1,103	$353
2002	$1,692	$1,164	$528
2003	$1,966	$1,223	$743
2004	$2,285	$1,281	$1,004
2005	$2,656	$1,337	$1,319

Figure 4.10
Scatter Diagram of Operating Income and Revenue

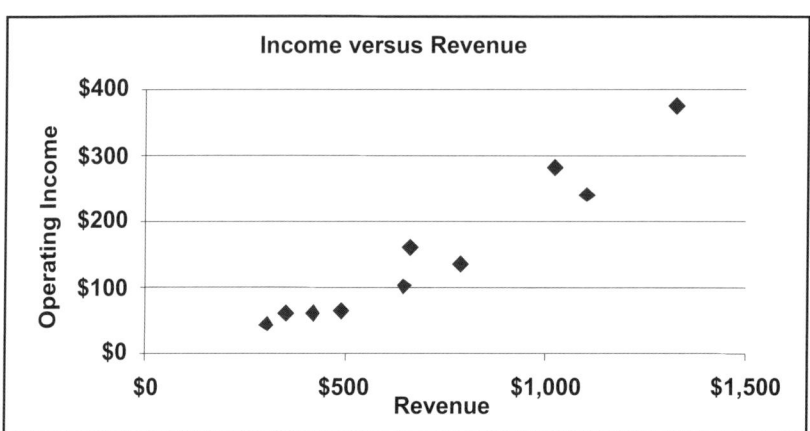

want to know). One can draw a best-fitting straight line through the data and establish a single value for operating income for any value of revenue. Obtaining the best-fitting straight line to a set of data points is what regression analysis is all about. The regression line allows us to predict operating income based on an assessment of revenue. Figure 4.11 is the result of running a regression analysis between operating income and revenue.

The adjusted R Square differs from the R Square in that it takes into account the amount of data. As the number of data points increases, the difference between the R Square in cell B67 and the adjusted R Square in cell B68 narrows. The R Square of 92% indicates a fairly good fit between the regression line values and the data points. The regression line intercepts the y-axis at −71.96 (cell B79) and has a slope of 0.315 (cell B80). Thus, the equation is Operating Income = −71.96 + 0.315*Revenue. Figure 4.12 compares the regression line with the actual data.

Of course, there is some uncertainty associated with the value of operating income for a specific value of revenue because nearly all of the data points constructing the best-fitting straight line do not lie on the line but close to the line. While there is a fairly good fit between revenue and operating income, there is also uncertainty that can be modeled as a normal distribution around the line value as a mean and with the standard error of 31.228 (cell B69) in Figure 4.11 as a fairly good proxy for the standard deviation.

Revenue in Figure 4.13 is the copied and pasted results of the formula for the power trend line contained in Figure 4.8. (The entry for time in the trend line formula is "1" for the first year, not "1991.") As mentioned, the forecast of future revenue need not be condemned to follow a particular trend line based on past data but can be modified to fit the circumstances. The past may be prelude to the future, but it does not determine the future.

Figure 4.11
Regression Analysis of Operating Income Versus Revenue

	A	B
63	SUMMARY OUTPUT	
64		
65	*Regression Statistics*	
66	Multiple R	0.965277743
67	R Square	0.931761121
68	Adjusted R Square	0.923231262
69	Standard Error	31.22820731
70	Observations	10
71		
72	ANOVA	
73		*df*
74	Regression	1
75	Residual	8
76	Total	9
77		
78		Coefficients
79	Intercept	-71.95993863
80	X Variable 1	0.315125469

Figure 4.12
Comparing Regression Line with Actual Data Points

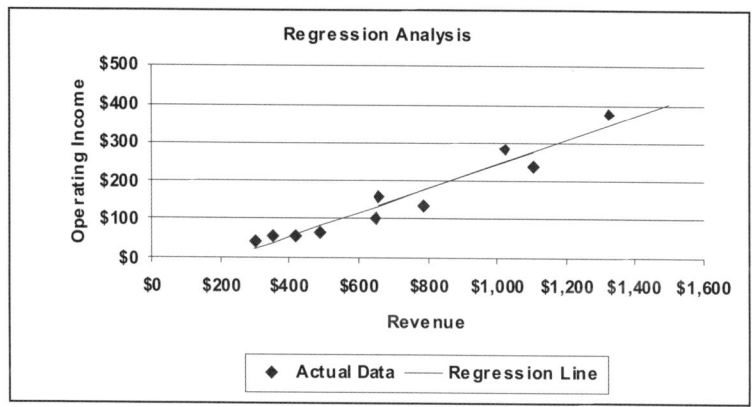

Figure 4.13
Revenue and Operating and Other Income

	B	C	D	E	F
50			Operating	Operating	Other
51			Income with	Income with	Income
52		Revenue	Certainty	Uncertainty	(Expense)
53	2001	$ 1,103.8	$ 275.9	$ 257.5	$ 1.8
54	2002	$ 1,164.7	$ 295.1	$ 299.3	$ (11.3)
55	2003	$ 1,223.8	$ 313.7	$ 328.0	$ (12.0)
56	2004	$ 1,281.2	$ 331.8	$ 357.9	$ 14.4
57	2005	$ 1,337.0	$ 349.4	$ 315.7	$ 33.5

The operating income with certainty, cell D53 in Figure 4.13, is the regression equation from Figure 4.11:

=$B$79+$B$80*C53

The operating income incorporating uncertainty is generated by a normal distribution whose mean is the line value of the regression equation in column D of Figure 4.13 with a standard deviation equal to the standard error in Figure 4.11. The formula in cell E53 of Figure 4.13 is:

=RiskNormal(D53,$B$69)

In this chapter, there are two columns—one reflecting certainty and one reflecting uncertainty. As a practical matter they can be combined into one column such as:

=$B$79+$B$80*C53+RiskNormal(0,$B$69)

The mean of the normal distribution is contained in the first part of the formula, and the second part provides the uncertainty reflected in the standard error of the regression output.

A scatter diagram of the variation in other income (column E of Figure 4.6) indicated no relationship with revenue. An arbitrary decision was made to model the projected values in column F with a triangular distribution with the following indicated values for the minimum, most likely (mode), and maximum:

=RiskTriang(–25,35,45)

@Risk/Model/Fit Distributions to Data could have provided the best-fitting distribution rather than relying on a visual estimate of the data. A modeler does have a choice in how a model is set up, and different individuals will not end up with the same model, which, incidentally, leads to different outcomes.

On a personal note, I've assigned a quantitative problem to graduate business students where about 95% of the requisite data are given and the remaining 5% are a bit fuzzy but can be derived or estimated from the available data. Students have to make assessments to model the fuzzy 5% and present their conclusions in the form of a consultant's report. I have found the diversity of results to be nearly astounding considering the rather limited leeway left to the student's discretion. Since the quantitative results vary with the modeler, one has to be careful about the general role of models in the decision-making process. Moreover, models cannot evaluate subjective assessments such as management's honesty and the integrity of an accountant's report upon which the model is built. Ultimately, models help managers to make decisions, but managers, not models, make decisions.

MOVING ON

Back to the problem at hand—the values in Figure 4.13 and in the remaining figures are generated in the *Monte Carlo* mode under *Simulation Settings/Sampling/Standard Recalculating*. The *Monte Carlo* mode promotes a better understanding of the impact of variation when constructing the model and is a better aid in detecting spreadsheet bugs than the *Expected Value* mode. Figure 4.14 is the projection of debt repayment and interest charges.

The future outstanding balances of the existing debt in column G of Figure 4.14 would be obtainable from the corporate financial officer. Here the ending balance of $855 in 2000 is assumed to be paid down to $800 in 2001 with remaining debt amortization of $50 per year. The projected future interest rate in column I was assessed to be between 4% and 8% and modeled with a triangular probability distribution:

$$=RiskTriang(0.04,0.06,0.08)$$

If it is desired to increase the interest rate over the outlook period, the interest rate could be modeled on a year-by-year basis where the minimum, most likely, and maximum interest rates have a narrow range at first but widen with time to reflect the growing uncertainty of assessing interest rates further into the future. The interest expense is calculated on the basis of the amount of debt outstanding less one-half of the annual amortization to approximate semiannual repayments of debt. The formula in cell J53 of Figure 4.14 is:

$$=(G53-0.5*H53)*I53$$

New debt for 2002 in columns K through M of Figure 4.14 is modeled with a 10-year repayment with interest figured on the same basis as existing debt. Figure 4.15 shows depreciation and before- and after-tax income. Existing depreciation in column N, like existing debt, is a known entity that can be provided by management. Here the entries in Figure 4.15 are assumed. New depreciation in column O

Figure 4.14
Debt Servicing

	G	H	I	J	K	L	M
50		Existing		Existing		New	New
51	Existing	Debt	Interest	Debt	New	Debt	Debt
52	Debt	Repayment	Rate	Interest	Debt	Repayment	Interest
53	$ 800.0	$ 55.0	7.2%	$ 55.5			
54	$ 750.0	$ 50.0	6.8%	$ 49.5	$ -	$ -	$ -
55	$ 700.0	$ 50.0	5.1%	$ 34.3	$ -	$ -	$ -
56	$ 650.0	$ 50.0	5.8%	$ 36.2	$ -	$ -	$ -
57	$ 600.0	$ 50.0	5.7%	$ 32.6	$ -	$ -	$ -

represents future capital expenditures, to be discussed shortly. Total depreciation of existing and new depreciation is in column P. Before-tax income in column Q is operating income plus other income less interest on existing and new debt and total depreciation. The formula in cell Q53 is:

=E53+F53–J53–M53–P53

The effective tax rate in Figure 4.15 does not include the low rates seen in the early 1990s. It is presumed that the conditions giving rise to these rates no longer apply and that the effective tax rate will be between 35% and 39%:

=RiskTriang(0.35,0.37,0.39)

Arbitrary assessments are being made for existing debt amortization and tax rates and in the depreciation schedule in Figure 4.15. In reality more accurate assessments would be made after conferring with management. It is possible to ignore depreciation and base taxes only on the effective tax rate that compares before-tax profits before depreciation with after-tax profits.

There is a small chance of a negative tax being generated. It is presumed that this becomes a tax refund for the year generating a cash inflow. Tax loss carryforwards are not necessary as tax losses can be refunded from the previous three years' taxes as long as tax losses are not too substantial. This company has historically generated sufficient revenue to keep it in a tax paying environment.

WORKING CAPITAL

A regression analysis was run between working capital as the dependent variable and revenue as the independent variable, with the results shown in Figure 4.16.

The adjusted R Square of only 30% suggests a poor fit between working capital and revenue. The standard error of $180 introduces enormous variation considering that working capital has frequently been under $100. The XY scatter diagram of working capital versus revenue is in Figure 4.17.

Figure 4.15
Depreciation and Taxes

	N	O	P	Q	R	S
50				Before	Effective	After
51	Existing	New	Total	Tax	Tax	Tax
52	Depreciation	Depreciation	Depreciation	Income	Rate	Income
53	$ 140.0	$ 15.5	$ 155.5	$ 48.4	36.4%	$ 30.8
54	$ 130.0	$ 42.1	$ 172.1	$ 66.4	36.5%	$ 42.2
55	$ 120.0	$ 66.3	$ 186.3	$ 95.3	37.2%	$ 59.8
56	$ 110.0	$ 91.4	$ 201.4	$ 134.6	37.3%	$ 84.4
57	$ 100.0	$ 122.5	$ 222.5	$ 94.1	36.8%	$ 59.5

Figure 4.16
Working Capital versus Revenue

	J	K
65	Regression Statistics	
66	Multiple R	0.61475402
67	R Square	0.377922505
68	Adjusted R Square	0.300162818
69	Standard Error	180.0472778
70	Observations	10
71		
72	ANOVA	
73		df
74	Regression	1
75	Residual	8
76	Total	9
77		
78		Coefficients
79	Intercept	-117.0948392
80	X Variable 1	0.383235551

Figure 4.17
Scatter Diagram of Working Capital and Revenue

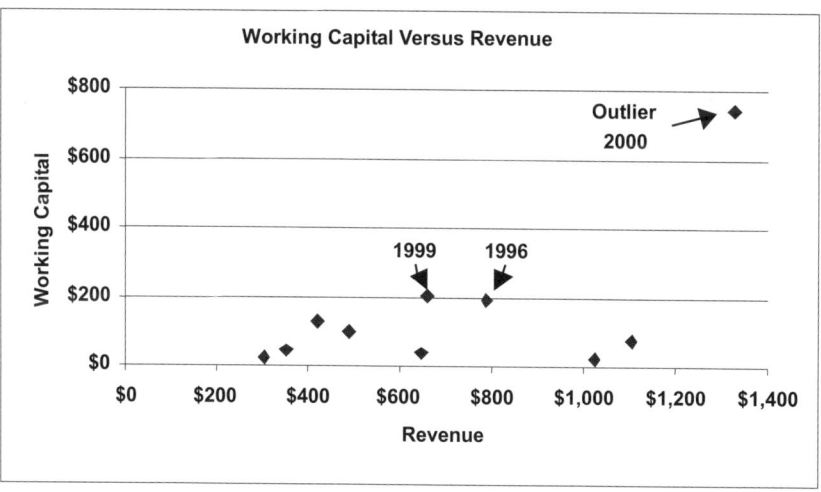

Some of the supposedly nonexplanatory variation in Figure 4.17 is explanatory. Proceeds from debt issues sit in working capital until they are consumed for their intended use of funding the retirement of existing debt and funding capital expenditures. Working capital was "artificially" inflated three times in 1996, 1999, and 2000 by issuing debt. These are explanatory variations. Removing these outliers reduces the variation, as seen in the scatter diagram in Figure 4.18.

The R Square value for Figure 4.18 is very close to zero. This means that there is no statistical relationship between revenue and working capital. The best-fitting straight line is basically flat with a slope close to zero, which means that knowing revenue is no help in predicting working capital. Thus, changes in working capital can best be modeled by a random probability function, which was arbitrarily selected as a triangular probability distribution with the indicated values visually derived from Figure 4.17:

=RiskTriang(50,75,125)

Again @Risk's capacity to fit distributions to data or management insight to what they expect for future working capital needs should be incorporated into the model. The spreadsheet is being formulated on the basis of new capital funds being excluded from working capital. Working capital is basically short-term cash needed to support company operations plus accounts receivable and inventory less accounts payable. Excess cash above the short-term cash needs of the company will be kept separately in a funds flow account.

Figure 4.19 shows the portion of the spreadsheet pertaining to working capital. The previous formula for working capital is in column U. Column V contains the annual changes in working capital. The change listed in 2001 is based on working capital previously shown for 2000, or =U53–P47. The huge amount of cash in working capital in cell U53 distorts funds flow in 2002 as the excess cash in working capital is reassigned to funds flow. Thereafter, funds flow reflects the adequacy of

Figure 4.18
Scatter Diagram of Working Capital without Outliers

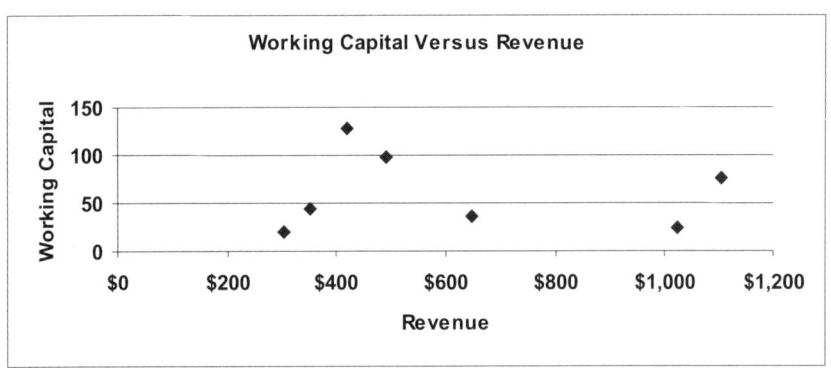

Figure 4.19
Working Capital

	T	U	V
50			Changes
51		Working	in Working
52		Capital	Capital
53	2001	$ 103.4	$ (433.0)
54	2002	$ 56.0	$ (47.4)
55	2003	$ 65.2	$ 9.2
56	2004	$ 77.6	$ 12.4
57	2005	$ 112.7	$ 35.0

after-tax earnings to support capital expenditures, debt repayment, and dividends. The change in working capital in 2002 and thereafter is =U54–U53, replicated down. Capital infusions after 2001 are assigned to funds flow, not working capital.

A positive change means that working capital is expanding and is a use of corporate funds. A negative change means that working capital is shrinking and is a source of corporate funds. It is important that the effect of changes in working capital on funds flow have the correct sign!

CAPITAL EXPENDITURES

The results of a regression analysis between capital expenditures and revenue are in Figure 4.20. The R Square of 83.7% is fairly good agreement between revenue and capital expenditures. This means that management is more apt to approve a request for capital expenditures when revenue and, hence, operating income are high than when they are low. This mirrors the shifting sands of management's optimism and pessimism as profits rise and fall. Capital projects have a greater chance of being funded when management feels good about the future. Falling profits have a negative impact on funding a capital project. This should not be interpreted as the fickleness of management as much as prudence. More than one company has failed because capital outlays were not cut or cut too late as its financial condition deteriorated. Figure 4.21 shows the capital expenditure portion of the spreadsheet.

As before, capital expenditures under certainty in column Y is the regression line derived from Figure 4.20:

$$=\$U\$79+\$U\$80*C53$$

and uncertainty in incorporated in column Z:

$$=RiskNormal(Y53,\$U\$69)$$

As previously mentioned, these two columns can be combined into one with the formula:

$$=\$U\$79+\$U\$80*C53+RiskNormal(0,\$U\$69)$$

Figure 4.20
Capital Expenditures versus Revenue

	T	U
65	Regression Statistics	
66	Multiple R	0.9248628
67	R Square	0.8553712
68	Adjusted R Square	0.8372926
69	Standard Error	41.0294512
70	Observations	10
71		
72	ANOVA	
73		df
74	Regression	1
75	Residual	8
76	Total	9
77		
78		Coefficients
79	Intercept	-40.5387401
80	X Variable 1	0.27248697

Figure 4.21
Capital Expenditures

	X	Y	Z	AA	AB	AC	AD
49		Capital	Capital				
50		Expenditures	Expenditures				
51		With	With	New	New		
52		Certainty	Uncertainty	Project	Depreciation		Dividends
53	2001	$ 260.2	$ 186.0		$ 15.5		$ -
54	2002	$ 276.8	$ 319.4		$ 42.1		$ -
55	2003	$ 292.9	$ 240.3	$ 50.0	$ 66.3		$ -
56	2004	$ 308.6	$ 251.5	$ 50.0	$ 91.4		$ -
57	2005	$ 323.8	$ 372.3		$ 122.5		$ -

In addition to the expected capital expenditures to maintain the current productive capacity of the company, a new capital project is slated for funding in 2003 and 2004 at $50 per year. If this project affects the revenue of the company, such as building a new plant, then the incremental revenue and costs of this project would have to be integrated into the model. Depreciation is an arbitrary 12-year average write-off of new assets. The formula for 2002 in cell AB54 is:

=SUM($Z$53:AA54)/12

This formula accumulates capital expenditures for the current and previous years during the outlook period and then writes them off over 12 years. The depreciation life of any asset must extend beyond the outlook period for this formula to remain valid. Again exact values for depreciation can be obtained from management; here an arbitrary assessment has to be made. The preceding formula is replicated down for the remaining years. The cells in column O, New Depreciation, references the corresponding cells in column AB. Dividend payments are in column AD, which for this company are nil.

FUNDS FLOW

Funds flow is after-tax earnings (column S) plus total depreciation (column P) less the repayment of existing and new debt (columns H and L) less working capital change (column V, where a positive change absorbs corporate funds) less normal capital expenditures (column Z) less extraordinary capital expenditures for the new project (column AA) less dividends (column AD) plus new infusions of debt (column AH) and equity (column AK). The formula in cell AF53 of Figure 4.22:

$$=S53+P53-H53-L53-V53-Z53-AA53-AD53+AH53+AK53$$

Column AG accumulates funds flow, which includes the issuance of new debt in column AH and new equity in column AK. Column AI calculates new debt repayment over 10 years, which is then reflected in column L. Column AJ is the outstanding balance for calculating new debt interest in column M. The formula in cell AG54 to accumulate funds flow is =AG53+AF54 replicated down. The cumulated funds flow gives a picture of where the company stands at the end of the outlook period. If the cumulated funds flow does not have a positive ending balance, then the company requires infusions of new debt or equity to remain solvent.

Interest coverage is earnings before interest and taxes in column Q plus adding back interest for existing and new debt in columns J and M divided by interest for existing and new debt. The formula in cell AJ53 is:

$$=(Q53+J53+M53)/(J53+M53)$$

Figure 4.22
Funds Flow

	AE	AF	AG	AH	AI	AJ	AK	AL
50			Cumulative	New	New	New		
51		Funds	Funds	Debt	Debt	Outstanding	New	Interest
52		Flow	Flow	Issues	Repayment	Balance	Equity	Coverage
53	2001	$ 383.8	$ 383.8					1.69
54	2002	$ (69.1)	$ 314.7	$ -	$ -	$ -	$ -	3.62
55	2003	$ (205.1)	$ 109.6	$ -	$ -	$ -	$ -	2.50
56	2004	$ (109.1)	$ 0.5	$ -	$ -	$ -	$ -	5.12
57	2005	$ (111.1)	$ (110.6)	$ -	$ -	$ -	$ -	3.32

STATUS QUO—NO ISSUANCE OF NEW DEBT

A @Risk simulation was conducted with the output cells being funds flow starting in 2002 (cells AF54:AF57), interest coverage (cells AL54:AL57), and the ending cumulative funds flow (cell AG57). The reason for starting the analysis in 2002 is to avoid the distortion on funds flow in 2001 with the transfer of excess working capital to funds flow. The summary graph in Figure 4.23 is the funds flow for no issuance of new debt from 2002 to 2005.

The center line is the mean of the simulation results. In 2002 the average funds flow is a deficit of about $85, in 2003 a deficit of about $125, in 2004 a deficit of $120, and in 2005 a deficit of $80 despite reporting positive after-tax earnings. The darker inner band includes simulation results that lie between the mean and plus or minus one standard deviation, representing roughly two-thirds of all results. The outer upper and lower bands represent simulation results that were between one standard deviation from the mean to 95% of all results, or approximately two standard deviations. Funds flow in 2003 has a mean of about –$125 with a 95% chance of being between –$40 and –$200. Despite a positive after-tax earnings, there is virtually no chance of the company generating a positive funds flow throughout the outlook period.

The company reports after-tax earnings but is actually cash-starved. After-tax earnings are insufficient to retire existing debt and fund the capital expenditure program, which is necessary for the company to maintain its productive capacity, plus pay dividends if dividends were being paid. Thus, the company must seek out-

Figure 4.23
Funds Flow—No New Debt

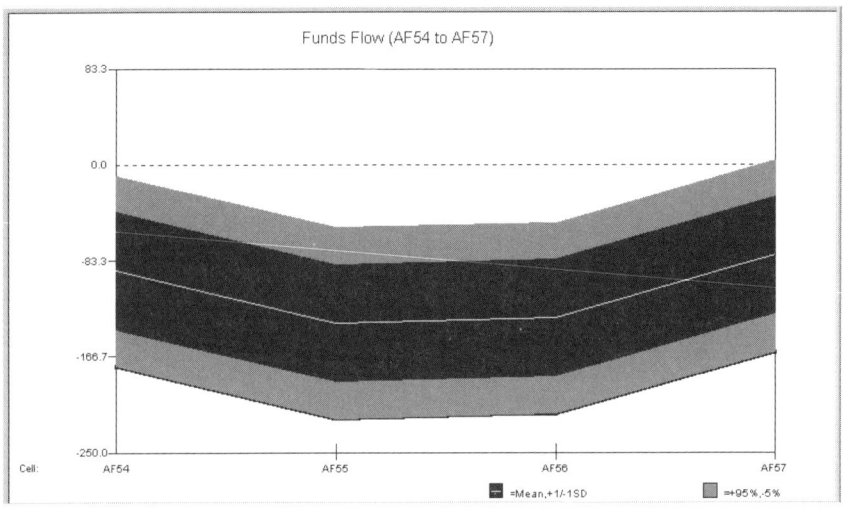

side sources of funds to remain solvent. The continual need to raise funds is not atypical for growing corporations. On the surface everything appears satisfactory as the company generates a positive after-tax earnings. Below the surface the company is actually generating a negative funds flow because of the magnitude of debt amortization, capital expenditures, and dividend payments with respect to after-tax earnings. This is not unlike the view of the *Titanic* from above the waterline that led the first-class passengers to conclude that the vessel was still unsinkable after striking the iceberg. The view of the vessel from below the waterline led the third-class passengers to a quite different conclusion.

Figure 4.24 shows interest coverage as the degree of protection afforded by before-tax profits. Interest coverage has an initial average of about 3.2 and increases thereafter as interest expense declines with the repayment of the existing debt. In 2002, two-thirds of the results for interest coverage were between 2.3 and 4.2 (one standard deviation from the mean), and 95% of all results were between 1.7 and 4.9. The expanding interest coverage is a bit misleading because more debt is necessary to keep the company solvent.

The ending position of the cumulative funds flow in cell AG57 in Figure 4.25 shows that there is an 81% chance of having a negative value in 2005.

Debt can be introduced to the extent necessary for a positive cumulative funds balance in 2005. Relying too heavily on new debt to support the funds flow of a company can become onerous if interest coverage begins to deteriorate. Interest coverage is closely watched by credit-rating organizations, and a deteriorating coverage may result in a lowering of a company's credit rating. A company may not always be able

Figure 4.24
Interest Coverage—No New Debt

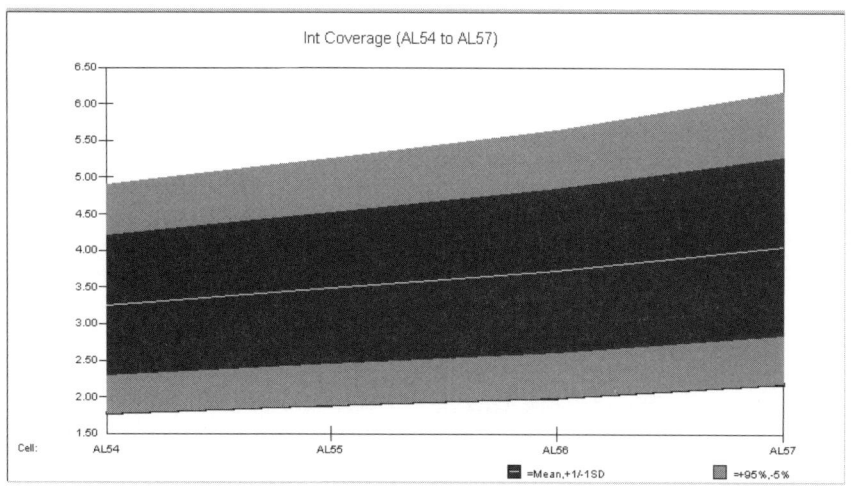

Figure 4.25
Ending Position with No New Debt

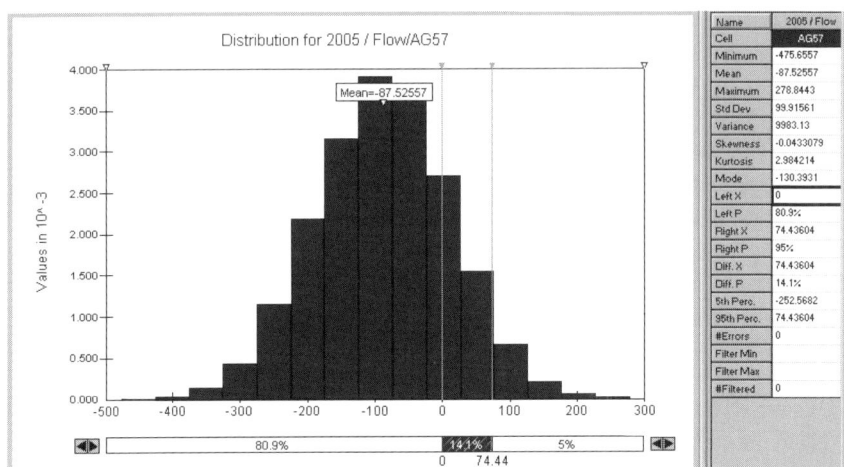

to raise debt as a sole source of new capital funds if the resulting deterioration of interest coverage adversely affects the creditworthiness of a company.

A @Risk simulation was done with capital infusions of $100 million in new debt in 2002 and 2003. This was sufficient to raise the average ending funds flow balance to a positive value and cut the probability of a negative balance in half. But the infusions were not enough. More has to be added, and if too great a reliance of debt results in weak interest coverage, then equity has to be raised. Thus, @Risk simulations of funds flow, the cumulative funds flow balance at some point in the future, and interest coverage can be used to assess the magnitude, type, and timing of new capital infusions under conditions of uncertainty.

WHAT HAPPENS WHEN COMPANIES DON'T EARN ENOUGH?

When companies don't earn enough money for whatever reason, after-tax earnings are no longer sufficient to cover debt retirement, capital expenditures, and dividends. If this deficit in funds flow is compensated by infusions of more debt and if the company's assets are earning a rate of return that is less than the cost of debt, then interest coverage will fall. This will be picked up by the credit-rating organizations and eventually result in a downgrade of a company's credit rating. A lower credit rating increases the interest rate as lenders seek a higher return to compensate for the greater perception of risk. This increases the cost of capital and widens the gap between what a company earns on its assets and what it pays to its shareholders and bondholders. This accelerates the fall in interest coverage, leading to another degradation in credit ratings and even higher interest rates. At some point lenders become reluctant to advance further funds. Being locked out of the credit market is a death knell for a company that depends on outside sources of capital to remain solvent.

Some actions can be taken when infusion of outside capital becomes difficult. One is to cut dividends, if being paid. This lowers the price of the stock and also the possibility of issuing new equity as a source of funds. The other is to cut capital expenditures. This can be a short-run solution, but the long-term implication is that the company may end up with an aged physical plant making increasingly out-of-date products. A company's financial position whose return on assets does not cover its cost of capital begins slowly to deteriorate, not unlike the slow, circular motion when a toilet is first flushed. As time goes by, the pace of the financial deterioration picks up until the company, like the contents of a toilet, is quickly flushed into financial oblivion.

The problem with government taxation based on before-tax profits is the perception that before-tax profits are the same as cash in the till. Taxation of profits appears harmless if it just reduces the size of a pile of cash. But this is not true at all. What really matters is funds flow. After-tax profits are merely a step in the process of determining funds flow that takes into consideration repayment of debt, capital expenditures, and dividends. If after-tax profits cannot sustain these outflows, then taxing profits has a deleterious effect on the financial well-being of companies. Taxation makes companies more dependent on outside sources of capital to fund capital expenditures needed to keep them as ongoing concerns. The favorite outside source of capital is debt because interest on debt is tax-deductible, and debt is easier to raise than equity. The problem is that too much debt can sink a corporation.

But all this is ranting and raving in the wind. To politicians and voters, corporations deserve to be taxed. No one can change this perception, and frequently corporations deserve this perception. A corporation that can afford to pay its executive officers millions can afford to pay taxes. If a top executive is paid $100 million per year, one is tempted to ask whether the executive is working any harder than if he or she were paid $10 million. If the answer is no, which is highly likely, then what are the shareholders getting for the extra $90 million? Paying $90 million "extra" to an individual in the form of a wage and bonus or to the government in the form of taxes makes no difference. It is still an outflow of cash that could have been supporting capital expenditures or retiring debt or (the gods forbid) providing a return to shareholders in the form of a dividend.

NOTE

1. Source of data is the *Statistical Abstract of the United States*.

5
THE RISK OF RUNNING OUT OF CASH

SYNOPSIS

Managing corporate cash is much like our managing our personal cash. There are outflows and inflows, the trick is to keep inflows slightly ahead of outflows to avert financial embarrassment or a cash crisis. The major difference between corporate and personal cash management is that personal cash management focuses on maintaining a minimum balance adequate to meet our needs. Corporate cash management is concerned with both the minimum and maximum balance. Cash management can be costly if too much money is being kept in the corporate checking account, forcing the company to utilize more expensive sources of cash, such as borrowings, to fund capital expenditures. Corporate cash management seeks a balance between a minimum and maximum amount of cash to be kept on hand to meet corporate obligations.

The chapter discusses the reasons behind the vagaries in cash inflows and outflows. These vagaries are buffered by two accounts. One account is a cash account earning little or no interest. The other is a short-term investment account that earns interest income but might also generate a charge when funds are transferred from the investment to the cash account. A spreadsheet is set up to describe the workings of these two accounts, and a RiskOptimizer simulation is utilized to determine the optimal maximum levels for both accounts plus a backup line of credit necessary to satisfy the variation in cash inflows and outflows.

CASH MANAGEMENT

Cash management is an important financial function. At the "risk" of oversimplification, it can be likened to managing a personal checking account except that the figures are much larger. A checking account has both inflows and outflows.

Most of us have a paycheck that generally means a regular and predictive inflow of money. But this is not true for those who are in business for themselves such as artists, retailers, doctors, dentists, and so forth. But even here there is a sharp differentiation in cash inflow between a doctor or dentist who can reasonably expect a daily parade of patients and an artist who makes a single sale every now and then. A company is more like a doctor or dentist whose services are offered or products are sold with invoices prepared and mailed out daily. It may not be enough business, but some business is being done continually. After a while—10 days, one month, or whatever the terms—the invoices are paid.

On the cash outflow side of the ledger, we pay bills from our personal checking account. Some are regular for known amounts such as the monthly rental or mortgage bill. Some are regular, but the amount varies such as telephone and utility bills. Some expenses are more discretionary such as the new suit, while others are less discretionary such as food. We prepare for the payment of a large quarterly property tax payment or an annual insurance premium by letting the balance in our checking account build up in anticipation of the receipt of the bill. We may defer paying the utility bill at the last minute to make sure that there is enough money to cover the check for the insurance premium. We may draw down on a line of credit to pay a portion of the bill, then spend the following months paying off the line of credit. These things we do at home also occur in companies under the aegis of corporate cash management.

RISK UNDER CONSIDERATION

The risk is the probability of running out of cash. This risk occurs even when there is a net positive cash inflow because of variation between inflows and outflows. Variation can swing in the right direction when outflow falls below inflow. Building up cash in the till to pay forthcoming bills is good. However, variation can swing in the wrong direction when outflow rises above inflow. An individual or a company can temporarily run out of cash, even though there is a net positive inflow. Running out of cash is bad unless one gets enjoyment in writing bad checks, as apparently some do.

MANAGING THE RISK OF RUNNING OUT OF CASH

All of us take the swings between cash inflow and outflow into consideration by maintaining a minimum balance in our personal checking accounts. This balance provides a sufficient degree of comfort that we can pay anticipated bills, even though we don't know the exact amount or due date. Moreover, the balance should be adequate to handle a bill for an unexpected automobile repair. We manage the risk of running out of money by having a little money lying around just in case it's needed. The objective we implicitly adopt when we determine the desired balance in our checking account is to minimize the risk of running out of cash. We can be a bit indifferent to the minimum balance as it does not represent a great deal of money.

This is not so in a corporate setting, where the balance in a checking account must handle inflows and outflows measured in millions of dollars. It does not make good sense to keep a lot of money in a corporate checking account earning 2% when it can earn 12% funding capital expenditures. Excess cash holdings can at least be used to prepay long-term debt costing 10%. This leads to a major difference between corporate and personal cash management. As individuals we worry about having too little cash lying around in our checking accounts, whereas corporate cash managers worry about having too little cash to pay the bills and too much cash tied up in assets earning a low return. Corporate cash management means having enough money to meet the cash needs of a company and that's all. It is not just the minimum balance that drives the system as in a personal checking account, but the minimum and maximum balances. When corporate cash holdings exceed the maximum desired amount, then they are free to be spent funding more profitable alternatives such as capital expenditures, stock buybacks, mergers and acquisitions. If a company lacks an immediate means to profitably invest excess cash holdings earning a low rate of interest, then the excess cash can be used to reduce borrowings costing a high rate of interest.

WORKING CAPITAL

Working capital has been alluded to in the two previous chapters. It consists of short-term cash plus accounts receivable and inventories less accounts payable, short-term bank debt, and maturities of long-term debt due within a year. Accounts receivable are inventory sent to, but not yet paid for, by the customer. Inventory is goods that have been made but not yet sold. Accounts payable are other companies' accounts receivable that have to be paid by some due date.

An expanding accounts receivable and inventory are drains on cash. Both represent goods that have consumed cash in their production but have not yet been paid for. The difference between the two is that there is a better chance of being paid for goods sitting in a customer's storeroom than goods gathering dust in the company's warehouse. Another cash drain is reducing accounts payable, which means that a company is paying its bills, thereby liquidating other companies' receivables. A company can always spruce up the balance in a checking account by not paying bills. Letting accounts payable expand is a temporary source of funds, although at some point they have to be paid.

Another source of funds is factoring receivables. Receivables can be sold to a bank or a factor at a discount to their face value. This gives a company an immediate source of cash at the cost of a discount. The factor makes money on the eventual payment of the receivable. If a receivable is paid sooner than expected, the factor makes more money than anticipated as the discount contains an implicit time period for repayment at a specified rate of return. Factors have to be careful to discount receivables only from creditworthy customers or make some arrangement with the client company to cover the potential for bad debt.

Any receivable can be factored. Life insurance is a receivable. The difference between life insurance and an account receivable is that payment is not within 30 days but at some indeterminate point in time known as the moment of death. Companies in the business of factoring life insurance policies discount the face amount by what they consider to be the appropriate period before the timely demise of the policyholder. This way the living rather than the heirs can squander the inheritance or pay for health care to prolong their lives, which is not in the overall interest of the factor.

The factor is an avid reader of the obituary column, for the sooner the departure of the loved one, the greater the profit. However, there are exceptions when death does not follow the mortuary tables. There is the occasional 60-year-old who has a serious heart condition that should bring about a visit from the Grim Reaper within four months but who somehow manages to postpone the visit for four decades. Too many of these and the factor is out of business. This, by the way, is a risk that can be managed by the appropriate selection of the discount based on the probability distribution for the demise of the sick and dying. The risk as always is in the tail of the probability distribution, where a few individuals survive a lot longer than expected. However, the probability distribution can change with advances in medicine that prolong the lives of the terminally ill. This may leave the factor holding the proverbial bag.

It is interesting how our personal perspective of an event can be so opposite. Here adding years to one's life is viewed as beneficial for the individual and detrimental to the factor. A rising price benefits one party (the seller) and can have a devastating effect on another (the buyer). A falling price reverses the roles. Much of the effort in risk management is to identify the two parties who are affected differently by the same event to create an instrument whereby one party may be willing to give up a portion of a potential benefit for protection against a portion of a potential loss.

Deferring accounts payable—not paying your bills—is another way to build up cash reserves, but cash reserves can also be enhanced by paying them in a way that delays the actual transfer of funds for as long as possible. Going back more than a few years when interest rates were high, one brokerage company delayed payment to its clients on the proceeds of a stock sale for as long as legally permissible. Then the check would be mailed from a location that would take the longest possible time to get to a client. The check would then be drawn on a bank that would also take the longest possible time for the check to clear after the client deposited the check in a local bank. A database was created where the input was the client's address and the output was the brokerage office for mailing the check and the bank for clearing the check. The system allowed the client's money to sit in the broker's account accruing interest for the longest possible time. The accrued interest income may seem small for an individual transaction, but when accumulated over untold numbers of transactions, incremental interest income amounted to many millions of dollars. Some of this flowed into the bonus check for the executive who thought of this learned example of sophisticated cash management. Banking reform placing time limits on banks' clearing checks, a lowering of interest rates, more speedy delivery of mail by the postal service, and an uproar among investors when the scheme was exposed by the press ended this pathway to riches.

SOURCES OF VARIATION

Certain types of cash outflows for corporations may exhibit little variation such as meeting the payroll, rent, insurance premiums, interest, and debt repayments. Others exhibit more variation but generally hold no great surprise such as communications, utility, repair, and maintenance bills. While corporations must deal with surprise expenditures from time to time, variation in cash outflows is normally less than variation in cash inflows.

As anyone in business knows; sales can vary greatly on a daily basis. Some days sales are robust; others are slow. But sales do not translate immediately to cash inflow. Sales by most companies are invoiced for payment within 15 or 30 or more days. Variation in payment of accounts receivable may not necessarily exhibit the same variation as sales volume. Appendix 5.A examines the variation between sales and receipt of payments. Sales follow a normal distribution averaging $100 per day with variation in sales equivalent to a standard deviation of $20 per day. Each day 10 customers buy 1/10th of the day's sales. Payment is spread over the subsequent 10 to 30 days after purchase. Figures 5.1 and 5.2 show the respective variation between sales and receipts.

In Figure 5.1, sales between $80 and $120 are one standard deviation away from the mean of $100. About two-thirds of sales should fall within this range. However, there are far more data points above $120 and below $80 in Figure 5.2 than in Fig-

Figure 5.1
Variation in Sales

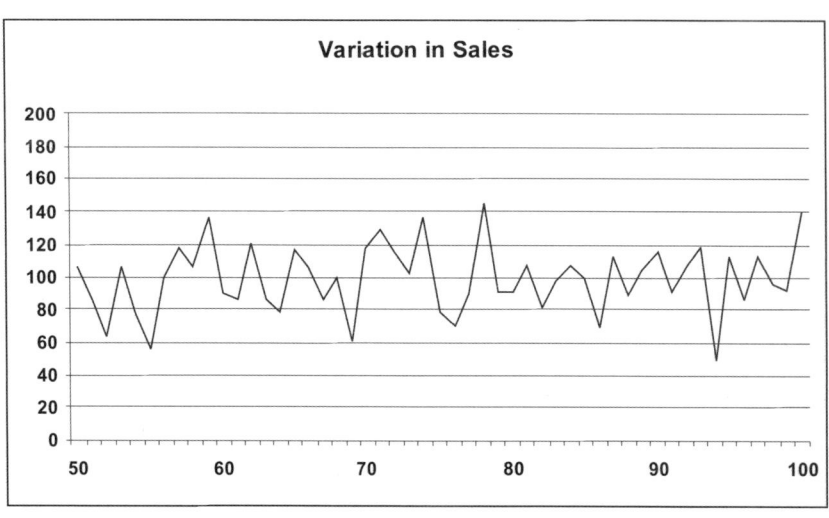

Figure 5.2
Variation in Receipts

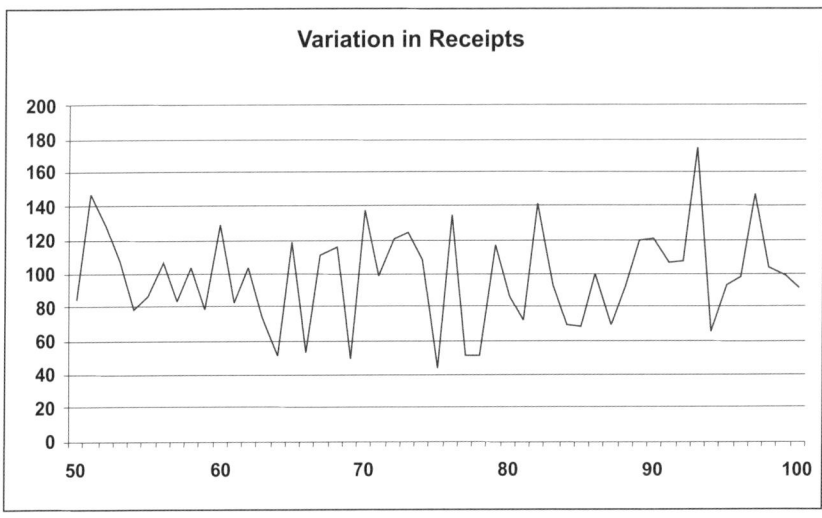

ure 5.1. This is visual confirmation that receipts have a larger standard deviation or greater variation than sales.

The difference in variation between receipts and sales increases when there are fewer customers making larger purchases and decreases for a greater number of customers making smaller purchases. Variation in receipts of payments approaches variation in sales as the number of customers becomes fairly large, with each purchasing a correspondingly smaller portion of a company's output. Variation in receipts is either the same or greater than the variation in sales depending on the number of customers.

Another factor affecting cash outflow is inventory. Suppose that sales average 100 units per day (not $/day) with a standard deviation of 20 units and the volume of production remains at 100 per day. What happens to inventory? Appendix 5.B demonstrates that this simplistic approach to inventory management of matching production with average sales doesn't work. Figure 5.3 shows the unremitting growth in inventory starting from 400 units, which is equivalent to four days of sales of matching production with average sales. This occurs when there is a period of time where actual sales are less than average sales.

Figure 5.4 shows the unremitting decline in inventory until it becomes insufficient to support sales. This occurs when there is a period of time where actual sales are greater than average sales.

Although sales average 100 per day, there may be extended periods when sales are above or below 100. If these last long enough, as they do in Figures 5.3 and 5.4, inventory either grows to excessive levels or no longer supports sales.

Figure 5.3
Inventory Becoming Excessive

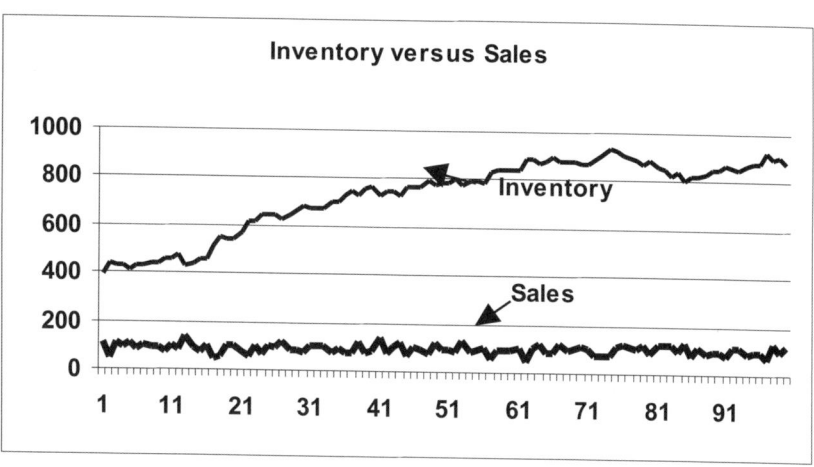

Bin levels can be established to reduce production when inventory rises above the high bin level and to increase production when inventory falls below the low bin level. Suppose that production increases to 105 when the inventory falls below a stipulated low bin level and decreases to 95 when inventory rises above a stipulated high bin level and is 100 when inventory is between the high and low bin levels. The factory can be manned for production of 105 units similar to grocery store chains that are manned for maximum demand. When demand rises, as seen by

Figure 5.4
Inventory Not Supporting Sales

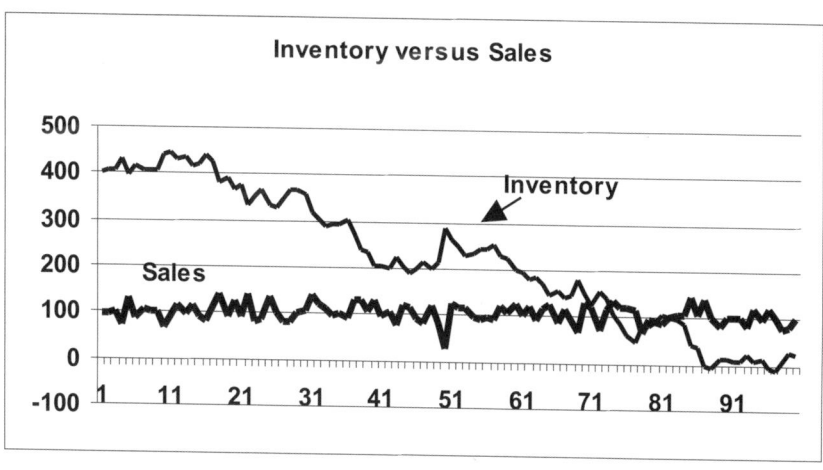

long lines beginning to form at the checkout counters, all the clerks are assigned to checking and bagging. When demand falls, some of the clerks are reassigned to sweeping the floors, and others to replenishing the shelves or working in the stockroom. The clerks are fully employed regardless of demand, with their assignments changing depending on the number of customers lining up at the checkout counters.

This same principle can be adapted to a factory. A factory can be manned for peak production of 105 units. The workers displaced when production falls to 100 or 95 can perform needed maintenance and repair on machines, sweep the floors, work in the warehouse, or meet in groups to discuss how to improve the manufacturing process. In other words, labor is not hired and fired as production varies between 95, 100, and 105 units. Labor costs remain constant, even though production is changing. What does change is the cash outflow for purchasing raw materials and shipping goods to customers. Thus, cash outflow is affected by production changes, even though average sales remain unchanged. Changes in production output introduce another layer of variability to cash outflow not present in cash inflow.

Cash outflows are also affected by changes in average sales. Suppose that average sales suddenly jump to 125 units. More workers have to be hired, more material has to be purchased, more goods have to be shipped, and marketing wants inventory increased from 400 to 500 units in order to preserve 4 days of sales in inventory. Cash outflow increases immediately. But what happens to cash inflow? Nothing; payments for the greater quantity of goods shipped today will not be seen for 15, 30, 45, or more days. A rise in production to match a sudden escalation of sales will increase cash outflow with little change in cash inflow. This, of course, is a drain on short-term cash funds and also affects the nature of the variability of cash outflows with respect to cash inflows.

Take the opposite tack: sales suddenly decline to a new average of 75 units per day. Now material and shipping costs fall sharply as production is temporarily cut not only to match production to the new level of sales but also to liquidate inventory to 300 units, the new 4 days of sales. What happens to cash flow? Cash outflow drops, but cash inflow remains unchanged because cash inflow is dependent on the payment of invoices issued 15–45 days prior when sales were at 100. Cash inflow does not fall until 15–45 days after sales dropped. An immediate drop in sales and production actually enhances near-term cash flow. This, too, affects the nature of the swings in cash outflows with respect to cash inflows.

THE OBJECTIVE

The risk is running out of cash to support a company's operations. The means to manage this risk is the amount of cash holdings. The cash holdings are in two different accounts. One is a checking account, referred to as the cash account that earns no or little interest and is used for disbursing funds. The other is a short-term investment account for parking funds to back up the cash account. The short-term investment account earns interest but lacks the complete liquidity of the cash account.

The short-term investment account may be invested in six-month financial instruments such as certificates of deposits (CDs) that mature on a fairly regular basis throughout the year. If the maturity of the instrument in the short-term investment account occurs before the proceeds are needed in the cash account, then there is a free transfer of funds from the short-term investment to the cash accounts. If the maturity of the instrument occurs shortly after the proceeds are needed, no fees need be generated if other disbursements can be temporarily postponed. Fees to transfer funds arise when there is a need to make an immediate disbursement without a sufficient balance in the cash account and without any near-term maturing of financial instruments in the short-term investment account. Now a short-term investment must be liquidated before its maturity date, generating a transfer fee in terms of brokerage fees and price discounts to conclude the sale. Too much reliance on the short-term investment account in comparison to the cash account may not be optimal when the transfer fees of moving funds from the short-term investment to the cash account are taken into consideration.

Unlike a personal checking account, where minimum balances are of primary concern, in a corporate setting, both minimum and maximum balances are of primary concern. A company wants to have enough money to pay its bills yet at the same time minimize cash holdings in order to put as much cash as possible to more profitable uses such as supporting capital expenditures, early retirement of debt, buying back company stock, proceeding with an acquisition or other cash expenditures in the financial interests of the company. As mentioned, it makes no sense earning 2% in the cash and short-term investment accounts if the funds can earn 12% by being invested in the company's future or paying off long-term debt costing 10%.

Thus, the cash manager practices a balancing act between the risk of running out of cash and the maximum amount of cash dedicated to protecting against this risk. The risk of running out of cash can be analyzed by setting up an infinite line of credit that serves as insurance for protecting the company from not being able to meet its cash obligations. The frequency and the size of drawdowns on the line of credit provide the means of measuring the risk of running out of cash for different maximum balances on the cash and the short-term investment accounts.

As a practical matter, most companies do have a line of credit just for this contingency. The cash manager must decide, in managing the risk of not running out of cash, not only the maximum limits of the cash and short-term investment accounts but also the appropriate size of the line of credit. Unlike personal lines of credit, banks normally charge a fee such as ½% for the unused portion of a corporate line of credit. Thus, the size of a line of credit does matter when determining the appropriate maximum limits on the cash and short-term investment accounts.

THE LIFE OF A CASH MANAGER

On a daily or weekly basis, the difference between cash inflow and outflow can be positive or negative. The first thing that a cash manager does when there is a net positive inflow is to check the status of the cash account to see if it is fully funded. If not, the net inflow remains in the cash account. If the cash account is above its maximum limit, then the excess cash—or all the inflow if the cash account is already fully funded—is assigned to the short-term investment account. Once the short-term investment account is fully funded, any excess cash is then assigned to the line of credit. Once the balance in the line of credit is paid off, any remaining cash is available for corporate use such as capital expenditures, acquisitions, mergers, stock buybacks, or early retirement of long-term debt. If the cash and short-term investment accounts are fully funded and there is no balance in the line of credit, the net inflow is immediately available for corporate use. Regardless of how this money is spent, it is no longer available to the cash manager.

If outflow exceeds inflow, then the cash manager draws down on the cash account to make up the difference. If this is inadequate, or if the cash account has already been exhausted, then the short-term investment account is drawn down. If this is not sufficient or already has been drawn down, then the cash manager writes a check on the line of credit. Drawing down the line of credit both in its frequency and in its amount is the risk of running out of cash. This risk varies for different maximum amounts assigned to the cash and short-term investment accounts.

Another way to look at this is that there are three rain barrels. Net cash inflows are first poured into the first rain barrel, the cash account, until it's full. Then whatever is left is poured into the second rain barrel, the short-term investment account, until it's full. Any further excess is then poured into the third rain barrel, the line of credit, until it is full (paid off). What's left is spilled on the ground, forever lost as far as the cash manager is concerned.

Net cash outflows work just the opposite. The first rain barrel is drawn down to support the net cash outflow. Once emptied, the second rain barrel, the short-term investment account, is drawn down, and when emptied, the third rain barrel, the line of credit, is drawn down. This rain barrel, as large as the Pacific Ocean, can never be emptied. Its job is to evaluate the risk of running out of cash.

Figure 5.5 shows the top portion of the spreadsheet that indicates the various interest rates associated with funds held in the cash account and in the short-term investment account and the interest charge on drawing down the line of credit. The fee associated with maintaining a line of credit has not been incorporated in the model as no size restriction is being placed on the line of credit. This can be incorporated, but the model would then have to be modified for a finite line of credit.

The transfer fee is basically an average fee to transfer funds from the short-term investment to the cash account. Sometimes the transfer is free when maturities match disbursements; other times investments must be liquidated to have immediate access to funds, generating a transfer fee in terms of brokerage commissions and discounts from face value to effect a sale.

Figure 5.5
Cash Account

	A	B	C	D	E
1	Cash and Short-Term Investment Account Manager				
2					
3	Interest Rate on Short Term Cash Account:				0.00%
4	Interest Rate on Short Term Investment Account:				4.00%
5	Transfer Fee From Investment to Cash Accounts:				0.25%
6	Interest Charge for Line of Credit:				10.00%
7					
8					
9	Minimum:	$ -	$ 80		
10	Most Likely:	$ 100	$ 90		
11	Maximum:	$ 200	$ 100		Preliminary
12					Short
13		Weekly	Weekly		Term
14		Cash	Cash	Weekly	Cash
15	Week	Receipts	Expenses	Difference	Account
16					
17	1	$ 52	$ 91	$ (39)	$ 44
18	2	$ 81	$ 89	$ (8)	$ 36
19	3	$ 77	$ 83	$ (6)	$ 30

Weekly cash receipts were modeled with a triangular probability distribution varying between $0 and $200 with a most likely value of $100. Weekly cash expenses were also modeled with a triangular probability distribution varying between $80 and $100 with a most likely value of $90. On average, inflows exceed outflows, which is necessary for a company to make a profit. But outflows can exceed inflows on a transitory basis. Moreover, the variance in cash inflows was arbitrarily chosen to be much greater than cash outflows to demonstrate the efficacy of the model to determine the optimal maximum amounts for the cash and short-term investment accounts. In practice, actual inflows and outflows could be modeled with the *@Risk Fit Distributions to Data* feature to obtain the best-fitting probability distributions. The model was set up to run over a 52-week period.

Figure 5.6 is the remaining portion of the spreadsheet showing the short-term investment account. Interest income and transfer fees and interest charges for use of the line of credit are in cells M3 through M6. The maximum balance or drawdown of the line of credit is in cell O3, the average balance in cell O7, and the number of drawdowns in cell O11. Column P contains moneys that pass through the cash management system and are available for corporate use. They can no longer be tapped to fund the short-term cash and investment accounts or pay down the line of credit.

Figure 5.6
Short-Term Investment Account

	H	I	J	K	L	M	N	O	P
1		Objective:	$ 179.23					Maximum	
2								Balance	
3	Interest Income on Short Term Cash Account:					$ -		$ -	
4	Interest Income on Short Term Investment Account:					$ 3.90			
5	Fees to Transfer from Investment to Cash:					$ (0.13)		Average	
6	Interest Charge on Line of Credit					$ -		Balance	
7	Net Expense:					$ 3.77		$ -	
8									
9								Number of	
10								Drawdowns	
11	Final		Preliminary			Final		0	
12	Short	Short	Short		Draw	Short			Funds
13	Term	Term	Term		Down	Term		Balance	Available
14	Cash	Investment	Investment		Line of	Investment	Funds	Line of	Corporate
15	Account	Inflow	Account		Credit	Account	Available	Credit	Uses
16	$ 83					$ 100			
17	$ 83	$ 59	$ 159	$ 100	$ -	$ 100	$ 59	$ -	$ 59
18	$ 76	$ -	$ 100	$ 100	$ -	$ 100	$ -	$ -	$ -
19	$ 83	$ 27	$ 127	$ 100	$ -	$ 100	$ 27	$ -	$ 27

RISKOPTIMIZER

@Risk simulations could be run for various maximum amounts assigned to both the cash and the short-term investment accounts to judge overall performance. But @Risk cannot determine the optimal maximum amounts, and old-fashioned trial and error would be too time-consuming. Selecting the optimal values for the two accounts is a job for RiskOptimizer. RiskOptimizer relies on "intelligent," not random, trial and error to determine the optimal maximum values for the two accounts. The "intelligence" in RiskOptimizer's optimization algorithms (rules) is to select new values for the variables (the maximum amounts for both accounts) based on the simulation results of previously assigned values. RiskOptimizer "learns" from the previous simulations in order to "evolve" an optimal solution over a series of simulation runs.

RiskOptimizer requires the assigning of an objective cell and adjustable cells along with an appropriate range of values and the incorporation of constraints. This particular model does not require any constraints other than those implied by the selected range on the adjustable cells. The objective is to minimize the sum of the costs (line of credit interest charges and transfer fees from the short-term investment account to the cash account less interest income on the cash and short-term investment accounts), the maximum amounts in the cash and short-term investment accounts, and the average use of the line of credit. A punitive charge of a factor of 10 was applied against the average use of the line of credit to reflect management's desire to minimize reliance on a line of credit to cover cash deficits. The RiskOptimizer menu is in Figure 5.7.

The objective cell J1 contains the aforementioned cost factors in formula format. The objective cell is to be minimized by varying the maximum amounts in the

Figure 5.7
RiskOptimizer Menu

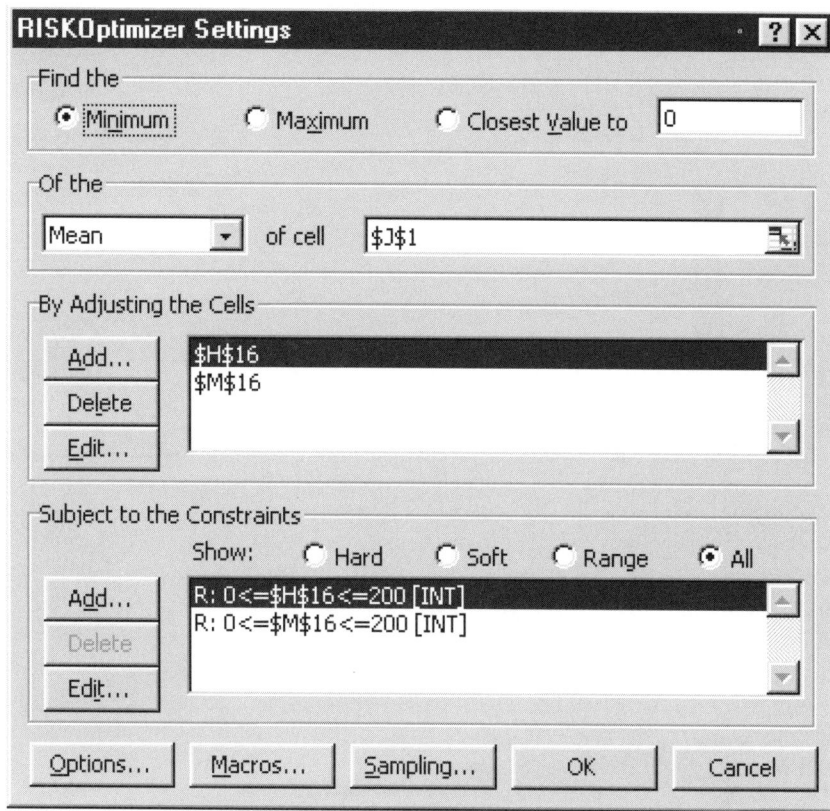

cash account (cell H16) and the short-term investment account (cell M16) with integers between 0 and 200. If the solution turns out to be near a range limit, it is advisable to rerun the RiskOptimizer with wider range limits. The optimal solution was for the cash account to have a maximum amount of $83 and for the short-term investment account to have a maximum amount of $100. This represents a little less than two weeks of cash inflow in both accounts.

EVALUATING THE RISK OF RUNNING OUT OF CASH

After RiskOptimizer determines the optimal values for the maximum amounts in the cash and short-term investment accounts, then @Risk simulations can be run in order to evaluate the risk of running out of cash. Designated output cells were the number of occurrences when the line of credit was drawn down over a 52-week period and the average and maximum amounts of drawdowns on the line of credit. Figure 5.8 shows the frequency of usage of the line of credit over the 52-week period.

Figure 5.8
Frequency of Occurrences

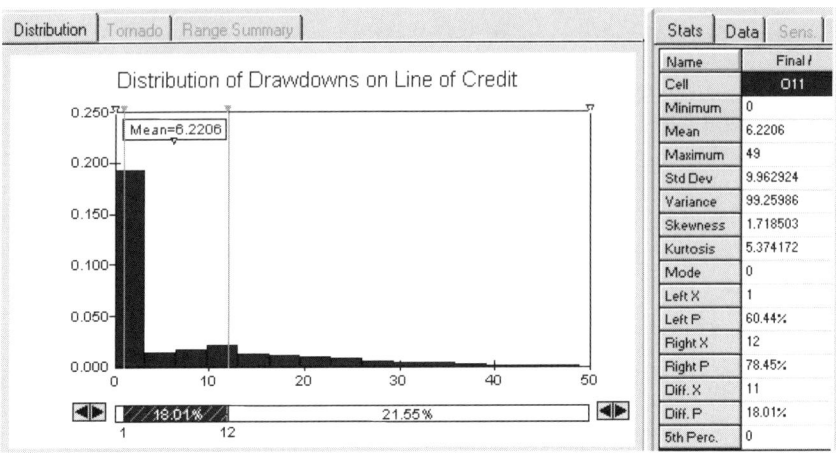

The probability of no drawdowns on the line of credit over the course of the year is 60.4%. Suppose that the cash manager does not want to tap the line of credit more than 12 weeks per year. From Figure 5.7 there is a 21.55% chance that drawdowns will occur more than 12 times per year. Drawdowns on the line of credit mean that both the cash and short-term investment accounts have been exhausted of funds for the selected maximum amounts for both accounts. These amounts can be increased to analyze the impact on the degree of reliance on the line of credit from the results of a @Risk simulation. The average annual drawdown of the line of credit is shown in Figure 5.9.

Figure 5.9
Average Drawdown on the Line of Credit

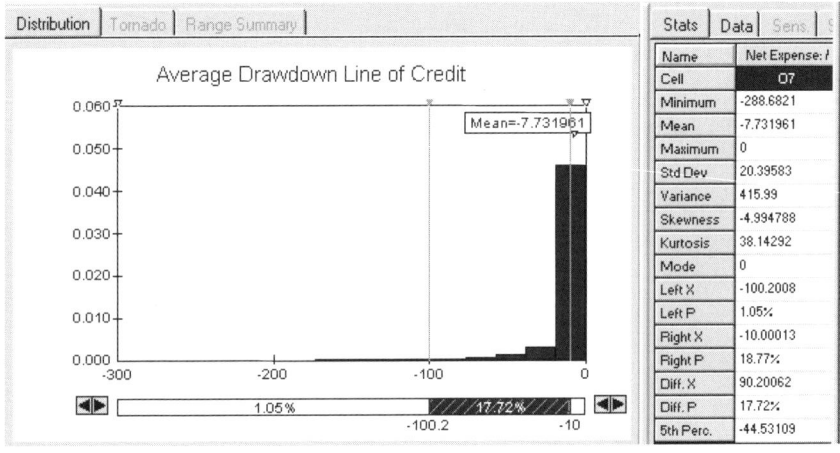

THE RISK OF RUNNING OUT OF CASH

The average annual drawdown on the line of credit is $7.70 (the negative values reflect the spreadsheet formulation of drawing down on the line of credit as a negative value). The low value reflects the line of credit not being drawn down 60% of the time. There are a 1.05% chance of the average drawdown being above $100 and an 18.77% chance of being above $10. A cash manager is in position to gauge average drawdowns for different maximum amounts to the two accounts by running and analyzing @Risk simulations. A better measure for analyzing the risk of running out of money is the maximum drawdown on the line of credit shown in Figure 5.10.

There are a 2.3% chance of the maximum line of credit having to be above $200 and a 9.53% chance of having to be above $100 to accommodate extreme variance in outflows with respect to inflows. Again a cash flow manager can vary the maximum amounts in the cash and short-term investment accounts to analyze the impact on the maximum line of credit.

A question that has to be dealt with is how to deal with the highly improbable cases where a very large line of credit is required to cover unusually long periods when outflows exceed inflows. These periods occur when the random process is consistently picking high values for cash outflows and low values for cash inflows. This can happen—not unlike consistently rolling even numbers with the cast of a die, but would one really have a line of credit of $584, the maximum result achieved in 10,000 iterations?

One way to deal with this is to utilize the @Risk filter feature to eliminate these highly improbable results. The problem, of course, is that the highly improbable result occurred. Another approach is to assume that the cash manager would respond to this situation by raising cash by factoring receivables, delaying payments

Figure 5.10
Maximum Drawdown on the Line of Credit

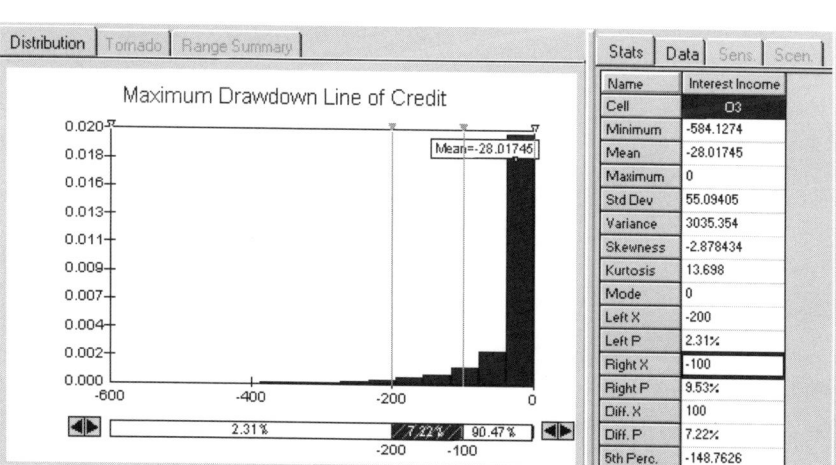

of current liabilities as much as permissible, and getting on the phone to badger customers about paying their bills. To the extent that the cash manager is not a passive observer and takes appropriate actions to raise cash, then there is no need for a line of credit to be sized to support the maximum drawdown of $584. Thus, a line of credit between $100 and $200 may be appropriate under the circumstances.

APPENDIX 5.A
VARIATION IN RECEIPTS VERSUS VARIATION IN SALES

The following spreadsheet does not set out to prove but to demonstrate that there may be greater variation in the paying of invoices than in the variation in sales that generated the invoices. Figure 5.A.1 generates invoices from daily sales and distributes the invoice payment dates to the subsequent 10–30 days after the sale.

Figure 5.A.1
Spreadsheet Setup

	F	G	H	I	J	K	L
1							
2							
3		0.502562	0.873777	0.570816	0.191201	0.992809	0.59121
4	Day:	1	2	3	4	5	6
5	Sales:	100.1	122.9	103.6	82.5	149.0	104.6
6		12	16	26	20	18	30
7		16	23	32	19	19	35
8		12	26	15	27	22	27
9		26	22	13	17	26	28
10		21	28	28	32	25	35
11		26	27	23	25	26	29
12		26	23	16	15	15	30
13		28	19	23	29	17	17
14		24	16	26	16	22	35
15		23	15	22	19	25	16

Row 3 is a random number generator, =RAND(), used to generate a normal distribution in row 5, which contains the formula, replicated to the right to the end of the spreadsheet (column IV):

$$=NORMINV(G3,100,20)$$

This generates a normal distribution with a mean of $100 in daily sales with a standard deviation of $20. The @Risk normal distribution could have been used, but Microsoft Excel also has the capability of generating a normal distribution. Each day 10 customers buy exactly 1/10th of daily sales in row 3. Each customer pays for the purchase anywhere between 10 and 30 days after the purchase. The days of receipt of payment of the 10 invoices are in rows 6 through 15, which vary between 10 and 30 days after the day of sale in row 4. The formula in cell G6 adds a randomly distributed 10 to 30 days to the day of the sale in cell G4:

$$=G\$4+INT(10+RAND()*20)$$

This is replicated down to create 10 purchases and replicated to column IV to create 250 days of simulation. Figure 5.A.2 shows a partial view of the collection of receipts for the first 17 days of the simulation period.

Column F indicates the days of the receipt of payment for the 10 individual sales. It starts with a value of 10 because that is the earliest possible payment for an item sold on day 1. As seen in Figure 5.A.1, day 1 sales are $100.10, and 1/10th of this is $10 (rounded). Two payments are due on day 12. On day 12 in Figure 5.A.2, there is a receipt of $20. There is a direct link between the assignment of the day of payment in Figure 5.A.1 and its receipt in Figure 5.A.2. The formula in cell G17 is set up for 10 customers buying 1/10th of the day's sales and is rather cumbersome in order to allow for multiple receipts occurring on the same day.

=IF($F17=G$6,G$5/10,0)+IF($F17=G$7,G$5/10,0)+IF($F17=G$8,G$5/10,0)+IF($F17=G$9,G$5/10,0)+IF($F17=G$10,G$5/10,0)+IF($F17=G$11,G$5/10,0)+IF($F17=G$12,G$5/10,0)+IF($F17=G$13,G$5/10,0)+IF($F17=G$14,G$5/10,0)+IF($F17=G$15,G$5/10,0)

Cell F17 is replicated to the right to column IV and down to row 287 to accommodate the 250 days of the simulation plus another 30 days for payment of receivables. Column D totals up daily receipts from column G through column IV. Figure 5.A.3 shows the results of the simulation, and Figure 5.A.4 shows the associated formulas.

Cell B3 totals sales, while cell B5 totals receipts to ensure that receipts cover sales. Average sales and receipts are contained in cells E2 and F5, respectively. Average receipts are less than average sales because the period of average receipts covers

Figure 5.A.2
Timing of Receipts

	D	E	F	G	H	I	J	K
16	Receipts		Day					
17	0.0		10	0	0	0	0	0
18	0.0		11	0	0	0	0	0
19	20.0		12	20	0	0	0	0
20	10.4		13	0	0	10	0	0
21	0.0		14	0	0	0	0	0
22	45.8		15	0	12	10	8	15
23	63.7		16	10	25	10	8	0
24	33.6		17	0	0	0	8	15
25	24.8		18	0	0	0	0	15
26	63.4		19	0	12	0	17	15
27	38.3		20	0	0	0	8	0
28	39.7		21	10	0	0	0	0
29	63.6		22	0	12	10	0	30
30	84.8		23	10	25	21	0	0
31	68.2		24	10	0	0	0	0
32	64.1		25	0	0	0	8	30
33	163.9		26	30	12	21	0	30

Figure 5.A.3
Simulation Results

	A	B	C	D	E
1	Variation in Receipts vs Sales				
2				Average sales:	98.0
3	Sales across:	24509.6		Std Dev sales:	20.2
4					
5	Receipts down:	24509.6		Average receipts:	90.4
6				Std Dev receipts:	36.7

Figure 5.A.4
Formulation of Figure 5.A.3

	A	B	C	D	E
2				Average sales:	=AVERAGE(G5:IV5)
3	Sales across:	=SUM(G5:IV5)		Std Dev sales:	=STDEVP(G5:IV5)
4					
5	Receipts down:	=SUM(D17:D287)		Average receipts:	=AVERAGE(D17:D287)
6				Std Dev receipts:	=STDEVP(D17:D287)

more days than average sales. In this respect average receipts are a bit misleading. The key to ensure the proper operation of the program is that total receipts (cell B3) equal total sales (cell B5). The standard deviations show that the variation associated with receipts is much larger than that of sales (doubling the standard deviation quadruples the variance).

Figures 5.1 and 5.2 show the difference in sales and in receipts for the same 50-day period of time. Receipts actually reflect sales that partly occurred before the selected 50-day period.

An experiment was done with only three purchasers buying exactly one-third of a day's sales. The resulting standard deviation of receipts was about $60, three times that of daily sales. This shows that variation becomes greater as the number of customers declines and the portion of daily sales sold to individual customers rises. Conversely, the variation of receipts approaches that of sales as the number of customers increases and the portion of sales sold to individual customers falls. A better experiment to compare the variation in sales with that of receipts would be a Basic program where the number of customers varies each day along with the portion of sales that each buys. This is more difficult to do in a spreadsheet environment. Nevertheless, this appendix illustrates the point that receipts can exhibit greater volatility than sales when the number of customers is relatively small.

APPENDIX 5.B
VARIATION IN INVENTORY

Figure 5.B.1 is the Microsoft Excel spreadsheet to create a simulation for inventory based on a constant production of 100 units and sales averaging 100 units with a standard deviation of 20 units.

Figure 5.B.1
Simulating Inventory

	A	B	C	D	E
1	Inventory Fluctuations				
2					Initial
3					Inventory
4	Day	Production		Sales	400
5	1	100	0.458935	98	402
6	2	100	0.41445	96	406
7	3	100	0.527837	101	405
8	4	100	0.095585	74	431

Column C contains random number generators, =RAND(), to generate integer values for sales in column D:

$$=INT(NORMINV(C5,100,20)+0.5)$$

Column E shows the state of the inventory. The current inventory in cell E5 is the previous day's inventory, here the starting inventory of 400 representing four days of sales, less sales plus production:

$$=E4-D5+B5$$

Individual simulations can be run by invoking *Tools/Options/Recalculation/Manual* and then pressing the F9 key. Columns D and E for appropriate iterations showing either a runaway inventory or one falling into negative territory appear in Figures 5.3 and 5.4. This model demonstrates that matching production to average sales will not work as an inventory control system. Production output has to bracket average sales in order to properly manage inventory. This model can be readily expanded to determine the low and high bin values to raise or lower production output, respectively, for optimal performance.[1]

NOTE

1. See Trigger Points and Production Run Length in *RiskOptimizer for Business Applications*, available at www.nerses.com.

6
EVALUATING RISK INHERENT IN PRODUCT DEVELOPMENT

SYNOPSIS

Chapter 3 dealt with the risk of a bank losing money in a project financing when the project did not generate sufficient revenue to support the underlying debt. A solvency loan was set up to measure this risk in terms of the frequency and the amount of drawdowns. The solvency loan also provided a tool whereby the terms of the debt could be revised in order to manage the degree of risk. Chapter 4 evaluated the risk of funds flow being inadequate to support a general corporate credit even with the company reporting an after-tax profit. This risk can be mitigated by the company raising outside sources of capital in the form of debt and equity to sustain its capital expenditure program. Chapter 5 examined the risk of a company running out of cash in its checking and short-term investment accounts. The degree of risk was measured by establishing a line of credit to measure the amount and frequency of drawdowns similar to evaluating the risk of financing a project. The degree of risk was managed by varying the maximum limits in the two accounts.

This chapter evaluates the risk of proceeding with a project that may or may not materialize and, if it does materialize, may not be profitable. While it may be understandable why some companies would shy away from such ventures for sound conservative reasons, it is to our benefit that some don't. R&D projects are inherently risky because there is no assurance of success, and failures can be costly. We would not have the benefit of drugs to treat illnesses if funds were not put at risk to find a cure or treatment for a disease.

The general methodology outlined in this chapter could be used as a basis for approving the commencement or continuation of any R&D project. However, to demonstrate the methodology, a situation was created concerning the introduction of a new drug. This was done in order to demonstrate the necessity of a venture overcoming two hurdles—success in developing a drug coupled with success in getting the necessary government approvals. However, this methodology could be applied to most business development ventures with the underlying spreadsheet tailored to fit the circumstances.

THE SITUATION

Some initial research has been done on a drug for veterinarians to treat horses for a certain malady with fairly promising preliminary results. The question now is whether to approve a $5 million request to proceed with a serious R&D effort. Top management has requested R&D, market research, operations, and finance to evaluate the prospects for profitability before proceeding with a full-blown R&D effort to try to bring this drug to market.

This exercise in judging imponderables is necessary to justify management support for the development of a new product. Top managers are not the only interested individuals. Marketing is interested in assessing the potential market for this product for internal planning purposes such as the amount to be spent on advertising, the choice of media, and the logistics of offering samples to veterinarians to introduce the product to the market. Production is interested in the results of a market research study in order to gauge the impact of a new product on existing production capacity, including the necessity of adding new capacity. Finance is interested in capital expenditures likely to be required by a new product in production facilities, in supporting the R&D effort, and in introducing a new product to the market. In addition, finance is interested in the new product's potential profitability or lack thereof in terms of return on investment and its long-term contribution to a company's financial well-being.

The individuals involved in making this judgment call are dealing with imponderables. This particular drug has two different applications, and it is not known whether the research effort is going to be successful for either one or whether government approval for either or both applications will be forthcoming. Other imponderables are the price and volume of sales and whether the drug will be restricted to the domestic market or be able to be sold globally.

To proceed with the analysis, knowledgeable individuals were assigned particular tasks. An expert within the company gave the assessment of the probability of success for the two applications of the drug based on the results of preliminary research. The individual was not associated with this drug development program and was instructed to be fair and impartial in making the assessment. The individual had a great deal of experience in research and was sufficiently knowledgeable to assess the chances of eventual success based on the findings of the preliminary research. An experienced cost accountant working with the R&D and marketing obtained the likely development costs for the two applications. A lawyer familiar with obtaining government approvals opined on both the chances of success and the cost of obtaining approvals in the domestic and global markets. Marketing provided estimates of the costs of introducing the drug to the domestic and global markets, much of which would be in the form of advertising expenses to acquaint veterinarians about the existence of the new drug and the cost of distributing free samples. Figure 6.1 lays out the portion of the spreadsheet for assessing development costs.

The expert felt that there was a 60–80% chance for the eventual success of application 1 alone. The expert was more sanguine about application 2 being successfully developed in the lab. The lawyer thought that there was an 80–90% chance of a successfully field-tested product getting through the regulatory process. Obviously, a drug that did not pass the development stage would not be presented for government approval.

Case 1 is the success and approval of application 1 only. Case 2 is the success and approval of application 2 only. Marketing feels that the success and approval of both applications would greatly widen the appeal of the product in the domestic market, which is covered in case 3. Case 4 is both applications being sold in the global market, which necessitates getting other government approvals.

The costs of failure and success of event 1 deal with development costs for both applications. In Figure 6.1, both case 1 and 2 are successfully developed in the lab. If both had failed, or one had failed, there would be different values in columns F and G. Event 2 is gaining government approval. Its costs involve the legal fees and testing costs associated with obtaining government approvals. There is no event 2 fee associated with a failed event 1. But there is a cost of failure for event 2 for a successfully developed product not gaining government approval. The underlying formulas in Figure 6.1 cover these contingencies. Cell G22 takes into account addi-

Figure 6.1
Estimating Development Costs

	A	B	C	D	E	F	G
1	Market Research/Financial Analysis						
2							
3		Case 1	Case 2	Case 3	Case 4	Cost of	Cost of
4		Use 1 Only	Use 2 Only	Use 1 & 2	Use 1 & 2	Failure	Success
5				Domestic Mkt	Global Mkt		
6	Event 1						
7	Min	60%	70%				
8	Most Likely	70%	80%				
9	Max	80%	90%				
10	Probability	70%	80%				
11							
12	Completed Event 1	1	1			$ -	$ 2,500,000
13							
14	Event 2						
15	Min	80%	80%		30%		
16	Most Likely	85%	85%		40%		
17	Max	90%	90%		50%		
18	Probability	85%	85%		40%		
19							
20	Completed Event 2	1	1			$ -	$ 1,300,000
21							
22	Final Case	0	0	1	0		$ 500,000
23							
24	Development Costs					$ 4,945,000	

tional costs for attempting to acquire global marketing rights. Total development costs in cell F24 contain a provision for a potential cost overrun of up to a maximum of 50% based on previous experience.

A number of hurdles have to be overcome. Success for case 1 means overcoming two hurdles (events 1 and 2 for success in the lab and gaining government approval). The same is true for case 2. Case 3 requires overcoming four hurdles (both case 1 and 2 must be successful). Case 4 requires overcoming five hurdles—the additional one being getting other government approvals for global marketing. Figure 6.2 is the effective probability distribution in overcoming the two respective hurdles for case 1.

There are an 81% chance that case 1 will not materialize and a 19% chance that it will. One might think that the probability of success should be higher since there are a 70% chance of making it through the laboratory phase of development and an 85% chance of gaining government approval. The probability of overcoming both hurdles of nearly 60% can be obtained by multiplying the two probabilities together. But a similarly high chance exists for application 2 (case 2) and if cases 1 and 2 are both successful, then case 3 kicks in, supplanting cases 1 and 2. In other words, the probability of success in Figure 6.2 applies for case 1 succeeding and case 2 failing. In the situation where both succeed, then case 3 or 4 applies, not case 1.

Row 22 signifies the final outcome, and there can be only one "win" (the values can either be a single 1 or all 0's). If cases 1 and 2 both have a value of 1 in row 20, indicating success for both applications, then the value for case 3 in row 22 is 1 and the corresponding values for cases 1 and 2 are set to zero. Table 6.1 shows the probability outcomes for the four cases.

Figure 6.2
Successfully Getting Application 1 to Market

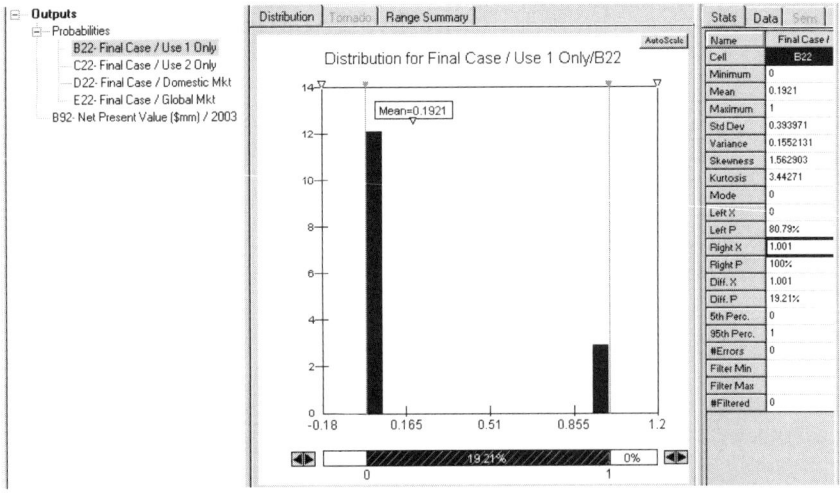

Table 6.1
Outcomes of Success and Failure

	Success	Failure
Case 1 alone	19%	81%
Case 2 alone	27	73
Case 3 (both cases 1 and 2 without foreign permission)	25	75
Case 4 (both cases 1 and 2 with foreign permission)	16	84

The chance of total failure where cells B22 through E22 add up to zero is only 13%; thus, the chance of success in terms of proceeding with this project is a very respectable 87%. This may seem high considering that Table 6.1 shows a high probability of failure associated with each individual event. But all four events must fail in order to have total failure.

Table 6.1 can be roughly approximated by a jar of jelly beans of four colors. There is a 25% chance of randomly picking a red jelly bean. Suppose a red jelly bean means success and the other colored beans mean failure. What are the chances of randomly picking four beans out of the jar of which at least one is red? The chance is obviously better than 25% since we have four tries to pick a red jelly bean. Manual iterations of the spreadsheet by pressing the F9 key in the *Monte Carlo* mode clearly show that total failure is not a common outcome. Relying on intuition to prejudge probabilities when events are contingent on one another can be dangerous to the decision-making process.

Figure 6.3 is the next portion of the spreadsheet. The launch year when this product is commercially available has a 10% chance of occurring in 2005, 70% in 2006, and 20% in 2007.

Market research contacted veterinarians to see if they would use the product if it performed as promised for a range of different prices. Veterinarians responded on the basis of the cost and effectiveness of the current practice for treating the malady compared to the alternative of using the new treatment at different prices. The result of the survey conducted by market research was that the product could be sold somewhere between $17 and $23 per application for optimal results. At higher prices, the veterinarians would remain with the present treatment; at lower prices, the volume of sales would not increase appreciably. The same sales price applies for all four cases.

Cases 3 and 4 have much higher volumes than cases 1 and 2. Production personnel concluded that different manufacturing technologies would apply, resulting in lower production costs for the higher-volume cases. The advantage of economies of large-scale production leads to higher unit profits for cases 3 and 4. Figure 6.4 generates the gross profit. The volume estimates for the total market were obtained from marketing based on estimates of the total number of veterinarians treating horses, the number of horses treated per veterinarian, and the frequency of the malady. Surveys by market research led to the estimates on the

Figure 6.3
Launch Year and Unit Profit

	A	B	C	D	E
26	Launch Year	0	0	2006	0
27					
28	Price				
29	Min	$ 17.00			
30	Most Likely	$ 20.00			
31	Max	$ 23.00			
32	Price	$ 20.00	$ 20.00	$ 20.00	$ 20.00
33					
34	Manufacturing Cost				
35	Min	$ 10.00	$ 10.00	$ 8.00	$ 7.00
36	Most Likely	$ 12.00	$ 12.00	$ 10.00	$ 9.00
37	Max	$ 14.00	$ 14.00	$ 12.00	$ 11.00
38	Manufacturing Cost	$ 12.00	$ 12.00	$ 10.00	$ 9.00
39					
40	Unit Profit	$ 8.00	$ 8.00	$ 10.00	$ 11.00

acceptance for case 1 and case 2 alone and in combination for both the domestic and global markets.

Market research obtained the likely market shares for the indicated price range. Gross profits look a bit anemic for cases 1 and 2 compared to cases 3 and 4. Figure 6.5 obtains net profit by netting gross profit of overhead. Estimates of overhead were obtained from production and finance.

The estimates in the investment in new production facilities were obtained from production based on the market assessment of volume. Figure 6.6 is the cash flow

Figure 6.4
Gross Profit

	A	B	C	D	E
42	Total Market Volume				
43	Min	500,000	300,000	1,500,000	2,500,000
44	Most Likely	750,000	500,000	1,750,000	2,750,000
45	Max	1,000,000	700,000	2,000,000	3,000,000
46	Total Market Volume	750,000	500,000	1,750,000	2,750,000
47					
48	Market Share				
49	Min	20%	30%	40%	50%
50	Most Likely	25%	40%	50%	60%
51	Max	30%	50%	60%	70%
52	Market Share	25%	40%	50%	60%
53					
54	Volume	187,500	200,000	875,000	1,650,000
55					
56	Gross Profit	$ 1,500,000	$ 1,600,000	$ 8,750,000	$ 18,150,000

Figure 6.5
Net Profit

	A	B	C	D	E
56	Gross Profit	$ 1,500,000	$ 1,600,000	$ 8,750,000	$ 18,150,000
57					
58	Overhead				
59	Min	$ 400,000	$ 300,000	$ 1,000,000	$ 2,000,000
60	Most Likely	$ 500,000	$ 400,000	$ 1,250,000	$ 2,250,000
61	Max	$ 600,000	$ 500,000	$ 1,500,000	$ 2,500,000
62	Overhead	$ 500,000	$ 400,000	$ 1,250,000	$ 2,250,000
63					
64	Net Profit	$ 1,000,000	$ 1,200,000	$ 7,500,000	$ 15,900,000
65					
66	Investment				
67	Min	$ 4,500,000	$ 5,000,000	$ 12,000,000	$ 20,000,000
68	Most Likely	$ 4,750,000	$ 5,250,000	$ 14,000,000	$ 22,000,000
69	Max	$ 5,000,000	$ 5,500,000	$ 16,000,000	$ 24,000,000
70	Investment	$ 4,750,000	$ 5,250,000	$ 14,000,000	$ 22,000,000

projection. The year to start is listed along with the investment, which includes the building cost of the new production facilities and the development costs, including government approvals and the initial marketing effort. The first year cash flow is the net profit for case 3, the applicable case in Figure 6.1. Once the project is onstream at 100% of its potential, then there is further long-term growth in net profit as the product increasingly gains market acceptance.

Row 84 in the lower portion of Figure 6.6 shows the outflow of the investment during the launch year. The investment could be spread over two or three years be-

Figure 6.6
Cash Flow Projection

	A	B	C	D	E	F	G
72	Year to Start	2006					
73	Investment	$ 18,945,000					
74	First Year Cash Flow	$ 7,500,000					
75							
76	Long Term Growth						
77	Min	2%					
78	Most Likely	3%					
79	Max	5%					
80	Long Term Growth	3%					
81							
82	Cash Flow Projection						
83		2003	2004	2005	2006	2007	2008
84	Investment	$ -	$ -	$ (18,945,000)	$ -	$ -	$ -
85		0	0	0	0.5	0.75	1
86	Operating Cash Flow	$ -	$ -	$ -	$ 3,562,500	$ 5,343,750	$ 7,125,000
87	Growth Rate	0%	0%	0%	0%	0%	0%
88		0	0	0	0	0	1
89	Growth Factor		0	0	0	0	1
90	Net Cash Flow	$ -	$ -	$ (18,945,000)	$ 3,562,500	$ 5,343,750	$ 7,125,000
91							
92	Net Present Value ($mm)	$15,671					

fore the launch year to better reflect the actual outflow of cash expenditures to cover development costs and the building of productive capacity. Row 85 is the phase-in period whereby half of the full potential is realized in the first year of operation, 75% in the second, and the full 100% in the third. The operating cash flow has an uncertainty factor of 90–110% associated with each year's cash flow contained in the underlying formula utilizing the @Risk function RiskUniform(0.9,1.0,1.1). The growth rate in row 87 applies after the first year (2008) of full operation (year 2009 is not shown in Figure 6.6). Rows 88 and 89 control the timing for applying the growth rate. Row 90 is the project cash flow without any allowance for depreciation, taxes, and interest charges. These obviously can be added. Cell B92 calculates the net present value of the project cash flow at a discount rate of 14%. Figure 6.7 is the net present value (NPV) of this project. The internal rate of return (IRR) cannot be used because there is no return on failure. An IRR for a single negative figure makes no sense. One can always calculate an NPV, but not always an IRR.

The average NPV is nearly $9 million. This signifies that proceeding with the project would, on balance, generate a return of greater than the corporate objective of 14%. Unfortunately, the average NPV is not representative of the potential outcomes. The chances of the outcome being around the average result are rather slim. There is a significant, 54% chance of a negative net present value, which signifies a return of less than of 14%. Included in this are the 13% chance of total failure and those instances of success for case 1 or case 2 where either the price or volume or both are insufficient to make this venture financially attractive. Part of the potential loss is under management control in that persistent losses associated with case 1 or case 2 can be terminated. Moreover, the investment in production facilities may be partially recouped in supporting other products.

Figure 6.7
Net Present Value

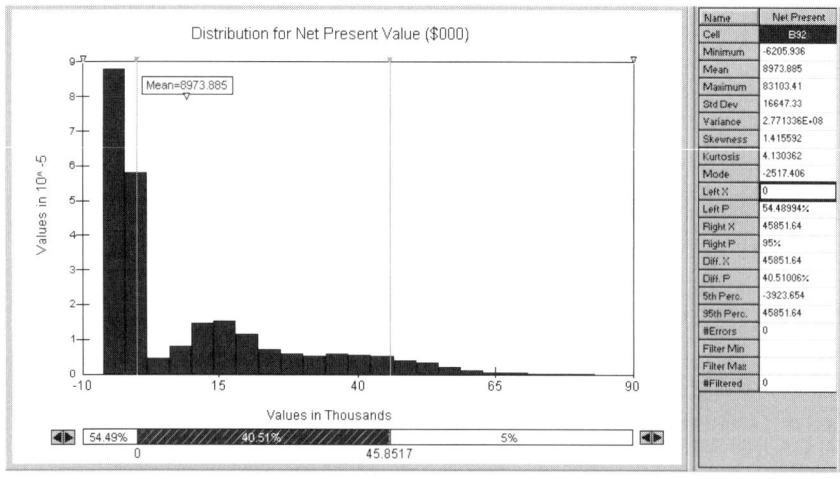

On the other hand, there is a 46% chance of the return being higher than 14%. In fact, there is a small chance of really cleaning up if high prices and volumes apply for cases 3 and 4. This venture is one of a high probability of losing money and a low probability of making a killing. But does this not aptly describe the drug business and many other industries on the cutting edge of technology?

WAS THE EFFORT WORTH IT?

Trying to quantify risk is frustrating because at the start of the day there are a number of outcomes each with a probability of occurrence, and at the end of the day there can be only one outcome. There is a probability of arriving safely at a destination before the trip starts. After the trip ends, there is only one outcome: you either made it safely or not. The drug company will either make or lose money in pursuing this new drug. There are a 46% chance of making it and a 54% chance of not making it. Will this really affect the decision to move ahead with the development of the drug? Probably not much.

If that's true, was the effort worth it? Put yourself in a management position. There is a request on your desk to spend $5 million to pursue a new treatment for a horse malady. What do you do? Signing it and having a nice lunch are not an uncommon seat-of-the-pants approach to management. A nice bonus might await you if the project is successful. If not, you may have to look elsewhere for a job. No one knows the eventual outcome, including the one authorizing the expenditure of funds.

One of the principal benefits of performing risk analysis for a new project is that it forces people to think. Someone has to do some hard thinking about the prospects of success in the company lab and in a government office. This is the only way the probabilities can be obtained. Maybe this will lead to a reassignment of personnel to buttress the probabilities of success.

Marketing has to get in touch with the customers to get a feel for price and volume and to start thinking about how to successfully launch the new drug if it overcomes the hurdles that stand in the way. This, too, is the only way the assessments on potential volume and price can be made. Someone in production has to think about current production capacities and what will be needed for the new drug in order to obtain the costs for adding productive capacity. Someone in finance ought to think about whether this project can generate a positive cash flow before the $5 million in development effort is authorized. The process of judging imponderables hardens the inherent softness of decisions for approving R&D budget requests. The probabilities of success and failure and the quantification of return can be useful in comparing competing projects where R&D funds are limited.

At the end of the day, the attempt to address the risk of product development simply becomes another input in the decision on whether to proceed, but at least it should be better than staring at the entrails of a disemboweled chicken for an answer.

EVALUATING PROJECTS WITH DIFFERENT VARIANCES

You just read the sentence: "The probabilities of success and failure and the quantification of return can be useful in comparing competing projects where R&D funds are limited." Were it so simple! Once it was simple when two projects were evaluated strictly in terms of returns. If one project had a return of 10% and the other 12%, then the decision would be to select the project with the higher return from a strictly financial point of view.

The decision-making process is not so simple when there are both risk and reward. Suppose that the former alternative with the average return of 10% can have a return as low as 6% and as high as 14% and the latter alternative with an average return of 12% can have a return as low as 0% and as high as 24%. Now which one do you select?

This depends on your attitude toward risk. A risk-averse individual will tend to pick the lower return with the lesser degree of risk as measured by the smaller spread in possible values. A risk seeker, on the other hand, may select the project for the higher average return on the basis not of a higher average return of 12% but of a higher possible return of 24%. A risk seeker tends to focus on the right-hand tail for potentially high returns and tends to ignore the left-hand tail of potentially disastrous returns. A risk-averse individual tends to do just the opposite. Risk is not an absolute but a perception that varies from individual to individual. One person's perception of risk may even be another person's perception of opportunity.

One way to try to come to terms with which project to select given a different risk and reward profile is to first determine a threshold of pain. Suppose that a return below 8% is the threshold of pain. The threshold of pain differs for individuals but could be linked to the cost of borrowing funds. A project that cannot support the interest payments on its financing would or should be the threshold of pain for its investors.

For the two probability distributions under consideration, both have a chance of the return being below 8%. The former alternative has a minimum return of 6%, and the other 0%. Presumably, the chance of falling below the threshold of pain is less for the project with the lower return. To handle risk averseness, returns below the threshold of pain can be "punished." For instance, a return of 7%, which is less than the threshold of pain of 8%, could be treated as equivalent to a return of 6%. An actual return of 6% could be treated as equivalent to a return of 4%. The operable rule here is to take the difference between the actual return and the threshold of pain, double it, and subtract the new difference from the threshold of pain. In the former case, the difference between 8% and 7% is 1%, and when doubled is 2%, yielding a return equivalent of 8% less 2% or 6%. The equivalent risk-adjusted return for the latter case is 8% less 6% or 2%, doubled 4%, and when subtracted from 8%, 4%. The greater the difference between an actual return and the threshold of pain, the greater the "punitive charge" placed against the equivalent return. This models an individual's growing distaste for low returns as they sink further below the threshold of pain. Another way of putting it is that the degree of pain becomes proportionately greater for returns that drop below the threshold of pain.

Now the two projects can be reevaluated using RiskOptimizer simulations to obtain a new average return for the riskier project whereby the probability of being below the threshold of pain in terms of risk-adjusted return equivalents is the same for both projects. If the actual return for the riskier project is higher than the calculated return for an equal degree of risk in terms of return equivalents, then select the riskier project. This means that the differential in average returns between the two projects is sufficient to compensate for the additional degree of risk. If not, select the project with lower risk because the spread between the returns of both projects is not sufficiently compensatory for the additional risk.[1]

Evaluating projects in terms of risk-adjusted return equivalents depends on both the individual's threshold of pain and the nature of the "punitive charge" placed against returns below the threshold of pain. The determination of the punitive charge is no mean feat. One approach might be to ask the individual for the actual return that would be equivalent to a zero return. If the individual responds that a 6% return would be equivalent in his or her mind with a 0% return, then the punitive charge would be a factor of 4. The difference between the threshold of pain of 8% less the actual return of 6% is 2%, which when multiplied by four is 8%, which when subtracted from the threshold of pain of an actual return of 8% is a risk-adjusted equivalent return of 0%.

The model can be modified for a threshold of pleasure where returns above the threshold of pleasure are rewarded in a manner opposite to the infliction of punishment, such as a 20% return being treated as equivalent to a return of 25%. A model with both a threshold of pain and a threshold of pleasure may seem contradictory, but think about it. Most of us are contradictory when looking at a potential investment, simultaneously fearing the pain of a potentially low return and anticipating the joy of a potentially high return.

NOTE

1. Detailed spreadsheet formulation can be found in Evaluating Projects with Different Variances in *@Risk Bank Credit and Financial Analysis*, available through www.nerses.com.

7
A NOT-SO-RANDOM WALK DOWN WALL STREET

SYNOPSIS

Price changes affect everyone. Rising prices hurt consumers, and falling prices hurt producers. A price change can be beneficial or adverse depending on which side of the table one is sitting. If a price change can help us, it can also hurt us. Most of the time there is no problem realizing whether we benefit or suffer from a price change. If we consume copper and copper prices begin to rise, it's going to hurt. Sometimes it's not absolutely clear. Suppose that your revenue is in British pounds and expenses are in U.S. dollars. You hear on the radio that the pound is strengthening with respect to the dollar. Does this enhance your profits, or are you facing a risk of loss from an adverse change in the currency exchange rate?

Before addressing the problem of adverse price changes, there is a need to create a means of assessing future prices. This chapter discusses what appears to be apparent randomness in price movements and constructs a model to illustrate how to mimic these movements. A model that mimics price changes can then be used to evaluate swaps and other means of controlling the degree of risk inherent in unpredictable price movements.

Any number of models can be constructed to mimic prices. The author experimented with several that created what appeared to be random price patterns. Building a model that best mimics future prices for a particular commodity or financial instrument is a challenge. The one proposed in this chapter was selected using a variant of Occam's razor. Occam's razor states that if there are several contending theories explaining an unknown phenomenon, assume the simplest is true. Among the several contending models that created quasi-random patterns, the simplest was selected.

CONFESSIONS OF A FORECASTER

A Random Walk Down Wall Street caused quite a stir when it was first published. It basically concluded that throwing darts at the Wall Street Journal to select a portfolio would most probably result in investment performance on a par with that of a professional manager. Fundamental knowledge about an industry and companies within that industry was of little use in selecting a stock portfolio or in predicting the future price of a stock or a commodity or currency exchange or interest rates or anything else. Randomly generated ups and down in daily stock or commodity prices could create head-and-shoulders and other stock price patterns that chartists interpret as buy-and-sell signals. Technical trading was deemed to be no better than a form of hocus-pocus: a modern-day version of the ancients staring at chicken entrails to decide whether to enter into battle. The only value to technical trading was not in the knowledge that a head-and-shoulders pattern was developing but in knowing what technical traders do when they see a head-and-shoulders pattern. If technical traders follow a herd instinct to buy or to sell when a certain pattern develops, then this knowledge is worth something to an astute trader. Thus, a technical sell signal does not create the selling; a sell signal causes traders who *believe* in technical trading to sell. Buy-and-sell signals become self-fulfilling prophecies because traders believe that certain chart patterns are buy-and-sell signals. Knowing that the herd is about to hit the phones to buy or sell does give value to paying attention to chart patterns.

Are stock and commodity prices guided by nothing more than random noise? My unequivocal response is sometimes yes and sometimes no. "Yes" when we are trying to divine the future and "no" when we review the past. As a consultant involved with marine planning, I have had the unenviable task of forecasting rates for tanker owners who profit when rates go up and for oil companies that save money when rates go down. The suppliers (tanker owners) are interested in a rate forecast to see how much money they'll be stuffing in their mattresses, whereas the consumers (oil companies) are interested in a rate forecast in order to take whatever actions they can to ensure that tanker owners don't stuff too much money in their mattresses.

Having done forecasts off and on for 30 years, I can attest that performing a forecast is a two-step process. The first step is to review the past. This entails generating an explanation of why the market price for tankers (tanker rates) rose or fell, and there always will be an explanation. It may be right, or it may be wrong, but there always will be an explanation. Figure 7.1 is the history of medium-sized tanker rates.[1]

"WS (Worldscale) Rates" is an industry term that can be looked upon as the price for employing tankers. The higher the Worldscale rate, the greater is the cost of moving a cargo for an oil company and the greater the owner's profit. Figure 7.1 shows that tanker rates hit bottom in 1999. From the perspective of post-1999, there is always an explanation of why rates sank so low. In fact, there were two explanations. First, demand for medium-sized tankers fell as a consequence of the

Figure 7.1
History of Medium-Sized Tanker Rates

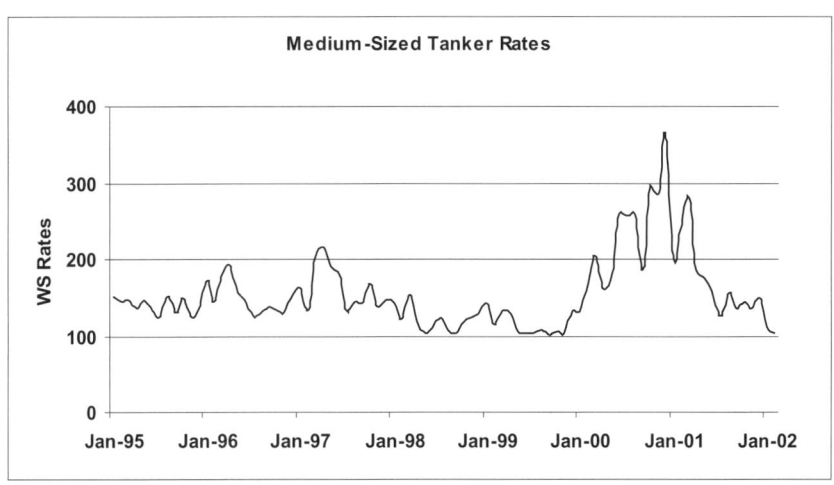

Asian flu, a significant fall in economic activity that hit Asia in 1998. As economic activity tumbled, so did Asian oil imports and demand for medium-sized tankers that move cargoes around the Pacific basin. Second, to make things worse for tanker owners, demand for medium-sized tankers also fell in the Atlantic basin. Exports from Venezuela, a major employer of medium-sized tankers, declined. Moreover, there was an explanation why Venezuelan exports were down. We need not consider the grisly details here but simply note that the falloff in Venezuelan exports in 1999 provided a needed explanation in 2000 of why rates were so dismal.

In 1998, a year before rates collapsed, what was my prediction? First I examined past trends for both economic growth and oil consumption for a batch of oil-importing nations. Then I looked at the past trends in oil production among importers and exporters. Armed with current news articles to make seemingly suitable adjustments, I extrapolated current trends of consumption and production into the future. A couple of steps later, this became a forecast of the international movement of crude oil, which was but one step away from a projection of tanker demand.

That one step was to look at the past trends in the supply of tankers. From this came another extrapolation that principally involved the building of new tankers and the scrapping of old tankers to obtain a projection of tanker supply. The final step was the comparison of the extrapolated trends of demand and supply of tankers to get a rate forecast.

As an old hand in this exercise, I would like to make two observations. One, small changes in growth rate assumptions for economic activity that can be related directly to oil consumption have a profound impact on oil consumption five or more years into the future. Want a strong tanker market? Let me increase U.S. annual economic growth from 3.5% to 4.0%, you want a weak market? Let me decrease U.S. economic growth from 3.5% to 3.0%. These percentage changes may seem small, but when extrapolated five or more years into the future, they have a significant impact on U.S. oil demand and hence U.S. oil imports. Am I being dishonest? Not really; both growth rates are entirely possible. Who can say with certainty which forecast for the growth rate of the United States is correct?

For the record I don't "jimmy" the forecast; I try to be unbiased. I'm just noting the ease of manipulating the output of a forecast by seemingly small changes in the basic assumptions. What this also means is that if I am off in my estimates by small amounts, the impact on the rate forecast will be significant. Put another way, the probability of being correct is small. But who's to say that my assumptions are wrong when I make them?

Two, the forecast of the supply of tankers, a step performed just before the final step of comparing supply with demand to get a rate forecast, is itself dependent on the rate forecast. Tanker owners tend to order fewer ships and scrap more ships when rates are low and order like crazy and cease scrapping when rates are high. Here I am trying to forecast the number of tankers to be built and scrapped as a prelude to a rate forecast when the number of tankers to be built and scrapped is rate-related. Thus, when I am forecasting supply, I need a rate forecast to figure out what the tanker owners are going to do with regard to ordering and scrapping. This affects the future supply of tankers that I need to compare to the future demand to get a tanker supply/demand balance and from that a rate forecast. Do you see the conundrum I'm in? I have to forecast rates to get a forecast of supply before I forecast rates. Think about the implications of a forecast being an input for a process where the output is the forecast. I don't blame you if you don't.

I've a friend who forecasted rates for liquefied petroleum gas (LPG) carriers. LPG consists mainly of butane found in cigarette lighters and propane that incinerates your steaks when you turn your back on the barbecue. While our personal use of LPG is minuscule, there are over 6 billion people on this earth. LPG is shipped around the world in vessels that carry up to 50,000 tons of the stuff. My friend would do an extremely detailed study on the demand for LPG and domestic production in order to arrive at an assessment of import demand for nearly every nation in the world. For reasons that need not concern us, the international trade in LPG was growing at a very nice pace for someone in the business of owning LPG carriers. Invariably, his conclusion was that although there was a current oversupply of LPG carriers because too many were ordered in the recent past, depressing rates, growth in the international trade of LPG was sufficient to absorb the excess tonnage in short order. This would lead to a strengthening in rates over the next two or three years, portending better days ahead for LPG carrier owners.

What did the recipients of this study do after they read it? Each had the same thought. If better days were just around the corner, what would be the harm in ordering just one more LPG carrier and profiting thereby? Nothing, if only one owner ordered one LPG carrier. But each owner ordered one LPG carrier, and collectively they managed to keep the industry in a state of surplus for years. The forecast turned out to be self-defeating. Rates never improved because the rate forecast that did conclude that rates would improve only induced owners to order more tonnage. This ensured that rates never did improve—it's all so convoluted.

Back in 1998, I muddled through the tanker forecast the best I could, trying to maintain some degree of integrity. When I was done extrapolating past trends into the future, I ended up with a rate prediction that was some sort of continuation of what rates were in 1995–1997. In 1998 I predicted a modest uptick in rates for 1999. In 1999 rates fell out of bed. What went wrong? I did not predict the tumbling of the Asian economies that began as the ink was drying on my forecast in 1998. I read press releases on Venezuela's intention to expand exports, and I certainly did not foresee certain events that had not yet occurred that led to a retrenchment in Venezuelan exports.

Hence, from the perspective of 1998 looking forward, I did not envision the dealing of two wild cards. Wild cards are unpredictable events that make a mess of forecasting the future by extrapolating past trends. After 30 or so years of continuously expanding economic progress, the Asian economies were about to be hit by the whirlwind of an economic downdraft that would play havoc with their stock and real estate markets, their currencies, and their political stability. Sitting comfortably in New York and examining the unremitting economic growth in Asia, how was I to know that a wild card was about to be dealt, making a shambles of my assessment that what had occurred over the past 30 years would continue uninterrupted into the future? How was I to anticipate the other wild card of events that would thwart Venezuelan intentions to expand exports?

Wild cards are in essence random events because they cannot be predicted. I could say that maybe I am incapable of foretelling the future, but I've been around long enough to realize that I'm not alone. Moreover, if by chance I were given the power to foretell the future, I would certainly not publish my findings. I would rent a little office on Wall Street, find some financial instrument that best matches my powers of prediction, and let the money roll in. I would try not to surround myself with too many sycophants and not be too ostentatious in choice of limousines. I'd pay some accountant from Arthur Anderson a small fortune to reduce my tax bill to nothing on my ill-gotten gains by forming foreign partnerships with my dog. Then after getting bored with my titillating lifestyle, I would contemplate whether this gift of prophecy came from above or below. If from below, I'd give 10% to charity and see if that would change matters.

From the perspective of 1998, my outlook for 1999 tanker rates and beyond was one of continuation of whatever trend was visible in the prior years. My prediction is on the basis of average annual rates. There is no way that I can predict daily, weekly, monthly rates with all their inherent fluctuations as clearly shown in Figure 7.1. As mentioned, events in 1999 proved me wrong. Now let's move forward in time to 2000; the wild cards of 1999 are in the past. From the perspective of 1998, the Asian flu and a downturn in Venezuelan exports were random events. In 2000 both are a part of history. They are no longer improbable possibilities; they are facts.

In 2000 the Asian economies were rebounding nicely from their slump, confounding those who extrapolated the initial downturn forever into the future. I remember economists' prognostications that once the Asian economies turned south, the logical extrapolation was for the flu to spread throughout the global economy, transforming the Asian flu to the Asian contagion. Did not the flu start in Thailand, spread to Malaysia and Indonesia, and then to Korea and Singapore? Why stop there? Just as the experts were predicting the worst, the sequential crumbling of the South American, Russian, European, and finally the North American economies, the Asian economies suddenly turned around, astounding everyone. Today few remember the Asian flu, and if they do, it has become a faded memory of an Asian hiccup.

From the perspective of 2000, oil movements in the Pacific basin were picking up, adding to demand for medium-sized tankers. Venezuela had overcome the circumstances leading to a decline in its exports, and rising exports were creating more demand for medium-sized tankers in the Atlantic basin. Armed with these facts and new extrapolations, my rate prediction for 2000 and beyond was an improvement in rates from the 1999 levels to something of the order of what they were in 1995–1997 plus a little boost.

In 2000 I did what I had always done before. First I explained why I was wrong in 1999—a detailed description of which wild cards upset my world of extrapolating past trends. Then I once again repeated my error of extrapolating past trends. It doesn't matter how many times I make the same mistake of assuming that extrapolated past trends are valid; I commit the same mistake over and over again because of my singular inability to forecast the timing and the nature of the Fates dealing the next wild card. From my perspective as a forecaster, the past is perfectly explanatory and the future is made up of indeterminable random events.

One other observation I would like to make is that rate forecasts always seem to have a built-in bias for a gently upward slope. I'm not sure why there is a bias for continual improvement in rates. One reason is that it gives hope to tanker owners who from time to time need a little shot in the arm as tanker rates tend to be depressed more often than not. "Sure rates are low, but they won't stay low forever" is a palliative such as "Your wife left you, but it won't be forever." There is this element of hope in the gently sweeping upward slope of a rate forecast. It cannot be blamed entirely on pleasing the clientele because oil companies are part of the clientele, and they prefer to see a gently sweeping downward slope on a rate forecast.

Back in 2000 my forecast was for rates in 2001 and beyond to be better than 1999, something modestly above the rates in the mid-1990s. Take a look at Figure 7.1 for 2001 to see how wrong I was. The tanker market in 2001 was the best market since the tanker boom of the early 1970s, nearly 30 years before. What happened to my forecast of things being a bit better than they were in 1999?

Another wild card was dealt called the *Erika*—not Eureka, *Erika*! In December 2000, about three or so months after publishing my rate forecast of a modest improvement in rates, a rust bucket of a tanker named *Erika*, whose owner could not be identified for weeks after the mishap, broke up in a storm and sank about 40 miles off the coast of France. Unexpectedly, a small part of its 35,000-ton fuel oil cargo reached the French shoreline.

This is not the first time European beaches were fouled by an oil spill, and this was by far a small spill compared to other mishaps, but for some strange reason, the public reaction was different. The uproar in Europe was so intense that the world's oil companies decided that it would be in their collective interests to charter only quality tonnage. Quality became mistakenly associated with age (those of you over 50 will appreciate this thought). This shift in charterers' preferences for younger tonnage effectively reduced the available supply of tonnage with respect to demand. To make things better for owners, tanker demand was growing as the Asian flu faded into the past and the collective economies of Asia and North America surged forward, taking oil imports along with them. The combination of these two factors caused tanker rates to take off like you wouldn't believe.

This became for me another wild card, upsetting, once again and invariably, the simple extrapolation of rates based on past trends. From my perspective, the *Erika* was just another random event that I was simply unable to foresee and incapable of foreseeing. Now, after all these years in planning, I have finally realized that I'm utterly doomed to failure in forecasting rates because the future does appear random. It is forever dealing wild cards that cannot be foreseen before the fact but can always be explained after the fact. Examining the past in order to extrapolate the future is a nonstarter. Why did it take so long for me to realize the futility of my life's work?

ARE PRICE MOVEMENTS RANDOM?

Absolutely not! They appear to be random when peering ahead and are perfectly explanatory when looking back. If price movements are purely random, that is if on any given day there are a 50% chance of rising and a 50% chance of falling, then we may eventually end up with a price falling below zero or rising to unrealizable heights.

Take the price of gold. If the price of gold is purely random, it is mathematically possible for gold to fall to $1 an ounce. Will it? Or do people, in seeing gold fall below $100 an ounce, recognize that this is an aberration and start buying to take advantage of the low price? This tendency to buy rather than sell when gold sinks below $100 prevents it from falling to $1 per ounce. Thus, the price of gold cannot be purely random.

Or if the price of gold were to go to $10,000 an ounce from purely random motion, might not there be a plethora of sellers and a scarcity of buyers? If there is a tendency to sell rather than buy, gold will not reach $10,000 per ounce. Random patterns may result in a negative price or a $10,000 price for gold, but we are defying reality if we construct a model that permits this to happen (by the way a $10,000 price of gold could happen, but I'm not sure I want to be around if it did). Moreover, if you read newsletters on gold, there is always a reason that the price of gold is where it is. To the extent that this is true, then the price of gold cannot be purely random.

WILL THE TRUE MEAN PLEASE STAND UP?

"Suppose that the future price of such and such can be modeled with a normal distribution whose mean is yyy and standard deviation is zzz." This sentence appears in erudite writings dealing with risk.

The first assumption is that future prices can be modeled with a normal distribution. This is certainly not true for tanker rates. Most of the time tanker rates are depressed because of the penchant of owners to order too much tonnage, ending up with a surplus of tonnage weighing down the market. Tanker markets are generally weak, and the average rate reflects a generally weak market. But there is a limit to how low rates can sink. At some point it pays for owners to lay up their vessels rather than continue moving cargoes. This occurs when the loss of continued operation exceeds the cost of laying up a vessel. Laying up becomes a means of minimizing losses.

There is a point below which rates do not sink. In other words, a zero rate or price for tankers is not possible. On the topside, rates can take off into the stratosphere, as seen in Figure 7.1. There is no upper limit other than tanker rates rising to a level that precludes the movement of oil. This has never happened except for traders involved with arbitrage. In arbitrage, traders are attempting to take advantage of price discrepancies in various parts of the world. If shipping costs are too high, the arbitrage cannot take place because shipping will eat up the profit of buying a cargo at a low price in one part of the world and selling it at a high price in another. For the remaining 99.9% of the world movement of oil, oil is shipped regardless of the cost of transportation. High shipping costs just end up in the price of gasoline. Consumers, not oil companies, ultimately end up paying for high shipping costs just as they do for every other cost associated with making petroleum products. Companies go broke if they cannot pass their costs on to consumers. Thus, tanker rates have a distribution that can be better described by a lognormal curve with a long and narrow tail to one side to model the occasional trips to the high end of the scale and a short stub of a tail on the other side to model that the average rate is closer to the low end of the scale.

But suppose that the future price or rates for tankers can be modeled with a normal curve. The challenge is in deciding on the mean and standard deviation to be used to model future prices. The glib answer is to calculate the mean and standard deviation from past data. Referring once again to Figure 7.1, what is the mean, or better yet, the true mean? Should the true mean cover the entire period of 6 years? Why stop at 6 years, as an argument could be made to go back 10 or 20 or more years, adjusting for inflation? Should the true mean ignore the 30-year high aberrations of 2000 and 2001? It is not at all clear what exactly the true mean is as it depends on the selected time period.

The same is true for the standard deviation. Figure 7.2 shows the daily rate swings in reported fixtures of medium-sized tankers. Clearly, there was greater volatility in rates in 2000 than in 1999. Volatility measured in terms of a range of values between the high and low or as the standard deviation was clearly not the same value throughout the 1990s or any other period of time.

Figure 7.2
Volatility in Rates

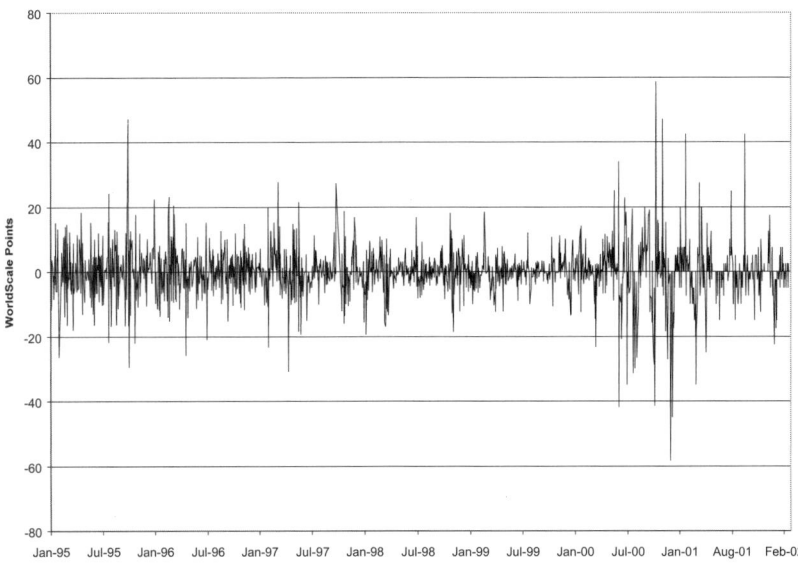

Table 7.1 lists the annual means and standard deviation based on daily rates. Regardless if tanker rates are to be modeled with a normal or lognormal curve, what are the true mean and the true standard deviation?

NOT-SO-RANDOM-WALK PRICE GENERATOR

The approach taken here is not to assume a probability distribution that applies at points in time such as one or two or five years in the future but to create a trail of

Table 7.1
A Choice—Pick One

	Annual Average Worldscale Rate	Annual Standard Deviation Based on Daily Rates
1995	139.3	15.0
1996	150.2	24.2
1997	163.5	31.6
1998	121.2	20.0
1999	115.1	18.1
2000	229.2	74.4
2001	174.3	48.7
Early 2002	108.9	15.9

prices throughout the period. I have to admit that it is possible to create different "guided" random price generators. I constructed a few models and then had to decide which one to use in this chapter. This actually was a major problem. One response would be to use a random price generator that best mimics daily, weekly, or monthly price changes of the commodity or financial instrument under scrutiny. But even this has the central flaw in assuming that the nature of the future pattern of price fluctuations is the same as in the past. The price generator discussed in this chapter and shown in Figure 7.3 was selected purely on its merits of simplicity. It is intentionally called a not-so-random-walk price generator to dodge philosophic criticisms on the true nature of a random price generator.

Suppose we want to model the price of a stock. Over the last 5 years, the stock price has varied between $30 and $80 per share. Looking forward, these limits appear reasonable. The stock is currently trading at $50. Its volatility as measured by the range between its yearly highs and lows averages around $30 per year. A purely random-walk-price generator could not mimic the future price of any stock because price could fall below zero or reach unsustainable heights. As will be seen, the formulation does not prevent price from exceeding $80 or falling below $30. All that the upper and lower limits in cells B7 and B8 do is change the formulation to mimic the increasing tendency to sell as prices rise above $70 and the increasing tendency to buy when prices fall below $40. Between $40 and $70, price is purely a random 50–50 chance of moving up or down. The bias factor of 3 in cell B11 increases the tendency to buy when price falls below $40 and to sell as price rises above $70, as shown in Figure 7.4.

Figure 7.3
A Weekly Price Generator

	A	B	C	D	E	F	G	H
1	Not-So Random Walk Price Generator							
2					Avg Price	Minimum	Maximum	Range
3	Desired Range	$30		Year 1	$46.01	$32.55	$62.46	$29.91
4	Start Price	$50.00		Year 2	$62.87	$43.72	$74.34	$30.62
5				Year 3	$67.34	$49.41	$84.95	$35.54
6	Highest	$ 80		Year 4	$72.77	$61.02	$84.41	$23.39
7	Upper	$ 70		Year 5	$62.73	$48.52	$77.88	$29.36
8	Lower	$ 40						
9	Lowest	$ 30						Avg Range
10				A Factor	15.551			$29.77
11	Bias Factor	3		B Factor	0.337			
12								Objective
13								-$0.23
14					Start			
15	Week			Weekly	Price	Month		
16	0		Up/Down	Change	$50.00			
17	1	0.50	1	$3.44	$53.44			
18	2	0.50	1	$4.79	$58.23			
19	3	0.50	1	$2.72	$60.95			
20	4	0.50	1	$1.50	$62.46	1		

Figure 7.4
Changing Bias to Buy and Sell (Factor of 3)

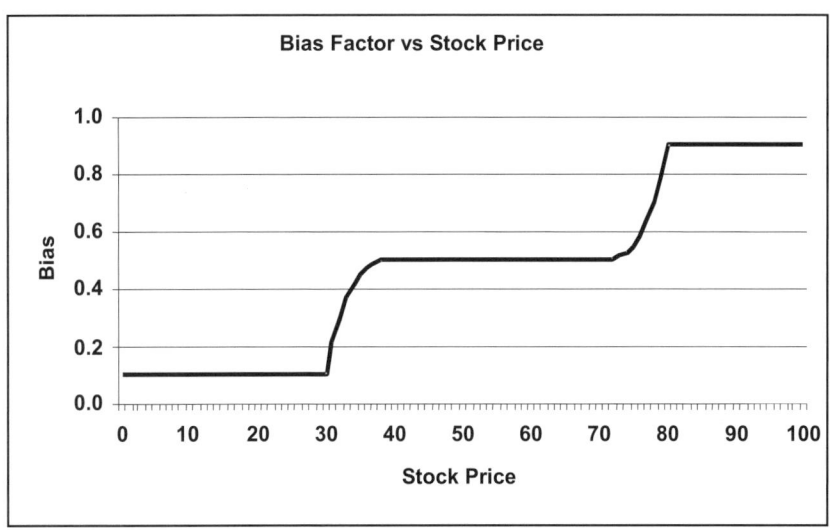

Figure 7.5 shows the changing tendency to buy and sell for a bias factor of 1. As price rises above $70, the bias factor climbs to a maximum value of 90%, meaning that there is a 90% chance of the change in price being negative and a 10% chance of the change in price being positive. This bias in selling does permit the price to exceed the upper limit as a relatively rare event. On the other hand, as price falls below $40, the bias factor declines to a minimum value of 10%, meaning that there is a 10% chance of the change in price being negative and a 90% chance in a price change being positive. Again there is a small probability of price falling below the lower limit. This bias to buy or sell is contained in column B in Figure 7.3. The value in cell B17 is 0.5 to start the process. The formula in cell B18 and following is:

=IF(E17>$B$6,0.9,IF(E17>$B$7,0.5+0.4*((E17−$B$7)/($B$6−$B$7))^$B$11,IF(E17>$B $8,0.5,IF(E17>$B$9,0.1+0.4*((E17−$B$9)/($B$8−$B$9))^$B$11,0.1))))

Column C simply generates +1 and −1 for an upward or downward movement in price based on the probabilities of generating +1 and −1 in column B. The formula in cell C17 and following is:

=IF(RAND()>B17,1,−1)

The size of the change in price is derived in column D. The A and B factors in Figure 7.3 apply to the following equation for determining the weekly price change:

$$AeBx - C$$

Figure 7.5
Changing Bias to Buy and Sell (Factor of 1)

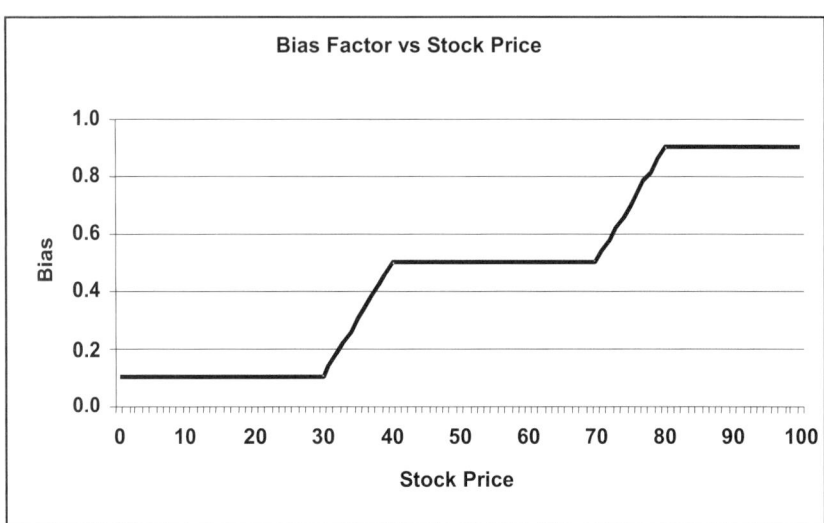

The A and B factors are determined by RiskOptimizer to generate price changes that work off a cumulative probability distribution that maintains a desired average price range. In Figure 7.3, the desired range in cell B3 is $30. The values for A and B are determined by maintaining the volatility in the stock price such that the average annual range in price between the highs and lows is $30. The constant C ensures that the change associated with a cumulative probability of x having a value near zero is zero. The cumulative probability is given by the variable x, which varies between 0 and 1. The values for A and B are in cells E10 and E11 of Figure 7.3, and the formula in cell D17 and below for generating the weekly price change is:

$$=\$E\$10*EXP((\$E\$11)*RAND())-\$E\$10*EXP(\$E\$11*0.00001)$$

A concave-shaped curve for the price change generator is desired because it reflects a higher probability of a small incremental change in price and a smaller probability of a large incremental change in price. This is what is normally seen in stock and commodity markets, illustrated in Table 7.2.

Figure 7.6 is the plot of the price change versus the cumulative probability using the X-Y scatter diagram. The concave shape indicates that the probability of a small price change is greater than the probability of a large price change.

The spreadsheet covers 260 weeks or five years. The minimum, maximum, and average price for each of the five years of the simulation are in cells D2 through H7 of Figure 7.3. The range between the high and low price for each year is the measure of volatility. The average range for all five years is in cell H10. The desire is to have an average five-year price range or spread in prices of $30 per year (cell B3). The av-

Table 7.2
Hypothetical Price Change History

Price Change	Discrete Probability	Cumulative Probability
$0	30%	30%
$1	25%	55%
$2	20%	75%
$3	10%	85%
$4	8%	93%
$5	5%	98%
$6	2%	100%

erage applies not to annual price ranges but to the entire period. The RiskOptimizer menu for deriving the price change curve is in Figure 7.7.

The objective cell H13 is the difference between the actual average five-year range and the desired range or spread in prices. This is to be set as close to zero as possible by varying cell E10 between 0 and 50 and cell E11 between 0 and 1. Figure 7.8 is the resulting price change generator for the stock.

The cumulative probability is fairly close to a straight line with a small degree of concavity. This means that there are nearly equal probabilities for each weekly incremental price change. While this somewhat flies in the face of reality of the probability of a small price change being greater than the probability of a large price change, nevertheless, this was the curve that was necessary to maintain the desired volatility in the price stock. With this price change generator, a new stock pattern

Figure 7.6
Concave Price Change Cumulative Probability Curve

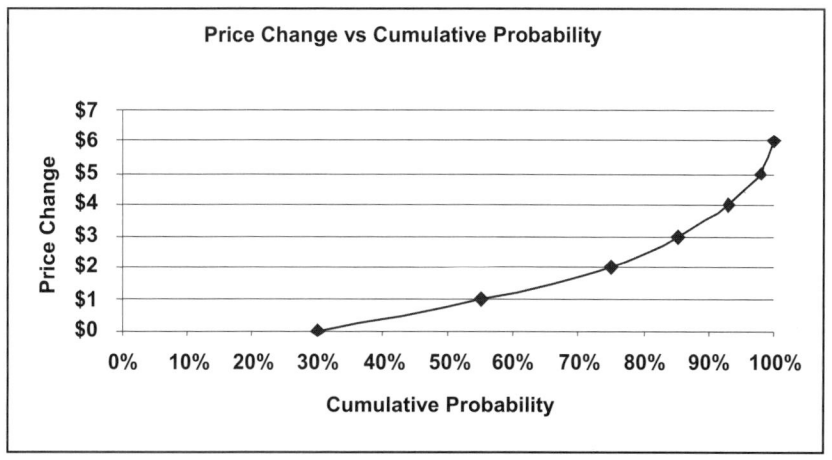

Figure 7.7
RiskOptimizer Menu

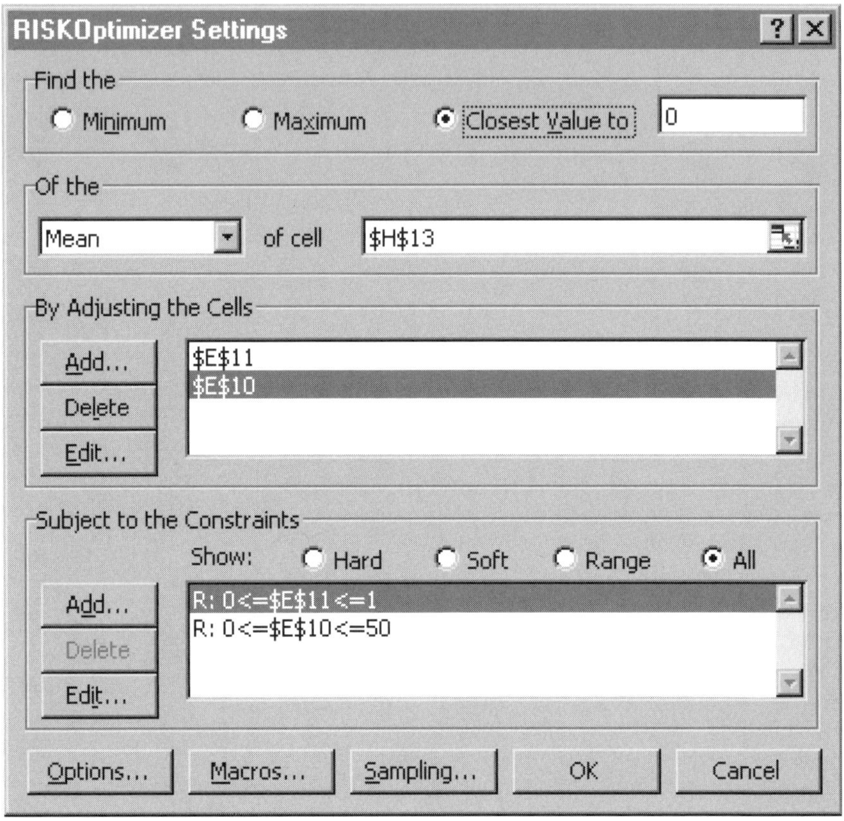

Figure 7.8
Price Change Generator

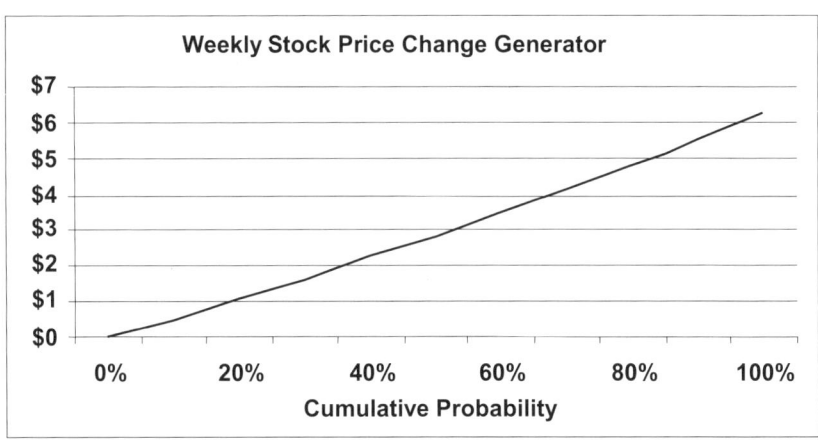

can be created in the *Monte Carlo* mode by striking function key F9 as seen in Figures 7.9 through 7.12.

Successive striking of function key F9 can create nearly every conceivable stock pattern one can imagine. After a while one begins to wonder about stock selection. We all want to buy low and sell high, but stock patterns have a penchant not to cooperate. Just as a little old lady may seem to have the knack of sucking quarters out of a slot machine in an Atlantic City gambling palace, so, too, do some individuals

Figure 7.9
Long-Term Buy-and-Hold Dream Pattern

Figure 7.10
Back to Where You Start Pattern

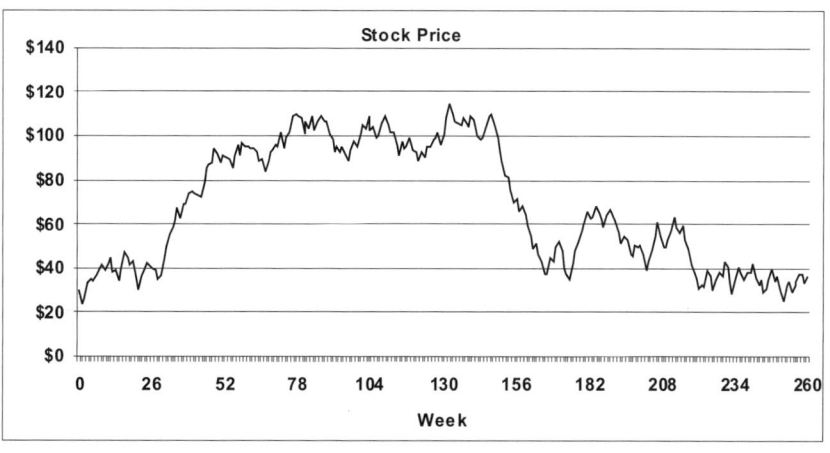

Figure 7.11
A Trader's Dream or Nightmare Pattern

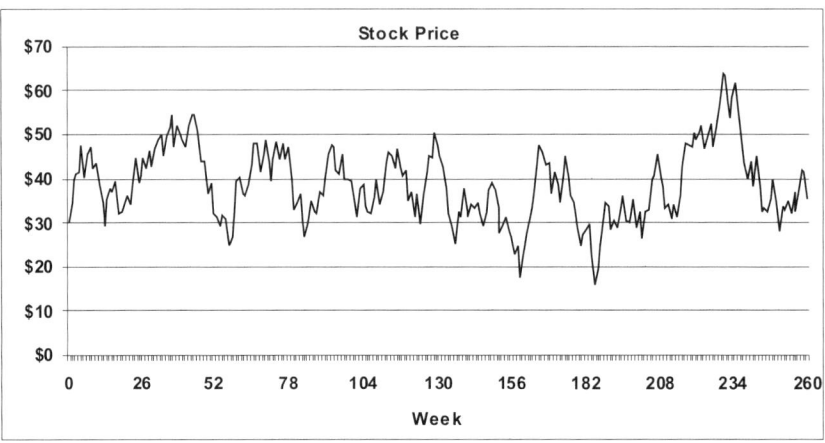

Figure 7.12
Watch It Go Up for Two Years, Then Buy Pattern

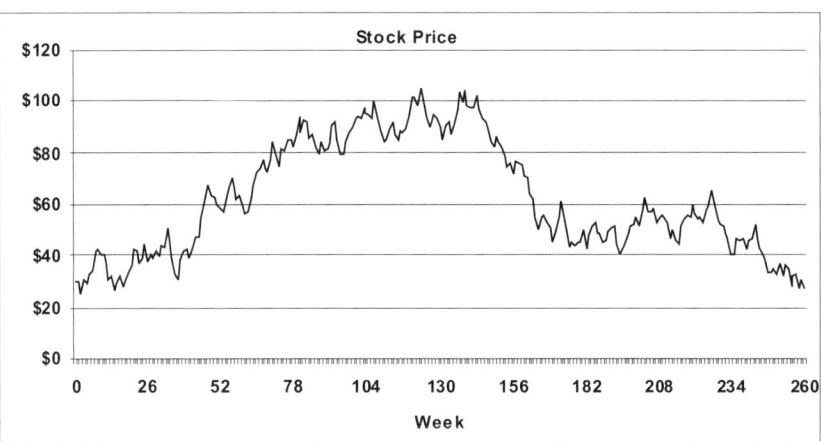

have the knack of picking the right stocks. But intuition or a pact with the Devil seems to play a role, or is this also random chance?

EVALUATING THE RESULTS

A @Risk simulation was run on cell H10, the average five-year range, shown in Figure 7.13. While the average five-year range clusters around $30, it was as low as $18 and as high as nearly $48 on individual runs. Figure 7.14 is the price distribution for week 52.

Figure 7.13
Distribution of the Average Five-Year Range

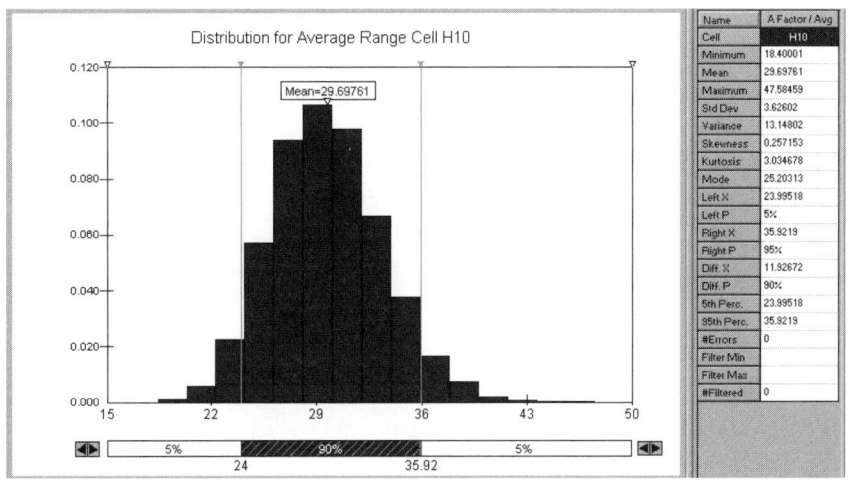

Figure 7.14
Year 1 Price Probability Distribution

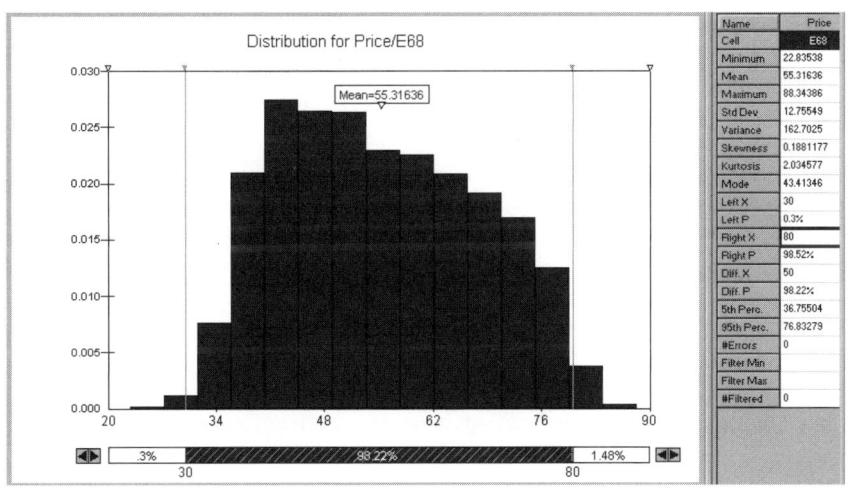

The rules established for the bias to buy and sell were sufficient to reduce the probability for price to exceed the upper limit to 1.5% and to 0.3% for price to fall below the lower limit. A certain flattening of the probability distribution is noticeable, which cannot be captured by the best-fitting curve in Figure 7.15.

The P-P curve matches up the discrete probabilities for various values between the actual data and the best-fitting curve while the Q-Q curve matches up the cu-

Figure 7.15
Best-Fitting Curve

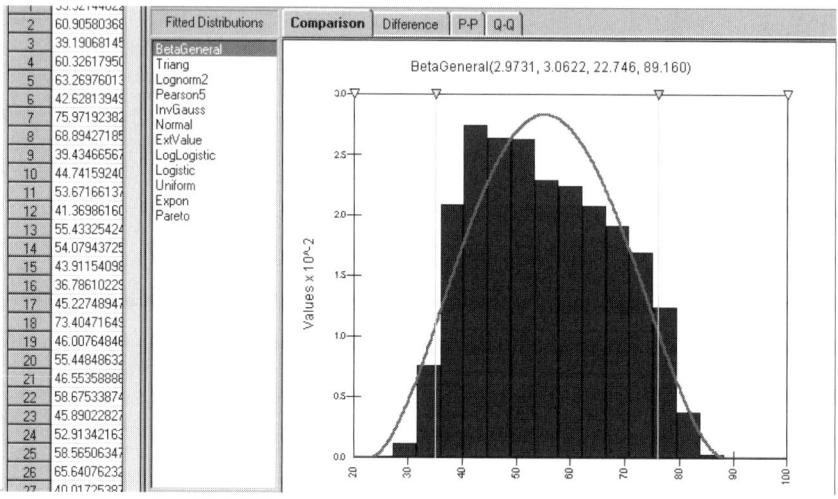

mulative probabilities between the two. A straight-line relationship for the P-P and Q-Q curves indicates a good match between the data and the best-fitting curve. Figure 7.16 is the Q-Q curve whose "jiggles" or departures from a straight line indicate a poor fit.

This flattening of the middle values of the distribution becomes more pronounced with time, plainly seen for the probability distribution for the price for year 5 in Figure 7.17. This phenomenon was experienced with other models for creating not-so-random-walk price patterns.

A flat distribution such as this increases the degree of risk of obtaining extreme values as compared to a more "peaky" or a higher kurtosis associated with a normal distribution. This result provides evidence, not proof, that modeling future prices with a normal distribution may actually be underestimating risk. Some practitioners in the arcane art of risk management have made the observation that modeling future prices with a normal distribution seems to underestimate actual risk. This is a critical point, as the normal distribution is frequently used for modeling future prices when assessing risk or pricing derivatives.

The contention that the normal curve may underestimate risk and that actual risk may be greater than the hypothetical risk contained in the tail of a normal curve is supported by the not-so-random-walk trail of prices from one year to the next. As the time period is extended, the probability distribution of future prices become flatter, indicating that the tails containing the risk are indeed getting fatter. If this flattening of the middle values and the fattening of the tails of a probability distribution are "normal," then none of the commonly accepted probability distributions is a good fit for prices based on a random walk. A better distribution seems

Figure 7.16
Q-Q Curve

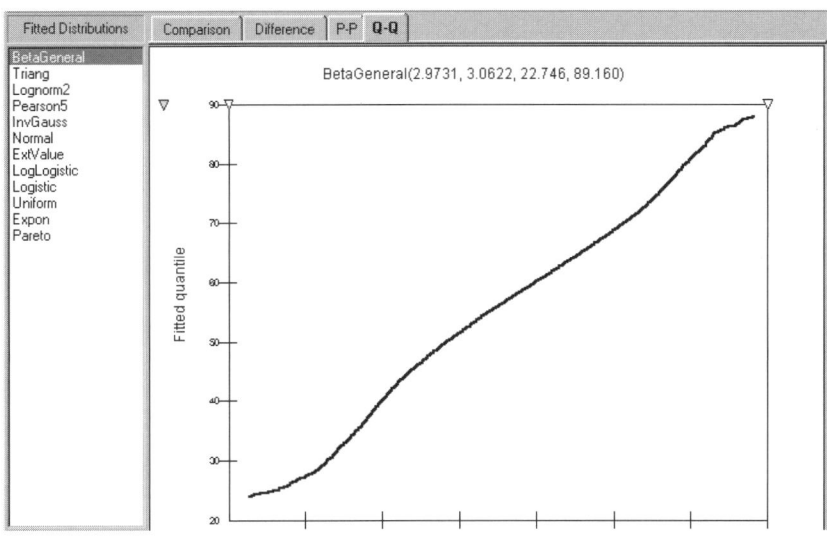

Figure 7.17
Year 5 Price Probability Distribution

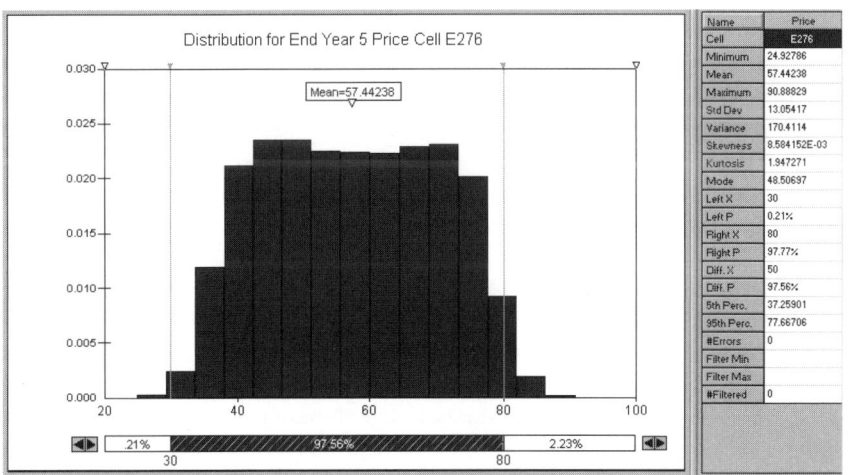

to be a uniform distribution for the middle values surrounded by two triangular distributions or perhaps some sort of logarithmic distribution to pick up extreme values. But normal it is not. Of course, this is not a proof, only an observation for this formulation and others of a not-so-random walk down Wall Street.

After this exercise I now look askance whenever I see the sentence, "Suppose that the future price of such and such can be modeled with a normal distribution whose mean is yyy and standard deviation is zzz." I don't think modeling future prices is quite so simple.

WRITING CALLS

An option is the right to buy or sell a stock at a stated or strike price for a specific period of time. The call option is the right to buy, and the put option is the right to sell. There are two types of options: European and American. The European option can be exercised only on its expiration date. This is far easier to analyze than the American option, where the option buyer is free to exercise the option at any time before or at its expiration date. The European call requires a probability distribution of the price of the stock at the expiration date. The American call requires a day-by-day price pattern because the call can be exercised at any time. The not-so-random-walk generator can create a daily price pattern. However, in this case, the weekly price change model has been adapted to evaluate an American call. Figure 7.18 is a modification to the not-so-random-walk spreadsheet to accommodate analyzing 90-day (13-week) calls.

Two new columns have been set up to evaluate writing an American call. Option investors rarely exercise an option simply because the price of the stock is above the strike price. Most investors wait until there is a clear profit before exercising an option or selling an option "in the money" to another investor. Column G is the premium over the strike price at which an individual who bought a call is likely to exercise or sell the option to another buyer. The premium erodes as the option life gets nearer the exercise date. On the expiration date of the option, an option holder will exercise as long as the price is above $50 to recoup at least a part of the investment in the option. Technically, there should be an increment to pay for the brokerage fees, but this could be built into the model by adjusting the exercise price to include brokerage fees.

The call option is exercised when the price of the stock exceeds the premium price for the first time. During the fourth week, the price of the stock exceeded the premium price, and the call was exercised. The amount received from the exercise of the call is the strike price of $50, which is deposited in a 4% interest-bearing account until the 90 days are over, yielding a total of $50.38. In addition, the $4.75 received in selling the call has been in the same 4% account for the entire 13-week period. The ending position for selling the call if the call is exercised is the proceeds from the sale of the call and the exercise of the stock at the end of the 13 weeks plus accrued interest. If the call is not exercised, then the ending position is whatever the stock is worth at the call's expiration date plus the proceeds of the call and its ac-

Figure 7.18
Writing Call Options

	A	B	C	D	E	F	G	H
1	Call Option Price Generator							
2								
3	Desired Range	$30			Initial Premium			$ 65.00
4	Start Price	$50.00			Strike Price			$ 50.00
5					Call Option Price			$ 4.75
6	Highest	$ 80			Ending Position With Call			$ 55.17
7	Upper	$ 70			Ending Position Without Call			$ 66.88
8	Lower	$ 40			Difference			$ (11.71)
9	Lowest	$ 30						
10								
11	Bias Factor		3		A Factor	15.551		
12					B Factor	0.337		
13								
14						Start		
15		Week			Weekly	Price	Month	Premium
16		0		Up/Down	Change	$50.00		$ 65.00
17		1	0.50	1	$5.66	$55.66		$ 63.85	$0.00
18		2	0.50	-1	$0.16	$55.50		$ 62.69	$0.00
19		3	0.50	1	$6.12	$61.62		$ 61.54	$50.38
20		4	0.50	1	$2.59	$64.21	1	$ 60.38	$0.00
21		5	0.50	-1	$3.54	$60.67		$ 59.23	$0.00
22		6	0.50	-1	$1.00	$59.67		$ 58.08	$0.00
23		7	0.50	1	$1.39	$61.06		$ 56.92	$0.00
24		8	0.50	1	$6.13	$67.19	2	$ 55.77	$0.00
25		9	0.50	-1	$1.42	$65.77		$ 54.62	$0.00
26		10	0.50	1	$1.30	$67.07		$ 53.46	$0.00
27		11	0.50	-1	$1.92	$65.15		$ 52.31	$0.00
28		12	0.50	-1	$2.94	$62.21		$ 51.15	$0.00
29		13	0.50	1	$4.67	$66.88	3	$ 50.00	$0.00

crued interest. If no call is sold, then the ending position is simply the value of the stock 13 weeks hence.

The evaluation of selling a call or not selling a call is done from the vantage point of 13 weeks in the future. This is not a strategy of rebuying the stock when a call is exercised and selling another call. This would require a great deal more effort in formulation. Here the simpler approach is taken of comparing the two alternatives of selling or not selling a call at the end of 13 weeks.

A RiskOptimizer run was made to set cell H8, the difference between writing and not writing a call, as close to zero as possible by varying the call price in cell H5 between $0 and $10. This resulted in a break-even value for writing a call of $4.75, or nearly 10% of the price of the stock, ignoring brokerage costs. Although this is the break-even rate to equate the returns of the two investment alternatives, the nature of the returns is radically different. As shown in Figure 7.19, the distribution of returns for the call writer is a cutoff of profits when the price of the stock exceeds the premium price and the call option is exercised. The call writer must bear the loss of value in the stock with the proceeds of the selling call as his or her only consolation.

In Figure 7.20 the distribution of returns for not writing the call gives the stockowner full access to the profitability if the stock price goes up and full exposure to a loss if the price goes down.

Note that there is no flattening of the probability distribution for the stock at the end of 13 weeks. The best-fitting curve appears to be a lognormal or equivalent

Figure 7.19
End Position in Writing Calls

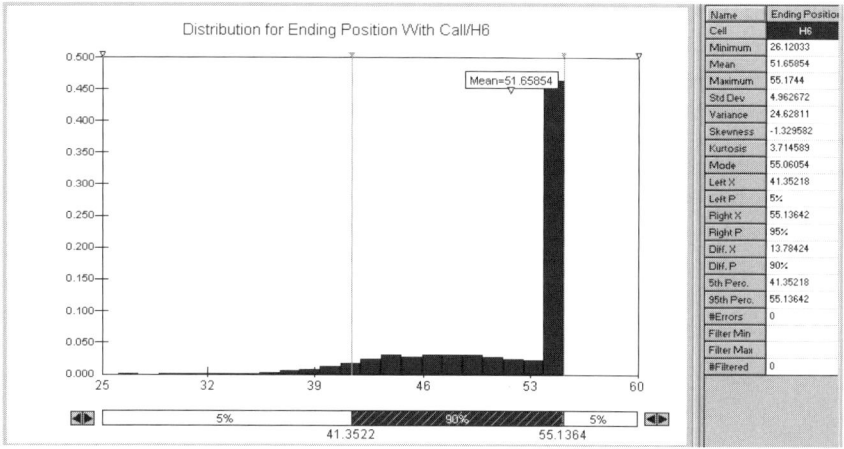

Figure 7.20
End Position in Not Writing Calls

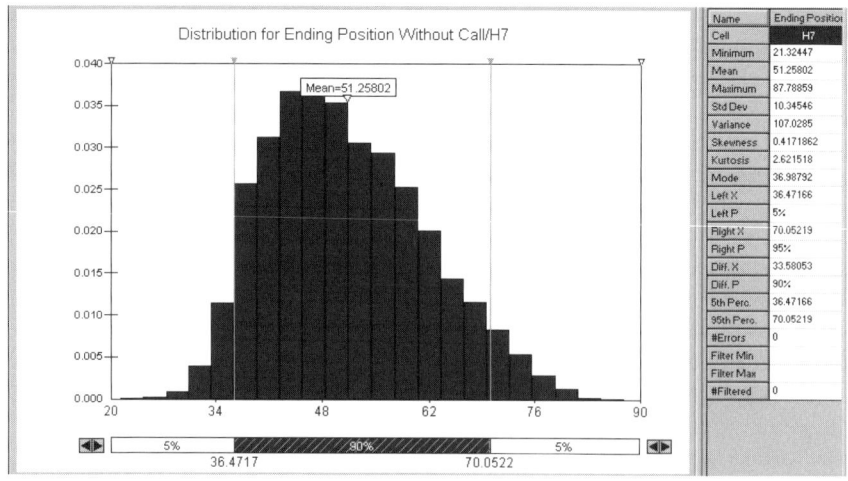

curve with an excellent fit. The flattening of the stock price distribution as seen in Figures 7.14 and 7.17 becomes more pronounced with time. I have no explanation for this other than noting its occurrence.

This evaluation for writing one call does not provide for any other action if the call is exercised except waiting until the end of the option period to evaluate the results. Other scenarios for writing options are possible. For instance, one strategy would be to hold 1,000 shares and write a call on 100 shares. If the call is exercised, immediately write another call. Continue this until there are no shares left. How does this strategy compare with simply holding the stock? One problem with evaluating this strategy and others is that the spreadsheet formulation becomes too complex, requiring a computer program to evaluate the strategy.

NOTE

1. Source of data is Poten & Partners, New York tanker brokers.

8
HEDGING WITH A SWAP

SYNOPSIS

The purpose of this chapter is to explore the use of a hedging technique to protect against the risk of financial loss. The hedging technique under scrutiny is a swap, a plain vanilla swap to be exact. This chapter discusses the use of a swap to mitigate the risk of loss in the financing of a copper mine. While the swap provides the benefit of reducing risk, it also carries a cost by sacrificing potential profits. A cost-benefit method is proposed to determine the appropriate volume and structure of the swap that best serve the interests of both lender and borrower. The principles of the proposed methodology for evaluating the cost-benefit relationship in this situation can be used as a model for evaluating others with suitable spreadsheet modifications.

THE SITUATION

A mining company is developing a copper mine primarily financed with debt. The anticipated debt servicing charges, when added to the operating costs, require a certain minimum price of copper for the mining company to remain solvent. Unfortunately, the history of copper prices shows a reasonable chance of falling below this price. An adverse price change in copper can threaten the company's financial viability. The bankers are rightfully concerned; so should be the mining company executives.

The lending institution is insisting on a loan covenant that the mining company enter into a swap to protect the lender's interests before advancing any funds. The mining company is reluctant to enter into a swap because its motivation in developing the mine is not to protect the lender but to profit from a high price for copper. While the mining company executives are not entirely gamblers at heart and realize that losing the mine is not in their best interests, the point is that they are not bankers either. They view the swap as an unavoidable evil in order to acquire the necessary funds.

WHAT IS A SWAP?

A swap stabilizes the price the mining company receives for its copper output. The benefit for the bankers is clear: a swap provides protection against an adverse price fluctuation. The cost for the borrower is also clear: a swap means giving up profits from a favorable price fluctuation. A cost benefit relationship can be analyzed to determine the optimal swap characteristics in type, price, and volume that satisfy the objectives of both lender and borrower.

A plain vanilla swap consists of two counterparties agreeing to exchange a money payment depending on the spread between an agreed published price that serves as proxy for the market price and a reference or swap price. The exchange of money between the counterparties depends on the direction of the price movement with respect to the swap price, and the amount of payment depends on the resulting spread and the associated swap volume. Swap payments are made at a stipulated frequency throughout the life of a swap such as the exchange of money at the end of every month for the duration of a swap period that may last from six months to 20 years.

In addition to commodities, swaps can be designed for interest rates. The swap interest rate is stipulated along with the swap volume in terms of a nominal amount of debt. Money is exchanged based on the difference between a published interest rate and the swap rate multiplied by the nominal amount of debt at stated frequencies during the swap period. Swaps can also be designed for currencies. The swap currency exchange rate is stipulated along with the swap volume in terms of a nominal holding in currency. Money is exchanged based on the difference between a published currency exchange rate and the swap exchange rate multiplied by the nominal holding of the currency at stated frequencies during the swap period. Neither the volume of the commodity nor the amount of debt nor the holding in currency is real; each merely provides a basis for calculating the exchange of money.

For this situation the swap counterparties are a copper-mining company and a manufacturing company that produces copper wire. Swap counterparties have divergent views on risk. The mining company fears the consequences of a low copper price that no longer supports the underlying debt servicing charges. A low price of copper may bankrupt the mining company. To obtain the benefit of protection against a low copper price, the mining company enters into a swap. Suppose that the copper swap is based on a swap price of $1,500 per ton for a quantity of 1,000 tons payable monthly. The price used to calculate the exchange of money is not actual market transactions but a mutually agreed, unbiased, and reliable source of copper prices such as the listed price in a financial publication or trade journal on a given day.

The exchange of money is the difference between the published price and the swap price multiplied by the swap volume. Suppose that sometime after entering the swap, the price for copper declines to $1,400 per ton. The mining company sells 1,000 tons of copper produced from the mine on the open market for $1,400 per ton and receives $1.4 million. Although the mining company receives what the market offers, the price used to calculate the exchange of money in a swap is referenced to a published price. The two need not be the same, although they ought to be close. Here they are assumed to be the same.

So in addition to the $1.4 million, the mining company receives the difference between the swap price of $1,500 and the market price of $1,400 or $100 per ton for the swap volume of 1,000 tons or $0.1 million from the swap counterparty. The net proceeds for the mining company are $1.5 million in revenue, even though the price of copper is below $1,500 per ton. The swap has done what it is supposed to do—it has stabilized the price of copper at $1,500 per ton, preserving the mine owner's revenue. Thus, the swap provides the bankers with the assurance that the financing charges on the debt used to develop the mine will be honored. The bankers can now sleep soundly knowing that the risk of default has been mitigated by the swap.

Why would the swap counterparty pay the mining company the difference between the market price of $1,400 and the swap price of $1,500? The swap counterparty entered into the swap for an entirely different reason than the mining company or, more exactly, an entirely different perception of risk. Suppose that the swap counterparty, a manufacturer of copper wiring, has a substantial, long-term contract to manufacture copper wire for a telecommunications company. Copper wire manufacturing is basically a commodity-type business, which means intense competition and low profit margins (the movie *Other People's Money* provides an in-depth analysis of the copper wire manufacturing industry).

The copper wire contract is desirable because it provides the manufacturing company with a base load of work. In securing a portion of its future revenues, the copper wire manufacturer has also exposed itself to an adverse fluctuation in copper prices. The company stands to lose a substantial amount of money if copper prices rise over the duration of the contract. The risk faced by the copper wire manufacturer is a price rise that could, if high enough, lead to its financial demise.

Now suppose that the price of copper rises to $1,600. The copper wire manufacturer buys 1,000 tons of copper on the open market for $1,600 per ton for a total of $1.6 million and receives from the counterparty the difference between the market price of $1,600 and the swap price of $1,500, or $100 multiplied by the swap volume of 1,000 tons or a total of $0.1 million. The net cost of the copper for the manufacturer is $1.5 million, even though the price of copper has risen above $1,500. Figure 8.1 shows the flow of money.

Figure 8.1 illustrates that either the mining company is receiving money to preserve revenue from falling too low or the copper wire manufacturer is receiving money to keep costs from rising too high as copper prices fluctuate about the swap

Figure 8.1
Flow of Money between Counterparties

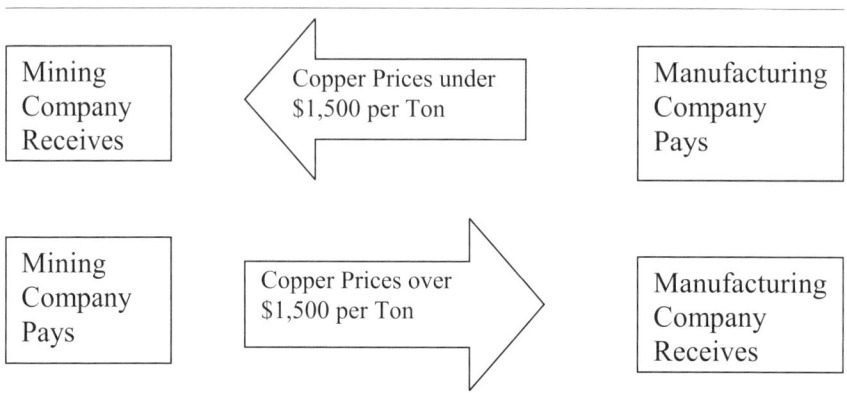

price. The swap matches the counterparties' diametrically opposed perceptions of risk for their mutual benefit.

BUT THERE IS A COST

In the world of business there is no such thing as a free lunch. The benefit of the swap to either party is not cost-free, and it is not a broker's commission but something far more costly. To attain the benefit of protection against a low price of copper through a swap, the mining company must give up the incremental profits when copper prices rise above the swap price. To attain the protection against a high price of copper, the copper manufacturer must give up the incremental cost savings when copper prices fall below the swap price. These can be substantial costs to the swap counterparties.

The benefit of a swap has been described in detail, now it is time to describe its cost in detail. With copper prices at $1,400, the mining company receives a payment from the copper wire manufacturer to maintain its revenue. The copper wire manufacturer purchases 1,000 tons of copper for $1.4 million to satisfy its needs and then pays $0.1 million to the mining company. This increases the effective cost of copper from $1,400 per ton to $1,500 per ton. The cost of protection for not paying more than $1,500 for copper is giving up the benefit of cost savings when copper prices are below $1,500. Similarly, when copper prices are $1,600 per ton, the copper wire manufacturer receives a payment from the mining company to preserve the manufacturer's costs at $1,500. To make this payment, the mining company has to give up the benefit of incremental profits from the higher price of copper.

The manufacturer is not benefiting from incremental cost savings as the price of copper falls below $1,500 for the amount of usage covered by the swap volume. Similarly, the mining company is not benefiting from incremental profits as the price of copper rises above $1,500 for the amount of output covered by the swap volume. In this sense the counterparties may pay a dear price for the protection provided by the swap. This is particularly true if the swap volume covers much of the mining company's production or the manufacturing company's needs. The analysis of the benefit of a swap in preventing a risk of financial loss for either the mine owner or the copper manufacturer must also include the cost of the swap in terms of foregone profits or cost savings.

COST-BENEFIT ANALYSIS OF A SWAP

It is possible to look at the evaluation of swaps or other hedging techniques in purely academic terms replete with a plethora of differential equations and multivariate regression equations. However, in the world of business, academic generalizations are of passing interest. Business deals with risk on a case-by-case basis. The reality of a specific situation is what interests businesspeople, not theoretical generalizations. The emotions of passing up potential profits or savings are difficult to capture in a partial differential equation. The issues that pertain to a cost-benefit analysis can be more easily understood using a concrete example. Hopefully, the thinking behind constructing a model for evaluating risk and in determining a cost-benefit relationship can establish the basis for analyzing other situations.

Suppose that the mining company owns only a single mine. Its return on investment and its capacity to honor the underlying debt obligations are contingent on the price of copper, not on the creditworthiness of a parent company. Mitigating the risk of ending up with bad debt provides the requisite motivation for bankers to insist on the mining company entering into a swap. The mining company is interested in evaluating swap alternatives in order to be in a position to initiate a dialogue with the bank. Without a dialogue, the mining company is left without any means to counter the demands of the bank. The bank, if not opposed, wants the entire production of the mine covered by a swap for the greatest degree of protection. This is understandable from the parochial interests of the lender but may not be in the best interests of the mining company as borrower. The mining company is not in the copper-mining business to preclude itself from profiting from high copper prices, yet this is what the bank wants. The mining company executives want to delight in high copper prices, not bemoan the fact that they have been stripped of the opportunity to enjoy the bonanza.

From the business perspective, the lending institution and the mining company sit on the same side of the table: they both want to develop the mine. But the risk perspectives of those sitting on the same side of the table are not congruent. The mining company executives are interested in minimizing the coverage of the swap in order to leave room for profits when copper prices are high. They want to go out some evening to celebrate being submerged in a deluge of money. The bankers are interested in ensuring that they sleep soundly at night, and they can sleep soundly if their debt obligations are protected by a swap that covers most of the mine's output. Risk analysis comes down to a difference on how the borrower and lender want to spend their evenings.

HERE WE GO

Figure 8.2 is the history of copper prices obtained from the London Metals Exchange (www.lme.co.uk).

There is a real danger that the bankers may be left holding the bag if $1,500 is the flash point in financing the copper mine. Suppose that the bankers ask the mining company executives for an opinion on the future price of copper. Can you guess their response? Let me tell you their response: there is no chance in all of creation that the future price of copper will ever again fall below $1,500 per ton. This will then be supported by a supposedly unbiased report found in some trade magazine or in a consultant's report replete with 101 reasons that it is impossible for copper prices to fall below $1,500 per ton, barring possibly the end of the world.

Some time ago I was a subscriber to a financial service that published a synopsis of what the gold gurus were saying about the future price of gold. Each month I read divergent views printed next to one another: the price of gold will go up, the price of gold will go down, or the price of gold will stay about the same. Each was accompanied by 101 reasons that validated their respective positions. This same financial service also published a synopsis of what the stock market gurus were saying about the future direction of the stock market. Can you guess what they said? In articles printed side by side I read that the market will go up, the market will go down, and the market will stay about the same. Each was accompanied by 101 reasons that they were correct.

Figure 8.2
Copper Prices

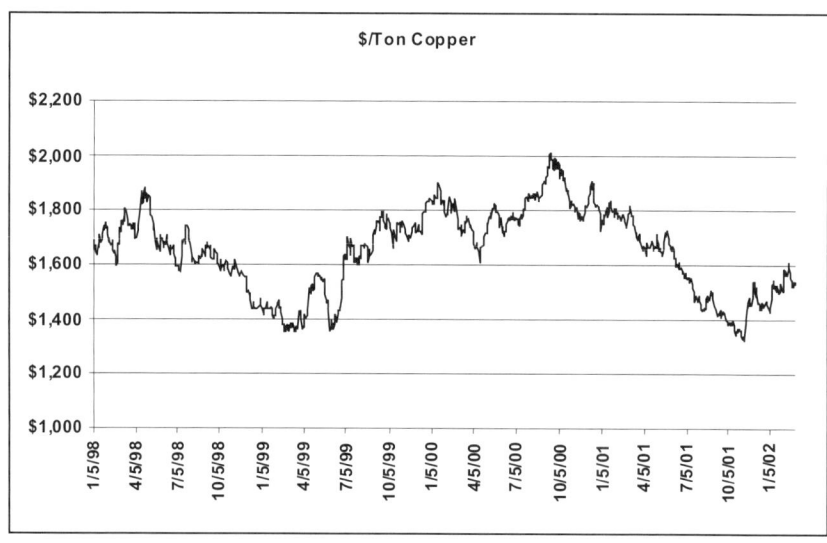

One gold service has predicted a return to a gold boom market ever since gold last spiked to $850 in 1980. The fact that the prediction has been wrong for over 20 years doesn't seem to matter. Subscribers still pay for the service. Maybe they're not the same ones, or maybe they're lifelong goldbugs akin to religious fanatics; it doesn't seem to matter. Each month for over twenty years the gold guru had some evidence, some graph, some glimmer of hope that gold was about to spike again.

Events in the 1970s that caused tidal waves in the price of gold caused barely a ripple in the 1990s. What changed were U.S. Treasuries rather than gold becoming the safe harbor refuge for the fearful and faint at heart. But one thing is certain; the prediction of high gold prices will be proven right. All we have to do is live long enough to see it.

I once had a conversation with an individual of a two-member team responsible for forecasting the price of a certain energy commodity. I had just discovered that one could trade futures in this commodity. I had visions of making a fortune trading futures since I had such a ready source of fundamental information about the commodity's price outlook. I queried one member of the team and received 101 reasons on why price would go up. With this information, how could I go wrong? Buy futures, sit back, and let the money pour in. But before I did this, I came across the other member of the team and queried her about the price outlook. Much to my surprise, I received 101 reasons on why the price would go down. I wondered how these two ever put out a forecast for their clients. It was a marriage of opposites. Maybe their forecast was that price would remain about the same. I gave up on my idea of getting rich on inside information.

Going back a really long time, I remember an issue of a leading magazine doing a front-page feature article on why the then-depressed price of copper would never recover. Alternative materials were being substituted for copper, forever depressing demand; new mines were opening, forever augmenting supply. Since there was no way for demand to absorb supply, the bloated inventories would forever remain bloated. With forever bloated inventories, a price recovery was out of the question. The copper-mining industry was finished for all time.

About a year or so later I was reading about the resurgence of copper prices. I remembered the article and the price of copper when it was published. Would you believe that the article was published just as the price of copper sank to its all-time low? The magazine's timing was perfect. Anyone who bought copper when the article was published would have made a fortune.

There are two axioms I've learned:

1. Those who predict can't.
2. Those who can don't tell.

Referring back to Figure 8.2, suppose that the borrower and the banker agree that the price of copper will not fall below $1,200 per ton or rise above $2,200 per ton and that the swing in copper prices over the next five years will average about

$400 per year. Figure 8.3 shows the RiskOptimizer solution for the Not-So-Random-Walk Generator from Chapter 7.

Figure 8.4 is the price change curve for the solution values. This is a more desired concave curve where there is a large probability associated with small price changes and a small probability associated with large price change. The cumulative probability of a weekly price change of $20 per ton or less is about 55%, whereas the cumulative probability of price changes between $20 and $100 per ton is 45%.

Figure 8.3
Not-So-Random-Walk Generator for Copper Prices

	A	B	C	D	E	F	G	H
1	Not-So Random Walk Price Generator for Copper							
2					Avg Price	Minimum	Maximum	Range
3	Desired Range	$400		Year 1	$1,565.71	$1,425.62	$1,685.36	$259.74
4	Start Price	$1,500.00		Year 2	$1,725.41	$1,571.12	$1,907.66	$336.54
5				Year 3	$1,449.42	$1,204.18	$1,818.50	$614.32
6	Highest	$ 2,200		Year 4	$1,334.99	$1,196.78	$1,451.94	$255.16
7	Upper	$ 2,100		Year 5	$1,743.06	$1,399.48	$1,963.10	$563.62
8	Lower	$ 1,300						
9	Lowest	$ 1,200						Avg Range
10				A Factor	7.261			$405.88
11	Bias Factor	2		B Factor	2.759			
12								Objective
13								$5.88
14					Start			
15	Week			Weekly	Price	Month		
16	0		Up/Down	Change	$1,500.00			
17	1	0.50	1	$3.70	$1,503.70			
18	2	0.50	-1	$14.00	$1,489.70			
19	3	0.50	-1	$18.29	$1,471.40			
20	4	0.50	1	$63.54	$1,534.94	1		

Figure 8.4
Copper Price Generator

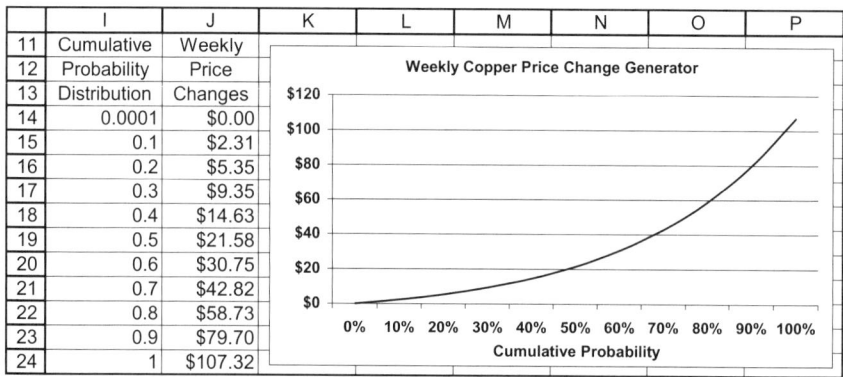

	I	J
11	Cumulative	Weekly
12	Probability	Price
13	Distribution	Changes
14	0.0001	$0.00
15	0.1	$2.31
16	0.2	$5.35
17	0.3	$9.35
18	0.4	$14.63
19	0.5	$21.58
20	0.6	$30.75
21	0.7	$42.82
22	0.8	$58.73
23	0.9	$79.70
24	1	$107.32

Moreover, the largest price change of a little over $100 per ton actually fits past price history in Figure 8.2 quite nicely.

Running an individual simulation (pressing function key F9 in the *Monte Carlo* mode) generated Figure 8.5, the future as seen by the mining company, and Figure 8.6, the future as seen by the bank.

The mining company sees robust prices in copper (why else would a copper mine be developed?). The bankers are not quite so sanguine (they stand to lose if

Figure 8.5
Mining Company's Perspective of the Future

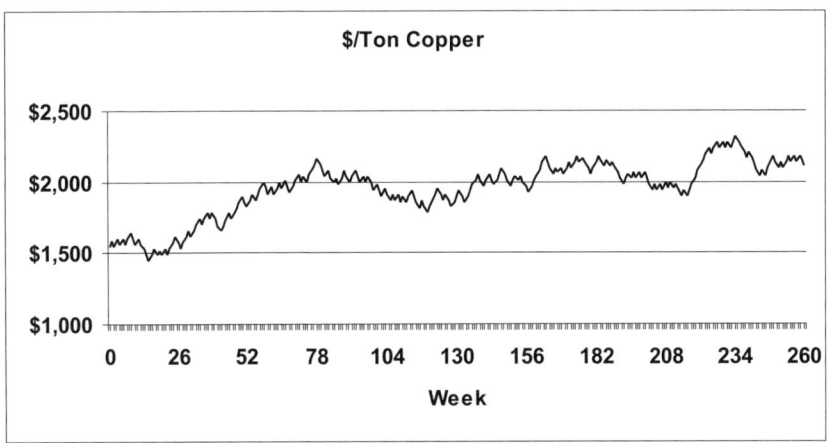

Figure 8.6
Banker's Perspective of Future Price

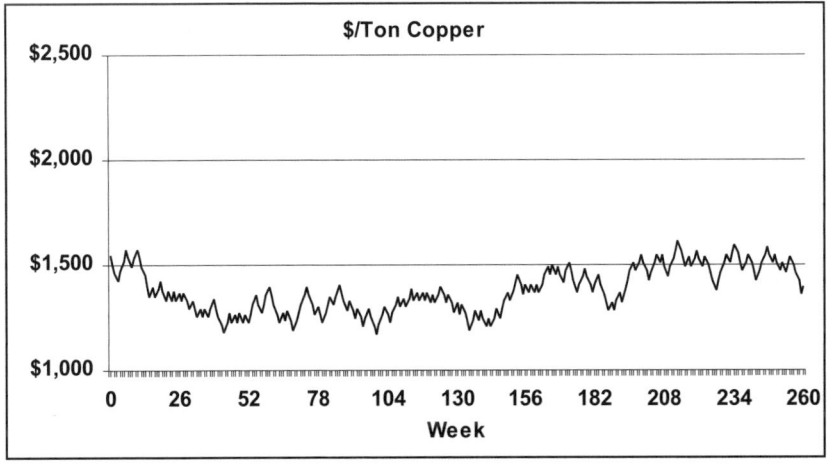

the mining company's price assessment is wrong). Both views are valid—who's to say with certainty what the future price of copper will be?

To complicate things a bit further, suppose that the financing of the mine is in British pounds (GBPs). This presents another risk because the revenue and operating costs are in U.S. dollars. Fluctuations between the currency exchange rates can work in favor of, or not in favor of, the mine owners. The history of the GBP in terms of the number of GBPs that can be purchased by one U.S. dollar in Figure 8.7 was obtained from OANDA Corporation (www.oanda.com).

Suppose that it is decided that the GBP/$ relationship would be no higher than 0.8 GBP to the dollar or lower than 0.5 and that the range would average 0.05 per year. The Not-So-Random-Walk Price Generator modified in Figure 8.8 for 100 times the GBP exchange rate for one dollar yields the appropriate A and B factors.

The resulting cumulative probability distribution curve in Figure 8.9 exhibits a small degree of concavity.

Having created a price generator for copper and a currency exchange rate for the number of GBP that can be purchased for one dollar, a spreadsheet can be created to evaluate having a copper and a currency exchange swap. Figure 8.10 shows the copper price portion of the spreadsheet.

Figure 8.10 creates the copper price for 260 weeks, and Figure 8.11 does the same for one hundred times the GBP/$ relationship.

Figure 8.12 covers the revenue for 60 months of mine operation. The minimum mine production of 1,000 tons per month ensures that mine production covers the maximum swap volume of 1,000 tons per month. The formulation of the spread-

Figure 8.7
GBP per $ Relationship

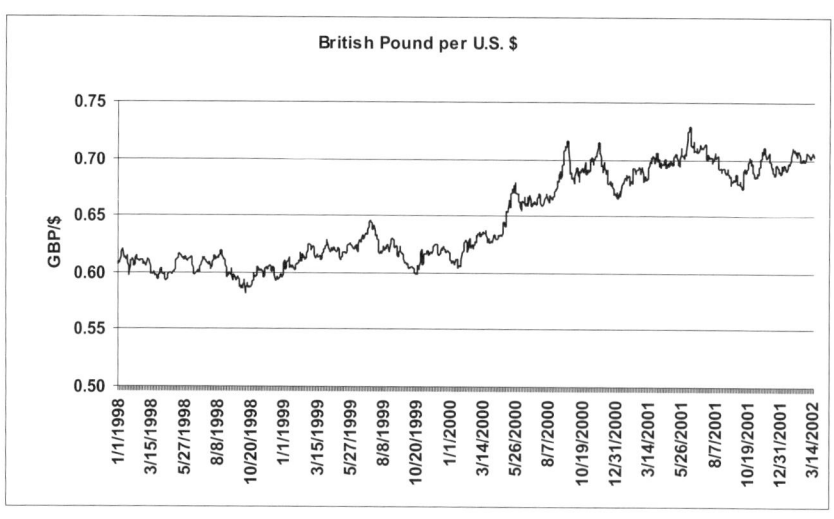

Hedging with a Swap

Figure 8.8
Not-So-Random Currency Exchange Rate Generator

	A	B	C	D	E	F	G	H
1	Not-So Random Walk Price Generator for 100 X GBP/$							
2					Avg Price	Minimum	Maximum	Range
3	Desired Range	5		Year 1	71.46	70.12	72.56	2.44
4	Start Price	70		Year 2	72.70	70.51	74.63	4.12
5				Year 3	69.63	67.59	71.43	3.84
6	Highest	80		Year 4	70.52	68.34	72.98	4.64
7	Upper	75		Year 5	68.63	67.02	71.26	4.24
8	Lower	65						
9	Lowest	60						Avg Range
10				A Factor	1.472			3.85
11	Bias Factor	2		B Factor	0.493			
12								Objective
13								-1.15
14					Start			
15	Week			Weekly	Price	Month		
16	0		Up/Down	Change	70.00			
17	1	0.50	1	0.12	70.12			
18	2	0.50	1	0.54	70.66			
19	3	0.50	1	0.69	71.35			
20	4	0.50	-1	0.26	71.09	1		

Figure 8.9
Currency Exchange Rate Generator

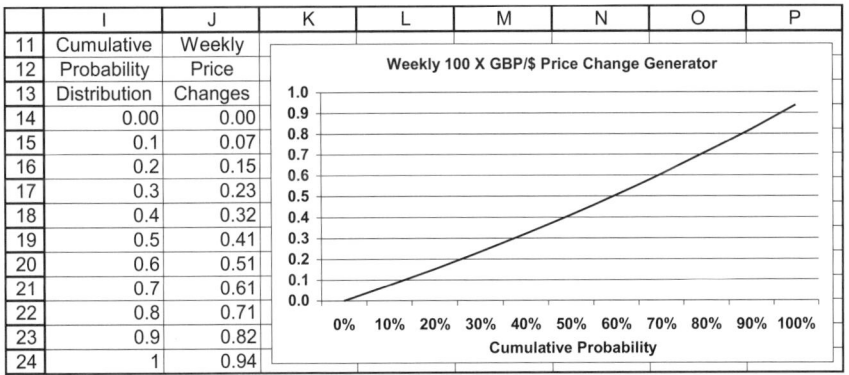

	I	J	K	L	M	N	O	P
11	Cumulative	Weekly						
12	Probability	Price						
13	Distribution	Changes						
14	0.00	0.00						
15	0.1	0.07						
16	0.2	0.15						
17	0.3	0.23						
18	0.4	0.32						
19	0.5	0.41						
20	0.6	0.51						
21	0.7	0.61						
22	0.8	0.71						
23	0.9	0.82						
24	1	0.94						

Figure 8.10
Copper Prices

	A	B	C	D	E
4	Start Price	$1,500			
5					
6	Highest	$ 2,200			
7	Upper	$ 2,100			
8	Lower	$ 1,300			
9	Lowest	$ 1,200			
10				A Factor	7.261
11	Bias Factor	2		B Factor	2.759
12					
13					
14					Copper
15	Week			Weekly	Price
16	0		Up/Down	Change	$1,500.00
17	1	0.50	-1	$9.62	$1,490.38
18	2	0.50	-1	$53.29	$1,437.08
19	3	0.50	-1	$46.60	$1,390.49
20	4	0.50	-1	$5.92	$1,384.56

Figure 8.11
GBP/$ Relationship

	F	G	H	I	J
4	Start Price	70			
5					
6	Highest	80			
7	Upper	75			
8	Lower	65			
9	Lowest	60			
10				A Factor	1.472
11	Bias Factor	2		B Factor	0.493
12					
13					
14					100 X
15	Month			Weekly	GBP/$
16			Up/Down	Change	70.00
17		0.50	1	0.13	70.13
18		0.50	1	0.34	70.46
19		0.50	-1	0.48	69.98
20	1	0.50	1	0.83	70.81

Figure 8.12
Determining Mine Revenue

	L	M	N	O	P	Q	R
4							
5							
6						Copper	Mining
7		Minimum	Most	Maximum	Actual	Price	Revenue
8	Month	Production	Likely	Production	Production	$/Ton	$MM
9	1	1000	1100	1300	1133	$ 1,546	$ 1,752
10	2	1000	1110	1310	1140	$ 1,689	$ 1,926
11	3	1000	1120	1320	1147	$ 1,922	$ 2,204
12	4	1000	1130	1330	1153	$ 2,046	$ 2,359
13	5	1000	1140	1340	1160	$ 2,111	$ 2,448
14	6	1000	1150	1350	1167	$ 2,158	$ 2,518
15	7	1000	1160	1360	1173	$ 2,070	$ 2,429
16	8	1000	1170	1370	1180	$ 2,092	$ 2,469
17	9	1000	1180	1380	1187	$ 1,989	$ 2,360
18	10	1000	1190	1390	1193	$ 2,039	$ 2,434
19	11	1000	1200	1400	1200	$ 2,095	$ 2,514
20	12	1000	1210	1410	1207	$ 1,971	$ 2,379

sheet does not cover the contingency of mine production falling below the swap volume.

Actual production in column P is a triangular distribution with the minimum, most likely, and maximum values listed in columns M, N, and O. The copper price in column Q references the corresponding weekly price in column E. For example, the formulas in cells Q9 and Q10 are =E20 and =E24, respectively. Revenue is price in column Q multiplied by volume in column P. Figure 8.13 is the cash flow from mine operations. Mine-operating costs in column S consists of variable costs of tons mined multiplied by $500 per ton plus or minus 10% and fixed costs of $600

Figure 8.13
Determining Mine Cash Flow

	S	T	U	V	W
4	Mining				
5	Costs				Cash
6	Without	Debt		Debt	Flow
7	Debt	Charges		Charges	w/o
8	Charges	GBP	GBP/$	$MM	Swap
9	$ 1,073	500	0.708	$ 706	$ (28)
10	$ 1,077	500	0.709	$ 705	$ 144
11	$ 1,080	500	0.701	$ 713	$ 411
12	$ 1,083	500	0.698	$ 717	$ 560
13	$ 1,086	500	0.691	$ 723	$ 639

(thousand) plus or minus 10%. Operating and financing costs were intentionally set up in order to ensure there would be negative cash flows for copper prices below $1,500 per ton.

The formula in column S is:

$$=P9*500*RiskUniform(0.9,1,1.1)/1000+600*RiskUniform(0.9,1,1.1)$$

Total debt charges of 500 GBP in column T cover both interest and principal repayment. Its corresponding dollar cost in column V varies with changes in the currency exchange rate. The formulas in column U are similar to those in column Q: cell U9 is =J20/100. The formula in cell V9 for the dollar cost of the financing is =T9/U9. Cash flow without the swap in column W is revenue less mining costs and debt charges; cell W9 is =R9-S9-V9.

Figure 8.14 measures the financial performance of the mine by determining the dividends that can be spun off from the mine and the state of the working capital account. Dividends can be paid only if the working capital account is fully funded. The minimum working capital requirement has a strong impact on the reliance of swaps to protect the mine from defaulting on its debt obligations.

Desired working capital is actually minimum working capital made up of cash plus accounts receivable less current liabilities. The bank loan sets up a minimum working capital as a source of cash in case there are shortfalls in cash generation such as from a low copper price or an adverse currency exchange rate. A value of $3 million is about two months' worth of expenses. Cash accumulated in excess of the minimum working capital requirement is spun off for other purposes such as funding capital improvements or paying a dividend. Whatever happens, the excess funds over the minimum working capital requirement are not available to save the bankers when times get tough. No cash can be spun off if there is a shortfall in working capital. The formula in cell X9 is =X5+W9, initial working capital plus the first month's earnings. Starting in cell X10, the formula is =X9+W10-Y10. Column

Figure 8.14
Financial Performance without Swaps

	X	Y	Z
2	Desired		
3	Working		
4	Capital		Lowest
5	$ 3,000		Balance
6			Working
7	Working		Capital
8	Capital	Dividends	$ 2,854
9	$ 2,999		
10	$ 3,071	$ -	Total
11	$ 3,051	$ 71	Dividends
12	$ 2,998	$ 51	$ 16,775

Y contains the dividends or funds spun off from the working capital account being in excess of the minimum requirement, or, in cell Y10:

=IF(X9>$X$5,X9–$X$5,0)

Figure 8.15 is set up to handle collars. A collar with a cap of $1,600 means that the mining company pays the swap counterparty only when copper prices exceed $1,600 multiplied by the swap volume. A swap floor of $1,400 means that the mining company receives funds from the swap counterparty only when copper prices are below $1,400 for the swap volume. Between $1,400 and $1,600 per ton, neither party exchanges funds. A collar swap becomes a plain vanilla swap when the prices for the cap and the floor are the same.

The formula in cell AB9 is:

=IF(Q9>$AB$1,($AB$1*$AB$3+Q9*(P9–$AB$3))/1000,
IF(Q9<$AB$2,($AB$2*$AB$3+Q9*(P9–$AB$3))/1000,Q9*P9/1000))

In Excelese, if the price is above the cap, the revenue is the cap price times the swap volume plus the market price times the sales volume less the swap volume. This is a reduction to the revenue depending on the size of the swap volume. If this condition is not true, and if the price is below the floor price, then the revenue is the floor price times the swap volume plus the market price times the sales volume less the swap volume. This is an addition to the revenue depending on the size of the swap volume. If neither of these conditions is true, then the market price must be between the cap and floor price, and revenue is the market price times the entire production volume. As mentioned, by having the same floor and cap price, the collar swap becomes a plain vanilla swap. The formula in cell AC9 is basically the same with regard to selecting the GBP/$ currency conversion rate.

Figure 8.15
Financial Performance with Swaps

	AA	AB	AC	AD	AE	AF	AG
1	Swap cap	$ 1,500	$ 0.72				
2	Swap floor	$ 1,500	$ 0.72		Desired		
3	Swap volume	500	0		Working		
4				Debt	Capital		Lowest
5		Revenue	Charges	Cash	$ 3,000		Balance
6		with	with	Flow			Working
7		Copper	Currency	with both	Working		Capital
8		Swap	Swap	Swaps	Capital	Dividends	$ (1,193)
9		$ 1,718	$ 715	$ (105)	$ 2,895		
10		$ 1,753	$ 737	$ (95)	$ 2,799	$ -	Total
11		$ 1,721	$ 766	$ (160)	$ 2,639	$ -	Dividends
12		$ 1,677	$ 755	$ (196)	$ 2,443	$ -	$ 587

=IF(U9>$AC$1,$AC$3/$AC$1+(T9–$AC$3)/U9,
=IF(U9<$AC$2,$AC$3/$AC$2+(T9–$AC$3)/U9,T9/U9))

Suppose there is no swap and the conversion rate is 0.75. Then the 500 GBP would convert to a dollar outflow of $667 (500 GBP divided by the conversion rate of 0.75 GBP per dollar). If there were a swap with a cap conversion rate of 0.72 for a swap volume of 300 GBP, then the dollar outflow would be 300 GBP/0.72 or $417 for the swap plus an open market transaction of 200 GBP/0.75 or $267 for a total outflow of $684. The mining company is giving up part of the benefit of a favorable currency exchange rate by having the swap. This is the cost of the swap.

Obviously, there has to be a benefit. Suppose that the conversion rate is 0.69. Without the swap, the mining company would pay out $725 to obtain the 500 GBP to service debt. With a swap of 300 for a conversion rate of 0.72, the outflow would be 300 GBP/0.72 or $417 plus 200 GBP/0.69 or $290 for a total of $707, a net savings from not being totally exposed to the spot currency exchange market. The impact of currency exchange rate swaps can best be interpreted by working out an example, as their inner workings are not as obvious as the copper swap.

The formula in cell AD9 is the cash flow determined by the revenue as affected by the copper swap on revenue and the currency exchange swap on financing costs less operating costs or =AB9-S9-AC9. The rest of the spreadsheet on working capital and dividends with a swap is formulated the same as without the swap.

IMPACT OF WORKING CAPITAL ON RISK

Risk has to be defined before it can be analyzed. Suppose that this company has a $2 million line of credit or some other form of outside support. Then the danger of default exists when the working capital falls below a negative $2 million. Cell Z8 keeps track of the minimum working capital balance without a swap, and cell AG8 does the same with the swap. Cells Z12 and AG12 keep track of total dividend payouts. Columns AA through AG could be replicated, and with some editing, to allow several alternatives on swap volumes and prices to be analyzed simultaneously in a single @Risk run.

Figure 8.16 is the minimum balance in the working capital account over the 60-month period with a requirement of having a positive $1.5 million balance before paying dividends.

If a negative balance of $2 million is the demarcation of risk, then there is a 36% chance of the minimum balance being below a negative $2 million and a 5% chance of being below a negative $6.2 million. Figure 8.17 shows the same situation except that the minimum working capital before paying dividends is $3 million.

By increasing the minimum balance in the working capital account to $3 million before dividends can be paid, the risk of a negative balance in the working capital account of a negative $2 million is reduced from 36% to 20.6%, and the 5% chance of having a negative balance of $6.2 million or less is reduced to a negative $4.7 million. Clearly, keeping a greater amount of cash reserves in the form of a minimum

Figure 8.16
Working Capital Account ($1.5 MM Minimum)

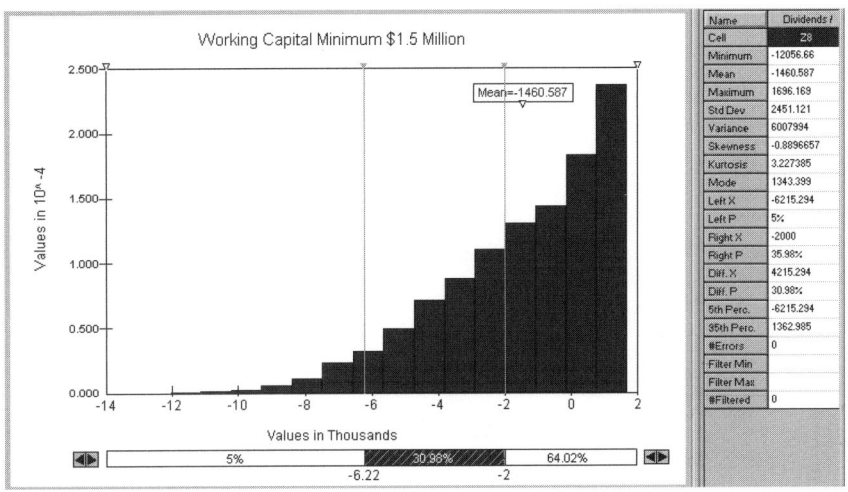

Figure 8.17
Working Capital Account ($3 MM Minimum)

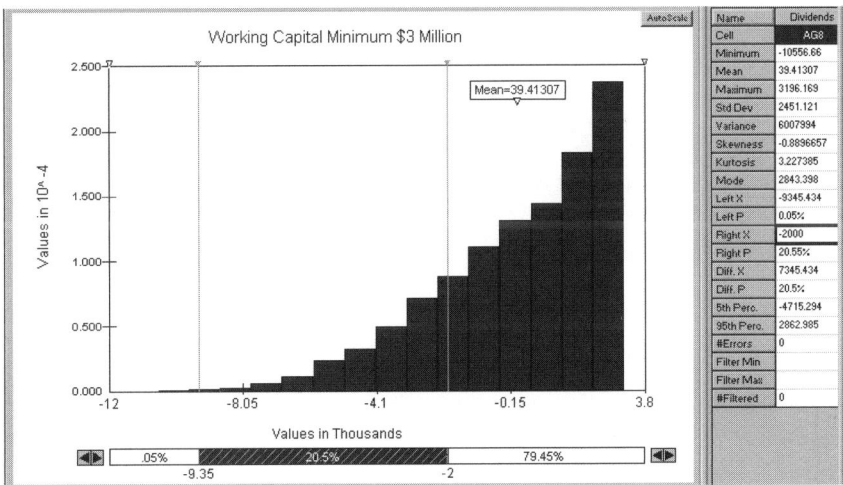

working capital requirement is a means to control risk. Further reduction of the risk of working capital balance falling below a negative $2 million will be the benefit of entering into swaps.

If minimum working capital before paying dividends is $3 million, then the total dividends paid out to the owning company of the mine is shown in Figure 8.18.

Figure 8.18
Total Dividend Payout

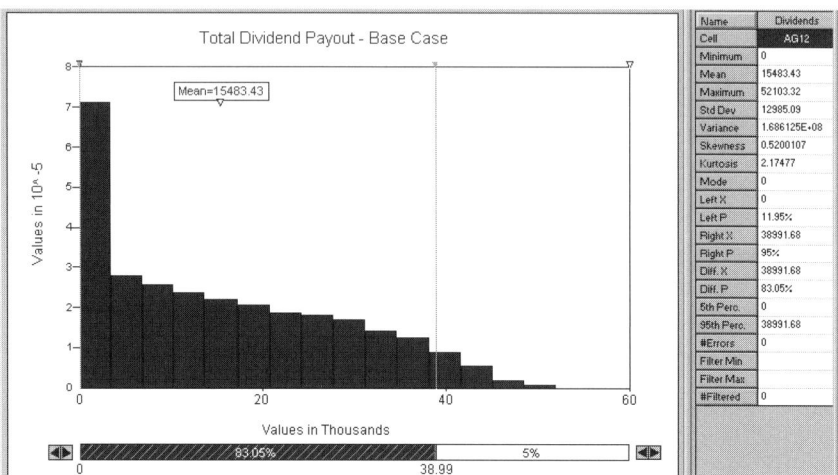

There is a 12% chance that no dividend will be paid out over the five-year period. This reflects horrible conditions in the copper market. The mean payout is $15.5 million, and the maximum is $52 million. Any degradation of the mean payout of $15.5 million will be the basis for evaluating the cost of swaps.

COST-BENEFIT ANALYSIS

Tables 8.1 through 8.3 record the mean of total dividend payout and the probability of the minimum working capital being less than –$2 million for different copper and currency exchange swap volumes. The swaps are plain vanilla swaps with a cap and floor price of $1,500 per ton for copper and a 0.72 exchange rate for GBP per dollar.

The examination of Table 8.1 shows that there is little incremental reduction in the risk of minimum working capital falling below a negative $2 million when the swap volume is increased from 750 to 1,000 tons. For this small benefit, the cost in a diminution of dividends is $2 million. This alone should convince the bankers that full coverage of mine output (a swap volume of 1,000 tons) is not necessary and certainly not desirable from the perspective of the borrower.

With a currency swap for 250,000 GBP, there is little benefit in having a swap volume over 500 tons of copper. The benefit of a swap volume of 1,000 tons versus 500 tons is a reduction in the risk from 1.9% to 0% for a cost of $3.8 million in the form of a reduction in total dividend payouts. Thus, a copper swap over 500 tons is of marginal value.

With a swap that totally covers the currency exchange risk, the copper swap can be reduced below 500 tons to cover the risk of working capital falling below a nega-

Table 8.1
No Currency Swaps

	No Currency Swap	
Swap Volume Copper	Mean of Total Dividends ($MM)	Probability of Minimum Working Capital Being Less Than -$2 Million
1000	$7.3	0.0%
750	$9.3	0.7%
500	$11.3	4.7%
250	$13.9	12.3%

Table 8.2
Currency Swap Volume 250,000 GBP

	Currency Swap 250,000 GBP	
Swap Volume Copper	Mean of Total Dividends ($MM)	Probability of Minimum Working Capital Being Less Than -$2 Million
1000	$8.0	0.0%
750	$9.9	0.0%
500	$11.8	1.9%
250	$13.9	8.4%

Table 8.3
Currency Swap Volume 500,000 GBP

	Currency Swap 500,000 GBP	
Swap Volume Copper	Mean of Total Dividends ($MM)	Probability of Minimum Working Capital Being Less Than -$2 Million
1000	$8.5	0.0%
750	$10.3	0.0%
500	$12.3	0.5%
250	$14.3	5.7%

tive $2 million with a relatively small sacrifice in potential profits. Tables 8.1 through 8.3 demonstrate the interplay between the currency exchange and copper swaps to control risk with different associated costs.

Figures 8.19 through 8.21 portray the information in Tables 8.1 through 8.3 as cost-benefit curves for various copper and currency swaps. The cost is the reduction in total dividends from the nonhedge total dividend payout of $15.5 million. The benefit is the probability of having less than a negative $2 million in the working capital account from a starting point of 20% without swaps. The size of the copper swap in tons is indicated in each figure.

196　CORPORATE FINANCIAL RISK MANAGEMENT

Figure 8.19
No Currency Swaps

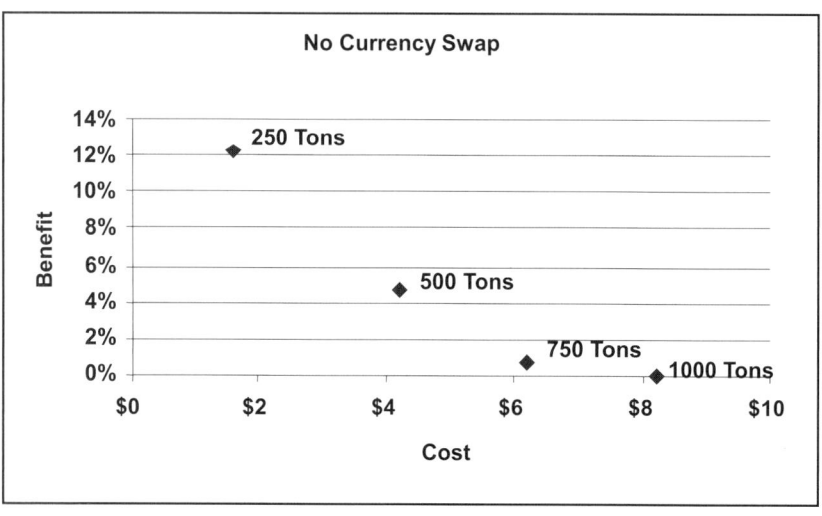

Figure 8.20
Currency Swap Volume 250,000 GBP

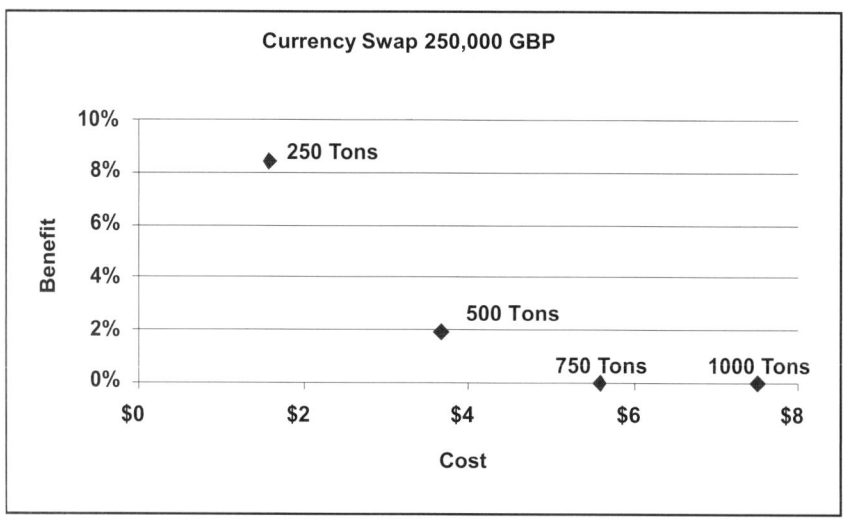

Figure 8.21
Currency Swap Volume 500,000 GBP

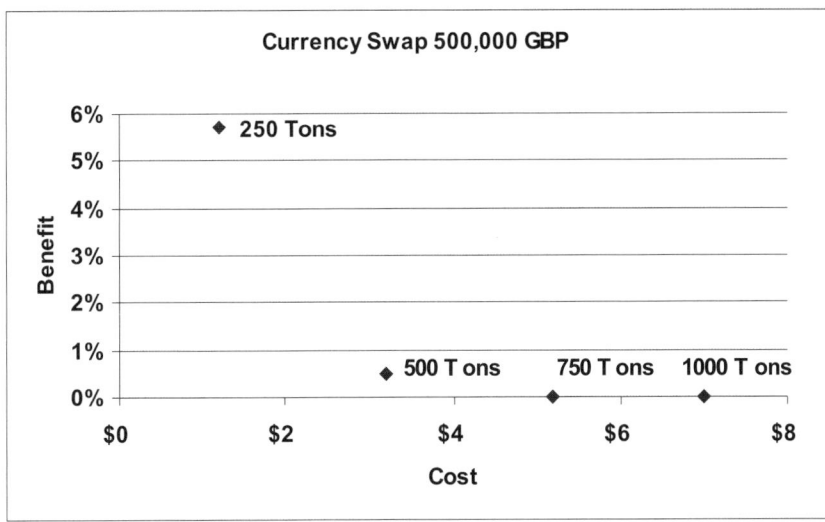

The efficacy of increasing the copper swap from 250 tons to 750 tons remains the same in the sense that the slope of the curve is constant. Equal increments to the copper swap have the same impact on reducing risk. After 750 tons, the curve flattens out, offering little incremental benefit for large increments in costs.

With a currency swap of 250,000 GBP, the efficacy of increasing the copper swap volume falls sharply after 500 tons. There is no point in having a swap volume greater than 750 tons.

With a currency swap of 500,000 GBP, there is virtually no benefit in having more than 500 tons of swap volume. These curves provide sufficient information for one to derive the optimal swap position such as a currency swap to fully cover the exchange risk coupled with a copper swap of about 300 or 400 tons. These swaps would significantly reduce the risk of working capital falling below a negative $2 million at a minimal cost of about a $2 million sacrifice in dividend payouts over the five-year period. From the lender's perspective a swap covering most or all of the production volume is unnecessary; from the borrower's perspective a smaller swap volume does not greatly inhibit potential profits. Thus, a cost-benefit approach can be used to determine the optimal level of swaps to provide the requisite degree of risk protection at a minimal cost.

TO UNDO A SWAP

Suppose that the copper mining is forced to enter into a swap that covers much of its production and the price of copper begins a sustained rise. Do managers sit idly by in their private suites bemoaning the loss of incremental profits, or do they take some sort of action? Humans find it extremely difficult to be unemotional about missing out on potential profits. Reporting to the shareholders that the company contained its losses when copper prices were low because of a swap is one thing, but reporting to the shareholders that the company managed to avoid making a bundle of money when copper prices were high because of a swap is another. A financial officer credited for preventing a loss in one year can lose his or her position the next for preventing a profit.

The way out of a swap is to enter into short-term futures contracts that "undo what the swap does." Suppose that copper prices begin to rise and management is convinced that this will be a sustained rise. The mining company can buy copper futures. As copper prices continue to rise, the profits in the futures position offset the money passed to the swap counterparty.

Taking an opposite position in futures when on the wrong side of a swap is a common practice among companies once they enter the fairyland of derivatives. This further enriches the investment bankers. First the investment bankers receive a commission on arranging the swap by incorporating a small spread between what one party pays and what the other receives. Then they figure out who is on the wrong side of the swap. If copper prices are going up, call the chief financial officer at the mining company and induce him or her to buy futures to offset the profit foregone by entering the swap. Oh, the price of copper is going down? Call the chief financial officer at the copper wire manufacturing company and induce him or her to sell futures to compensate for the cost savings foregone by entering the swap. Either way the investment bankers are making a bundle in commissions in buying and selling futures in addition to the swap spread.

The problem is that futures are effective only in preserving either profits or cost savings if the rise or fall in copper prices is sustained over a period of time. Futures usually are settled 90 days after entering into a contract, although futures with a shorter life span can be bought and sold. If there is an adverse price change when the futures contract is about to be liquidated, an anticipated profit can become a real loss. A choppy wave pattern for prices can generate continual losses in future contracts.

Let's put "futures can undo a swap only when there is a sustained rise or fall in the price of the underlying commodity" into practice. Referring to Figure 8.2, a sustained rise in the price of copper started in April 1999. If you were a financial manager in charge of taking a position in futures to undo the damage to earnings incurred by being a counterparty to a swap, at what point would you realize that the price of copper was indeed in a sustained rise? Please do not respond with April 1999. Look at the plunge in copper prices in June; how would that impact your decision?

At some point you start buying futures. Everyone considers you a hero as the price of copper continues its relentless, if erratic, rise. Now look at December 2000. Presumably you are still buying futures, which from that point forward will be generating losses. Actually, futures purchased after October or November would likely end up as losses. When do you stop buying futures? Please do not tell me December 2000.

If you feel confident that you can make timely decisions on the sustained rise or fall of copper futures, I have one last question. Pretend it is early 2002. Referring to Figure 8.2, the price of copper hit a low near the end of 2001. At that time the swap counterparty was sending you money. All was well with top management. A few weeks later, the price of copper rose above $1,500. The investment banker told you how much money to send to the counterparty. Top management queried you how long this lamentable situation is going to continue.

Now you are sitting at the extreme right-hand end of the price curve in Figure 8.2. The chart looks as if a sustained recovery in copper prices may be in the making. Tomorrow you are to advise top management whether the company should take a futures position and, if so, how large it should be. Please respond in memo form. Now open up the financial section of the newspaper and see if you were right.

Those responsible for taking futures positions to augment a company's profits or cost savings with or without the existence of a swap must live and breathe the commodity in question every moment of the working day. In the case of copper futures, supply, demand, mine openings, mine closings, labor disturbances and strikes, the ups and downs of the economy, swings in inventories, and the machinations of speculators contribute to minute-by-minute fluctuations. These in turn generate phone calls from brokers to buy on the dip ("a technical correction; price is bound to go up") or sell on the dip ("looks like a market collapse in the making"). Or if the price goes up, the advice is to sell ("you can't go wrong taking a profit") or buy ("you can't win if you don't play"). No one cares whether you're right or wrong in buying or selling as long as you buy or sell. Meanwhile, at the end of the day, some top manager, knowing the closing price of copper, asks you why you were so stupid for not buying or selling more than you did.

Now you can go home and dream or have nightmares, as the case may be, about the political climate in Zaire and its impact on copper production. You can spend your weekends and holidays watching your children grow up wondering what will be the opening price of copper on the next business day. You live and breathe copper. Such is the life of those who rely on derivatives to augment a company's profits or contain its costs.

TRIPLE RISKS

The spreadsheet could also be adapted to cover interest rate risks. Here the 500,000 GBP financing charge would be broken down into its components of interest payments and loan amortization. The impact of floating interest rates for loans denominated in GBP on the interest expense then becomes another risk to be evaluated. Care has to be exercised to ensure that the swap volume does not exceed the outstanding amount of debt. A similar procedure of generating a random walk pattern would be used to model floating interest rates for GBP loans as in modeling fluctuating currency rates.

Adding layers of risks affects the dividend payout. Dividend payout increases as copper prices rise, interest rates fall, and currency exchange rate moves in the direction that reduces dollar outlays on financing charges. Risk increases when there are a simultaneous fall in copper prices, a hike in interest rates, and a currency exchange rate that increases dollar outlays. However, when dealing with multiple risks, favorable changes in one risk factor can compensate for adverse changes in the others. For instance, a high price in copper partially or totally covers the adverse impact of a high interest rate and an unfavorable currency exchange rate. Some experimentation is necessary to obtain the optimal mix of swaps that provides the requisite degree of protection to keep working capital from falling below a prescribed point at the least cost in the form of a sacrifice in dividend payout. But the same methodology for evaluating a double risk can be applied to a triple risk.

9
INSURING AGAINST BUSINESS RISKS

SYNOPSIS

The previous chapter dealt with using a swap to hedge against a low copper price and an adverse change in the GBP/U.S. dollar exchange rate. In this chapter the model is expanded to include the risk of an adverse change to interest rates if the loan were tied to a floating interest rate.

The copper-mining company now faces the triple risks of a low copper price, an adverse currency exchange rate, and a high interest rate. Rather than utilizing swaps, this chapter explores the alternative of insuring against a business risk. An insurance company will be paid a premium to protect against the risk of a commercial loss using bonds as reserves to cover claims. The big difference for the copper-mining company is that an insurance premium has to be paid annually to cover the triple risks, whereas swaps, on the surface, do not represent a cost. But as already covered, there is a cost in terms of foregone profits or cost savings. If the cost of the insurance premium is less than the amount of foregone profits or cost savings, then insurance may be a preferable alternative. The chapter ends with a new situation on insuring against the business risk of high heating oil costs to discuss model-building techniques.

THOUGHTS ON SELF-INSURING

Rather than entering into three different swaps or writing a premium to a third party, suppose that the copper-mining company sets up a self-insurance subsidiary that is paid an annual premium by the parent. The subsidiary pays the parent only when a low copper price, an adverse currency exchange, and high interest rates work together to cause cash flow to fall below a stipulated minimum. Payout is contingent on a negative cash flow that exhausts working capital, not on specific levels of copper prices and currency exchange and interest rates. Thus, a high price in copper may compensate for an adverse currency exchange rate and a high interest rate. While the reward of one imponderable may compensate for the risk of another, there is a possibility of a simultaneous occurrence of a low copper price, an adverse currency exchange rate, and a high interest rate. This creates a long, narrow left-hand tail to a probability distribution of a company's profitability harboring a significant risk for financial loss.

The subsidiary would have to be initially funded at some prudent level just in case a drawdown is necessary soon after its formation. The company could sell an issue of stock and place the proceeds into a special fund within the subsidiary that then invests in debt instruments. The subsidiary now has two sources of income—the interest income on the bonds and the insurance premium from the company. These accumulate until the day comes when a withdrawal must be made to honor a claim. The insurance premium should be sufficient to cover the risk of negative working capital over a period of time. The risk of loss lessens with time as the repayment of debt reduces the potential losses associated with an adverse currency exchange rate and a high interest rate.

Companies are generally reluctant to issue stock, as this dilutes earnings per share. New stock issues are generally used to fund expansion plans such as capital expenditures and mergers, not provide an insurance fund for business risks. Moreover, funds raised by an equity financing could have been used to substitute for the debt incurred in financing the project, thus reducing the currency exchange and interest rate risks. Most companies prefer to issue bonds rather than equity since the interest paid on bonds is tax-deductible. The company could issue bonds and place the proceeds into a fund that is invested in other debt instruments in order to act as reserves to cover losses. In a way this is a bit self-defeating in that the company has increased its risk of insolvency by issuing more debt, although the fund does provide a source of funds when working capital turns negative. Moreover, the issue of bonds might have an adverse impact on a company's credit rating, which is based, in part, on the amount of debt within its capital structure and the degree of coverage of interest expenses.

A THIRD-PARTY PROVIDER

While some companies have joined together to set up mutual insurance organizations to insure themselves against specific risks, a more common practice is to seek the services of a third party to provide such coverage. A financial intermediary holding a portfolio of bonds might be willing to assume a business risk for a premium. The premium augments the interest income of a portfolio of bonds while the portfolio itself acts as reserves to honor claims. The premium should be more than the break-even rate to cover potential claims against the portfolio of bonds in order for the premium to augment the portfolio's income over time. Even with a premium that exceeds the break-even rate, the portfolio of bonds is still exposed to the risk of partial liquidation in order to honor claims.

One may argue that it doesn't make sense for a company to pay a premium to a third party that is greater than potential claims over a period of time. First among the counterarguments is that the insured doesn't know the break-even rate. Second, the company seeking the protection of insurance probably doesn't have the reserves against which to honor claims, particularly if claims occur early on. Third, a company may be more than willing to pay an insurance premium that is higher than the break-even rate if that premium permits the company to obtain the necessary financing to support a capital expenditure.

Insurance generally covers a catastrophic loss such as fire, earthquakes, and other natural and now-a-days man-made disasters. Companies that specialize in this area sometimes issue "catastrophe" or cat-bonds. Buyers are attracted to cat-bonds because of their higher yield. These bonds act as reserves to satisfy claims from catastrophic occurrences. What is being discussed in this chapter is insurance coverage not for a catastrophe but for a commercial loss.

DETERMINING THE RISK PROFILE

Figure 9.1 is the spreadsheet from Chapter 7 adapted to generate an interest rate. Suppose that interest rates for loans denominated in British pounds are expected to be between 4% and 9% with an average swing of 2%.

The A and B Factors in Figure 9.1 generate nearly a linear relationship between changes in interest rate increments and the cumulative probability distribution as

Figure 9.1
Not-So-Random-Walk Interest Rate Generator

	A	B	C	D	E	F	G	H
1	Not-So Random Walk Interest Rate Generator							
2		%			Avg Price	Minimum	Maximum	Range
3	Desired Range	2		Year 1	5.6	4.2	7.0	2.8
4	Start Int Rate	4.5		Year 2	6.2	5.2	7.4	2.1
5		%		Year 3	6.6	5.7	7.5	1.8
6	Highest	9		Year 4	6.3	5.8	6.9	1.2
7	Upper	8		Year 5	7.2	5.7	8.4	2.8
8	Lower	5						
9	Lowest	4						Avg Range
10				A Factor	1.453			2.1
11	Bias Factor	2		B Factor	0.233			
12								Objective
13								0.1
14					Start			
15	Week			Weekly	Price	Month		
16	0		Up/Down	Change	4.5			
17	1		0.50	-1	0.3	4.2		
18	2		0.12	1	0.3	4.5		
19	3		0.20	1	0.1	4.6		
20	4		0.25	1	0.1	4.7	1	

seen in Figure 9.2. The discrete probability for equal interest rate increments is essentially a uniform probability distribution. Figure 9.3 is the first portion of the spreadsheet to determine the price of copper as per the previous chapter. Figure 9.4 establishes the conversion rate between GBP and the U.S. dollar as per the previous chapter. Figure 9.5 establishes the interest rate set up in Figure 9.1. Figure 9.6 is the same as in the previous chapter other than being relocated within the spreadsheet.

Figure 9.7 generates debt servicing charges. An average interest rate of 6% was assumed to apply to the total debt charges of 500 GBP in column Z. Total debt charges were arbitrarily split between debt repayment in column AA and interest expense in column AB. The interest rate in column AC references those generated in column Q with the formulas in cells AC9 and AC10 being =Q20/100 and =Q24/100, respectively.

The interest expense in column AD is the presumed 6% interest expense in column AB multiplied by the ratio of the actual to the presumed interest. The formula in cell AD9 is =AB9*AC9/0.06. Column AE totals debt repayment and interest expenses, which are then divided by the conversion rate in column AF to obtain the equivalent dollar expense in column AG.

Figure 9.8 generates the cash flow in column AH as revenue less operating costs and the dollar equivalent of the financing charges plus any insurance claim receipts from the previous year.

The formula in cell AH10 is =X10–Y10–AG10+AK9. The first-year cash flow has no claim from a prior year. Minimum working capital requirements have been increased to $6 million. This provides a means for the company to reduce the business risk insurance premium by having deeper pockets to support operations when copper prices, currency exchange, and interest rates conspire against the financial welfare of the company. The working capital and dividend formulation is the same as in the previous chapter.

Figure 9.2
Interest Rate Generator

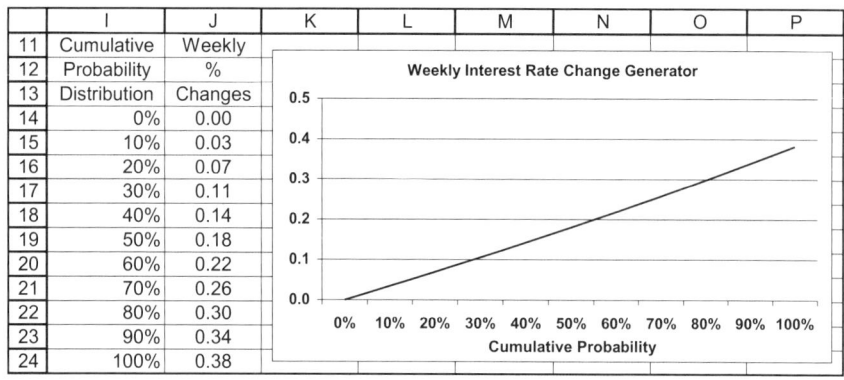

Insuring Against Business Risks

Figure 9.3
Determining the Copper Price

	A	B	C	D	E
1	Insuring a Business Risk				
2					
3					
4	Start Price	$1,500			
5					
6	Highest	$ 2,200			
7	Upper	$ 2,100			
8	Lower	$ 1,300			
9	Lowest	$ 1,200			
10				A Factor	7.261
11	Bias Factor		2	B Factor	2.759
12					
13					
14					Copper
15	Week			Weekly	Price
16	0		Up/Down	Change	$1,500
17	1	0.50	-1	$6.92	$1,493
18	2	0.50	1	$11.72	$1,505
19	3	0.50	1	$43.54	$1,548
20	4	0.50	-1	$5.80	$1,543

Figure 9.4
Determining the Currency Conversion Rate

	G	H	I	J	K
1					
2					
3					
4	Start Price	70			
5					
6	Highest	80			
7	Upper	75			
8	Lower	65			
9	Lowest	60			
10				A Factor	1.472
11	Bias Factor	2		B Factor	0.493
12					
13					
14					100 X
15	Month			Weekly	GBP/$
16			Up/Down	Change	70.00
17		0.50	1	0.68	70.68
18		0.50	1	0.61	71.30
19		0.50	-1	0.80	70.49
20	1	0.50	1	0.01	70.50

Figure 9.5
Determining the Interest Rate

	M	N	O	P	Q
1					
2					
3					
4	Start Price	4.5			
5					
6	Highest	9			
7	Upper	8			
8	Lower	5			
9	Lowest	4			
10				A Factor	1.453
11	Bias Factor	2		B Factor	0.233
12					
13					
14					%
15	Month			Weekly	Interest
16			Up/Down	Change	4.50
17		0.50	-1	0.27	4.23
18		0.12	1	0.15	4.38
19		0.16	1	0.12	4.50
20	1	0.20	1	0.22	4.73

Figure 9.6
Determining Revenue and Operating Costs

	R	S	T	U	V	W	X	Y
4								Mining
5								Costs
6						Copper	Mining	Without
7		Minimum	Most	Maximum	Actual	Price	Revenue	Debt
8	Month	Production	Likely	Production	Production	$/Ton	$MM	Charges
9	1	1000	1100	1300	1174	$ 1,456	$ 1,709	$ 1,106
10	2	1000	1110	1310	1066	$ 1,322	$ 1,409	$ 1,064
11	3	1000	1120	1320	1069	$ 1,375	$ 1,469	$ 1,054

Figure 9.7
Debt Servicing Charges

	Z	AA	AB	AC	AD	AE	AF	AG
2	Debt							
3	Charges							
4	With		Interest			Total		
5	Constant		Payment		Interest	Debt		Debt
6	6%	Debt	at 6%	Interest	Expense	Servicing		Charges
7	Interest	Repayment	GBP	Rate	GBP	GBP	GBP/$	$MM
8	GBP	GBP						
9	500	100	400	4.5%	$ 301	401	0.703	$ 571
10	500	101	399	5.0%	$ 330	431	0.705	$ 611
11	500	102	398	5.2%	$ 347	449	0.705	$ 637

Figure 9.8
Annual Cash Flow

	AH	AI	AJ	AK	AL
2		Desired			
3		Working			
4		Capital			
5		$ 6,000			
6					
7	Cash	Working			Total
8	Flow	Capital	Dividends	Claim	Claims
9	$ 32	$ 6,032			$ 955
10	$ (266)	$ 5,734	$ 32	$ -	
11	$ (222)	$ 5,511	$ -	$ -	

The claim in cell AK10 compensates for having negative working capital:

$$=IF(AI10<0),-AI10,0)$$

Cell AL9 totals up claims over a 60-month period. A simulation with cell AL9 as output was run to obtain a loss probability distribution from which an insurance premium can be derived. The best-fitting loss probability distribution in Figure 9.9 was obtained by the *Fit Distributions to Data* command.

The resulting distribution has a poor fit because of the prevalence of times with no claims as seen in the sample data to the left of Figure 9.9. The *Detailed Statistics* window with a *Target Value* of 0 showed that there were no claims 84.51% of the time. To obtain a probability distribution of the nature of the claims when they actually occur, the sample data were selected and copied using the Control C key and pasted in column A of a new spreadsheet. Zero dollar claims were eliminated in column B through the formula =IF(A1=0,"",A1). The best-fitting probability distribution in Figure 9.10 is based on values in column B, obtained by selecting @Risk/Model/Fit Distributions to Data. There are no zero claims in the sample data on the left-hand side. The average claim in column B for a five-year period is $2.565 million with a maximum of $13.2 million as compared to the maximum claim with the best-fitting curve of $17.2 million.

The P-P probability curve in Figure 9.11 is close to a straight line, suggesting a good fit between the beta general probability distribution and actual claims.

The best-fitting distribution is a discrete function that generates a zero value 84.51% of the time coupled with the beta general probability distribution in Figure 9.10. The formula is truncated at $13.2 million and divided by five to reflect a single year rather than five years of claims. Figure 9.12 is the spreadsheet to evaluate a break-even insurance premium to cover the triple risks of low copper prices, adverse currency exchange rates, and high interest rates.

208   CORPORATE FINANCIAL RISK MANAGEMENT

Figure 9.9
Not the Best-Fitting Distribution

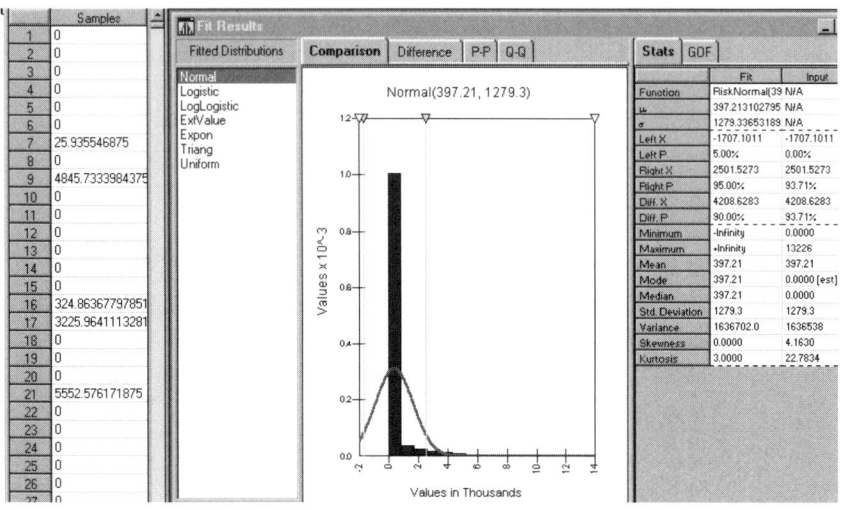

Figure 9.10
The Best-Fitting Distribution

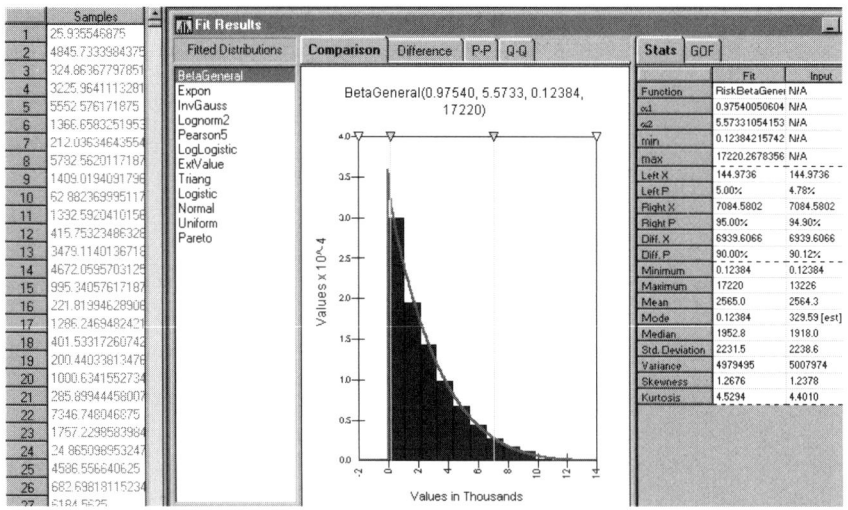

Figure 9.11
P-P Probability Curve

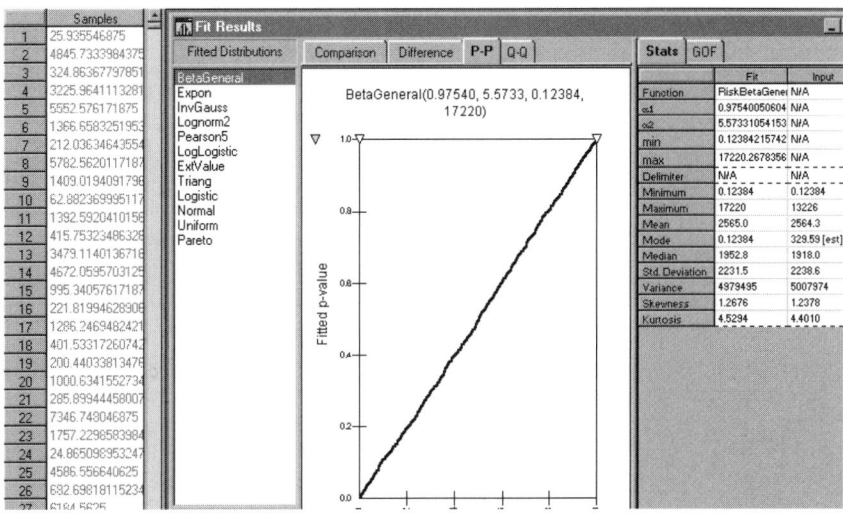

The average annual loss calculated by the beta general function is $2.5 million, but this occurs 15% of the time. Thus, an estimate of the premium to cover the average annual loss is about $75,000 as compared to the break-even insurance premium from a RiskOptimizer run of $90,000. This is higher than the estimate in order to be able to cover the low probability of having an exceedingly high claim. As an order of magnitude, $90,000 per year is about 15% of the firm's financing costs of the project. The premium rises to $120,000 if reserves fall by $20,000 from their initial amount and declines to $60,000 if reserves rise by $20,000 from their initial amount. The adjustable cells are cells D3 and D4 where cells C3 and C4 are fives times the values of the adjustable cells. The $20,000 increment was arbitrarily selected. The solution values are based on the objective of the initial reserves and the mean of the ending reserves being the same.

The selection of $100,000 in initial reserves is also arbitrary. The actual reserves can be obtained by running a @Risk simulation on ending reserves. As seen in Figure 9.13, there is a 0.12% chance of the initial reserves of $100,000 falling below $75,000. Reserves are much too high. Reserves could be reduced to $25,000 ($25 million) with a 0.12% chance of being exhausted. The chance of reserves falling below $85,000 ($85 million) is 1.93%. Hence, initial reserves could be $15,000 ($15 million) with a 1.93% chance of being exhausted. This information can be used to select whether reserves should be $15 million or $25 million or somewhere in between.

Reserves of $15 to $25 million are necessary to take care of those times when there are back-to-back claims for large losses. Even though there is a small probability of a triple witching period of low copper prices, an adverse currency exchange rate, and high interest rates, they can and do occur. Instead of having a high

Figure 9.12
Determining the Break-Even Insurance Premium

	A	B	C	D	E	F	G
1	Determining an Insurance Premium						
2							
3	Base Insurance Premium		$ 90	18			
4	High Premium		$ 120	6			
5	Low Premium		$ 60				
6	Start reserves		$ 100,000				
7	Upper Trigger		$ 120,000	20			
8	Lower Trigger		$ 80,000				
9							
10	Objective:		$ 6,628				
11							
12							
13			Reserves				
14		Annual	Earnings		Reserves		Ending
15	Year	Premium	Rate	Reserves	Income	Claims	Reserves
16	1	$ 90	6.0%	$ 100,000	$ -	$ -	$ 100,090
17	2	$ 90	6.0%	$ 100,090	$ 5	$ -	$ 100,185

copper price covering the risks of an adverse currency exchange and high interest rates, the three risks can work in tandem, making a bad situation worse.

While the operating costs are increased by the insurance premium, the insurance premium should not be part of operating costs. The insurance premium comes out of funds spun off from the operation. Having insurance to protect against a negative working capital that became negative by the presence of the insurance premium is like insuring the premium. The insurance premium should be viewed

Figure 9.13
Probability Distribution for Reserves

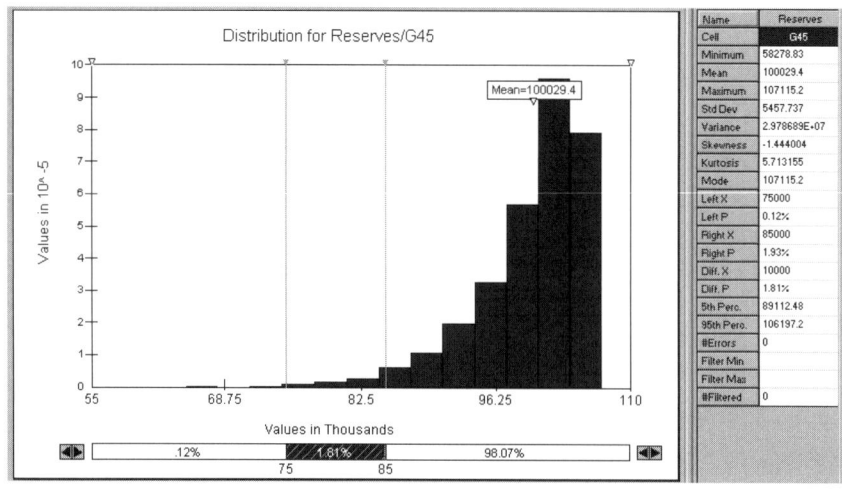

as a diminution of total dividends payouts similar to evaluating swaps. It is the cost portion of the cost-benefit analysis for insuring a business risk.

In insuring a business risk, care has to be taken to prevent management from using the insurance to cover its carelessness or ineptitude in controlling operating costs. Claims should be limited to exogenous factors not under the control of management such as copper prices and currency exchange and interest rates. Endogenous factors such as operating costs are under management control. The insurance premium as structured contains both exogenous and endogenous risks because compensation is based on a negative working capital. A negative working capital could result from management carelessness in controlling costs, not from an adverse combination of copper prices or currency exchange or interest rates. Placing a maximum limit on operating costs for evaluating claims on negative working capital would make sure that claims are not compensating management for its carelessness. Moreover, management is still rewarded if it takes actions to better control costs in the form of increased profitability. Thus, the value used for working capital in the submission of a claim is probably not actual working capital.

Now management has a choice of swaps or a business insurance policy to protect itself from a combination of low copper prices, adverse currency exchange rates, and high interest rates that could put the company into danger of a financial default. Business insurance policies to cover commercial risks such as explored herein are not readily available, certainly not to the extent of swaps. Even though the insurance premium of $90,000 is the break-even rate and an insurance company would charge a higher rate, on the surface insurance appears more economical than swaps. The annual insurance premium will be something in excess of $90,000, or a diminution of dividend payouts of something in excess of $0.5 million over a five-year period. While swaps "cost" nothing, there is a cost in the form of a diminution of dividend payouts, which was in excess of $0.5 million. The results of business insurance and swaps should not be directly compared as different minimum working capital requirements were used. The spreadsheets outlined in this and the previous chapter could be used as a basis for whether to utilize insurance premiums (were they available) or swaps. Moreover, the spreadsheets could be modified to evaluate a risk program covered partly by swaps and partly by insurance.

A NEW SITUATION

Agnes and Henry are a happily married couple well on their way to retirement. Their children are grown up and on their own. Henry is presently head maintenance man for the local school district in a northern state. Agnes spends her day running the household and, when the mood strikes, baking butterfingers for Henry and the neighbors. Agnes and Henry sit on a little nest egg of $250,000, partly savings and partly inheritance, which is invested in 8% bonds. Henry finds out that the school board is interested in insuring against high heating costs. Heating costs are an uncontrollable budget item that depends on the severity of the weather and the price of heating oil. The school board does not know what cost for heating oil to put in the budget because no one can predict next winter's weather. When winters are severe, the school board must go to the town council for more money, which in itself causes a problem in that the town is financed primarily through property taxes, a fixed source of revenue. Padding the heating oil budget is not a doable course of action in getting the town council's approval.

It is in the interests of the school board to pay an insurance premium to protect against high heating oil costs in order to stabilize the budget, that is, transform uncertainty to certainty. From the point of view of the school board, high heating oil costs can be looked upon as a commercial risk, although technically it is really a budgetary risk.

Agnes is intrigued by the prospect of becoming an underwriter. Henry is in a position to ensure that the schools in the district do not waste energy from careless opening of windows and doors during cold weather. Moreover, he has some influence over the temperature in the schools, although lowering the temperature to the mid-40s isn't going to fly. In Agnes' mind there is no risk of the school district, having insured itself against high heating oil costs, becoming careless about heating oil usage. As mentioned, the insured exercising due diligence for factors under its control is a vital consideration when providing insurance against a commercial loss.

Agnes knows that she has to somehow devise an appropriate premium to charge the school board. The first step would be calculating the break-even premium that covers her for the risk of unusually cold weather and high heating oil prices. If she can calculate a break-even premium, then she would be in a position to offer a higher premium and, in so doing, augment the income from the family nest egg.

Agnes initially gave up making butterfingers to concentrate on this project, but that didn't last long. She found she could think about the issues better while mixing the dough and shaping the butterfingers. Then she could do the number pushing during the 20 minutes for baking butterfingers. With time Agnes was baking a whole lot of butterfingers. Luckily, Henry had a ready means of disposal: hundreds of hungry schoolkids.

ANALYZING PRICE

Agnes thought about what influences the price of heating oil. One has to be the price of crude oil as a raw material, and the other must be the temperature because, as anyone knows, the colder the winter, the higher the price of heating oil. Agnes obtained data from the Internet on both heating oil and crude oil prices from the U.S. Department of Energy (www.eia.doe.gov). Figure 9.14 is a scatter diagram of the daily wholesale price of heating oil versus crude prices between 1995 and 2001.

With certain exceptions in the form of outliers, Agnes decided that there was a good correlation between the wholesale price of heating oil and crude prices. Specifically, she could model the wholesale price as a 23.7% premium over the crude oil price in terms of cents per gallon less 4.287 cents per gallon plus something for

Figure 9.14
Wholesale Price of Heating Oil versus Crude Oil Prices

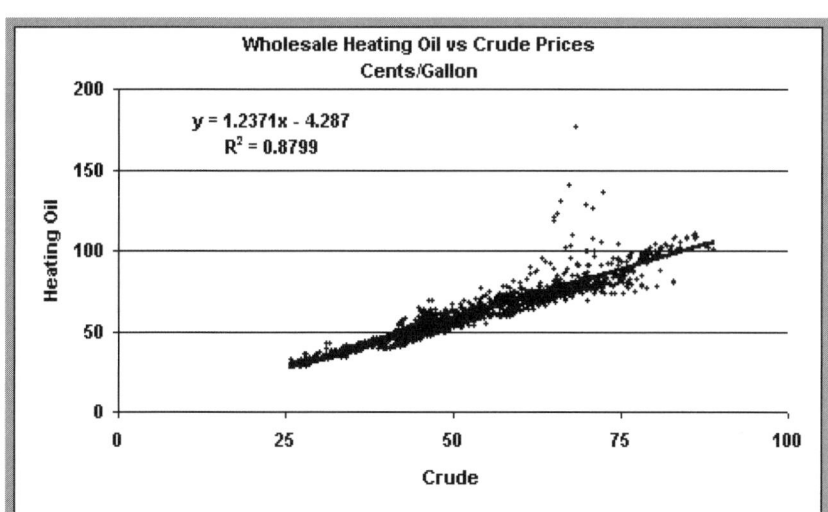

uncertainty. The outliers in Figure 9.14 troubled her. There appeared to be a small probability that heating oil prices might diverge significantly from crude oil prices.

Agnes next thought about the nature of heating oil prices during the winter season. Figure 9.15 is the scatter diagram of retail heating oil prices for five and a half months from the beginning of October to mid-March. There are roughly 22 days to the month in Figure 9.15, as the number of days after October 1 excludes weekends and holidays, when heating oil prices are not published.

Agnes was taken a back. Other than the winter of 1999/2000, heating oil prices were relatively flat throughout the winter season. She thought that heating oil prices would escalate as the winter season progressed, but this was clearly not the case. With the exception of the winter of 1999/2000, rising heating oil bills stem mostly from increased consumption of heating oil as the weather became colder, not from higher prices.

Agnes did a little research. She learned that there was essentially no seasonality in demand from the point of view of refinery operators, even though there are a peak during the summer in gasoline consumption and another peak during the winter in heating oil consumption. Refinery operators basically see constant demand adjusting their production slates to make more gasoline in the summer and more heating oil in the winter. Between peaks their output is still relatively constant as they build up inventories in gasoline during the spring and heating oil during the fall. With refinery operators more or less at constant output, crude oil producers see essentially constant demand with relatively little seasonal fluctuations. What affects the price of heating oil is not how cold the winter but the underlying cost of crude oil.

Figure 9.15
Winter Retail Heating Oil Prices

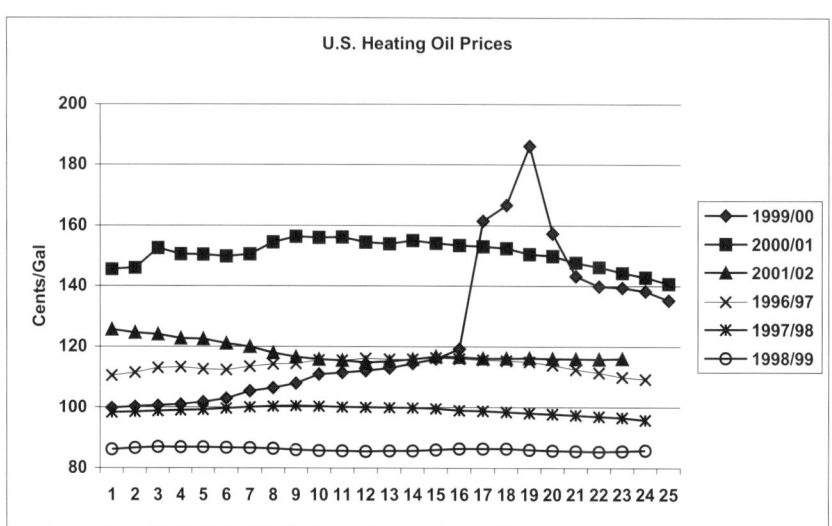

Before exploring oil prices, Agnes decided to first examine the relationship between the wholesale and retail price of heating oil by creating the scatter diagram in Figure 9.16 linking the two.

There is a fairly close relationship between retail and wholesale heating oil prices. The retail price can be approximated by multiplying the wholesale price in cents per gallon by 1.0365 and then adding 51.1 cents per gallon plus something for uncertainty. This relationship held even during the winter of 1999/2000, when the outliers occurred in Figure 9.14. The outliers were more of a departure from the relationship between the wholesale price of heating oil and crude oil than from the relationship between retail and wholesale prices. This meant that the wholesalers, not the retailers, profited from the outliers.

ANALYZING OUTLIERS

At this point in her analysis of the situation, Agnes was more concerned over the outliers than the underlying price of crude. She went to the public library to peruse newspaper articles in the archives on heating oil during the winter of 1999/2000. She read an article on the change in oil company attitudes toward inventories. In the good old days, the bad old oil companies kept a whole lot of inventory on hand just in case it was needed. Fluctuations in demand such as peaks in heating oil usage from extremely cold weather or in gasoline usage from Americans hitting the road in massive numbers or interruptions in production or problems with pipeline operations could be compensated for by inventory drawdowns. Lots of inventory

Figure 9.16
Retail versus Wholesale Heating Oil Prices

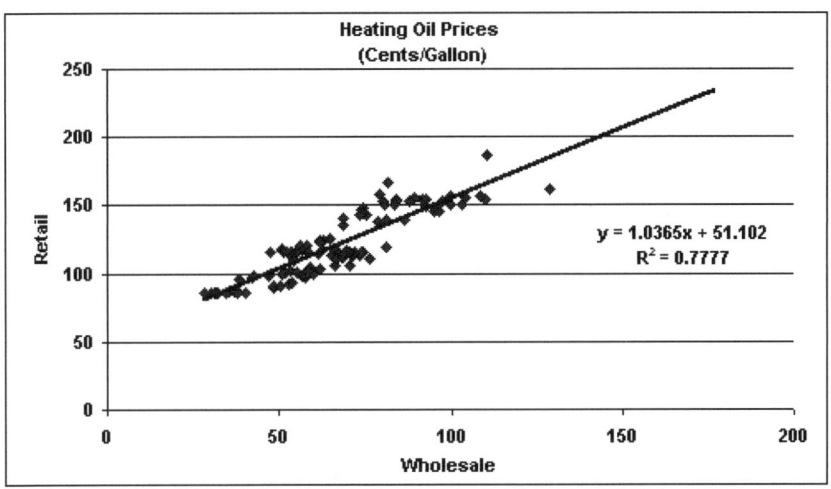

acted as a buffer that subdued price changes during times of extreme fluctuations in demand or interruptions in the supply chain.

Then there was a change in attitude toward inventory when the financial wizards discovered that tying money up in inventory was wasteful. Reducing inventories freed up capital that could be put to better use in reducing the indebtedness of the company or funding capital expenditures. Just-in-case inventory gave way to just-in-time inventory. Inventories were reduced to bare minimum levels to ensure a smooth operation during times of normalcy. The less gasoline, heating oil, and crude oil kept in tanks, the greater the amount of money freed up for other corporate uses. The days of inventory coverage with respect to consumption dropped year after year. But smaller inventories also meant less tolerance to departures from normalcy such as extreme fluctuations in demand, problems in the supply chain, and interruptions in refinery operation.

The birds came home to roost during a cold streak in the winter of 1999/2000. Inventories of retail heating oil supplies became dangerously low in certain areas of the nation. This started a bidding war for wholesale heating oil shipments, resulting in much higher prices for wholesale heating oil. This bidding war temporarily broke the traditional relationship between wholesale heating oil and crude oil prices, plainly visible in the outliers in Figure 9.14. The retailers apparently just added their normal markups, as there was apparent little departure between wholesale and retail prices at any time, as seen in Figure 9.16.

In the good old days there would have been plenty of inventory to cover the spike in demand. Now having experienced the havoc wrought by minimizing inventories to a point where there was marginal coverage for a spike in demand, what did the bad old oil companies do? Did they continue the practice of reducing inventories or revert back to the good old days of swimming in inventory? Agnes obtained data on heating oil inventories and heating oil consumption and plotted the equivalent days' coverage of inventory to consumption shown in Figure 9.17.

Agnes looked at the continued dropping of inventory with respect to days' coverage of demand and concluded that the oil companies did learn something in the chaotic conditions of the winter of 1999/2000. The spike in heating oil prices from inventory getting too low did wonders for their profits. The financial wizards were proven right twice over: once in the savings of inventory carrying costs by having smaller inventories and twice in being able to easily hike prices during times of threatened stockouts.

Threatened stockouts are much better than actual stockouts. Actual stockouts may result in hospital patients freezing to death in their beds. This makes for really bad press for the oil companies. Threatened stockouts that are more of an inconvenience rather than a reality are just great for the profit statements as heating oil retailers panic and bid up prices to secure supplies from wholesalers, who for the most part are the oil companies. Agnes felt that she better incorporate something for runaway prices when heating oil demand peaks with plunging temperatures, even though the government had set up a strategic supply of heating oil to prevent such a reoccurrence.

ASSESSING FUTURE PRICES

Agnes came to the conclusion that the principal driver for heating oil prices was not the weather but the price of crude oil. It didn't take long for Agnes to come to

Figure 9.17
Days Heating Oil Inventory Coverage

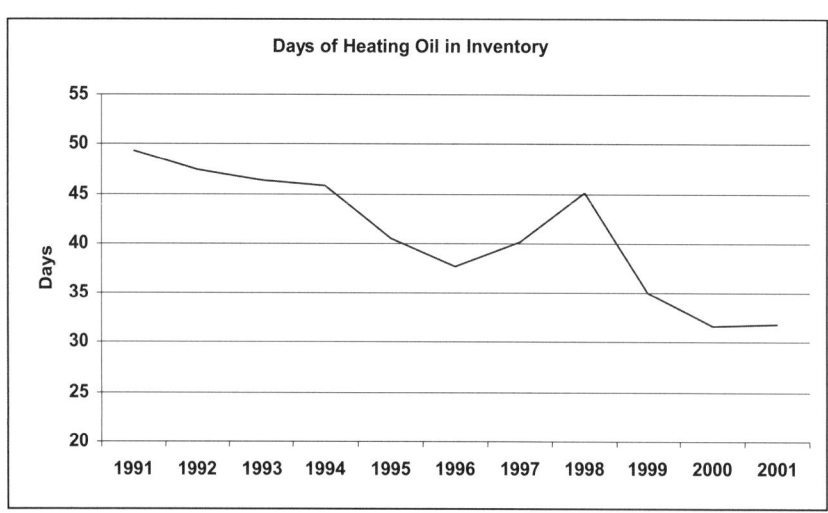

the realization that the principal driver for crude oil prices was the Organization of Petroleum Exporting Countries (OPEC). As she understood the situation from press articles, OPEC controls price by varying production. If price is weakening too much, OPEC closes the spigot on production, forcing prices up. If price is strengthening too much, then they open the spigot to lower price. Of course, there is also the matter of individual nations within OPEC cheating by exporting more than they're supposed to under their production quotas. This sometimes causes prices to fall below the desired range.

Agnes decided to take a closer look at the price of crude oil shown in Figure 9.18. Crude prices are generally quoted in $ per barrel where one barrel represents 42 gallons. A barrel goes back to the origins of the oil business when oil was shipped in barrels loaded on railroad cars. A barrel was sized to be handled by men. Anyone who has lifted a 5-gallon can of gasoline can appreciate what it must have been like to handle a 42-gallon barrel.

In viewing past oil prices, Agnes thought about OPEC's capacity to control price. All in all, she thought that they don't deserve a high grade. She found out that other forces are at play in influencing price besides OPEC members sitting around the table squabbling about production quotas. The global economy plays a major role. A soft economy, which lessens oil demand, was partly responsible for the low prices in 1999, and a more robust economy, which increases oil demand, was partly responsible for the high prices in 2000. The burst of the New Economy bubble in early 2001 and a resulting cooling of the global economy in 2001 and 2002 were partly responsible for the fall in oil prices. War jitters in the Middle East during the spring of 2002 caused oil prices to jump. Agnes wondered how she was going to be

Figure 9.18
Historic Price of Crude Oil

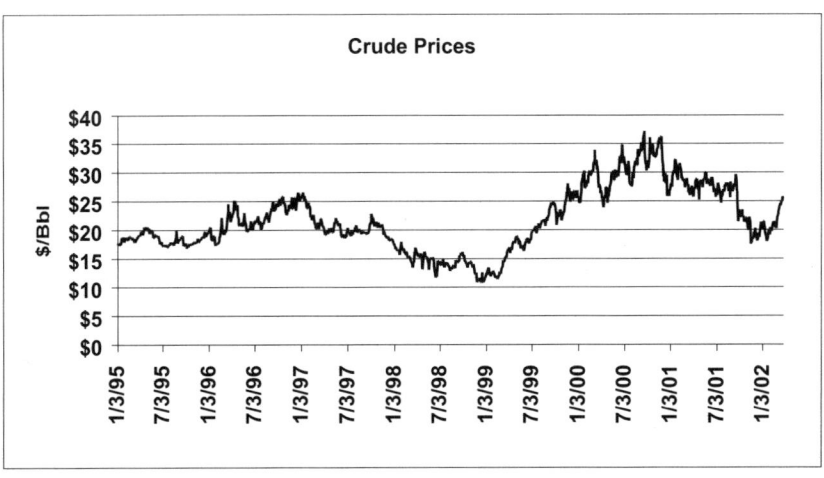

able to assess future crude oil prices when it was apparent that those dedicated to controlling its price seemed incapable of doing their job.

Agnes came across an interesting article on the problems facing OPEC. The article described technological progress in reducing the costs of bringing new oil fields into production. Three-dimensional seismic technology had decreased the probability of drilling a dry hole, lessening exploration costs. Rather than building 1,000-foot platforms from the ocean bottom to its surface to handle production as in the North Sea, the new way was to have far less costly floating production, storage, and offloading vessels remaining on station by various means with drilling pipes connecting the floating platform with the ocean bottom. These pipes then extend into the ocean bottom first vertically, then horizontally, to tap different oil fields from one vessel. A pipe passing horizontally rather than vertically through an oil field can extract more oil. When an oil field is exhausted, the floating vessel can be relocated and reused at another oil field, whereas a fixed platform must be abandoned or in some cases removed for environmental reasons, which is a very expensive undertaking. Moreover, floating platforms can work in waters deeper than 6,000' and getting deeper with time.

The comeuppance of all this is that new offshore oil fields can be brought onstream for crude prices of $8 to $15 per barrel depending on the circumstances. OPEC, in maintaining oil prices in the mid-$20s, is virtually guaranteeing a profitable return for the development of non-OPEC oil fields. OPEC control over the oil market is threatened by non-OPEC oil field development in Russia, the Caspian Sea region, offshore West Africa, South America, and elsewhere, whose return hinges on OPEC maintaining crude prices in the mid-$20s per barrel.

Agnes asked herself, Why doesn't OPEC lower the price of oil to stop development of competitive sources of oil? It turns out that mid-$20s per barrel oil is necessary to sustain their local economies, particularly OPEC members with high populations such as Nigeria, Venezuela, and Indonesia. Even Saudi Arabia is no longer a desert kingdom of wandering nomads but a nation of over 20 million, mostly living in towns and cities. Saudi Arabia needs a large oil income to sustain itself. But how long can OPEC sustain high prices when its volume is doomed to fall as a consequence of non-OPEC production? This in Agnes' mind would be an argument for a long-term decline in oil prices.

Agnes read about another possible outcome in the form of a robust global economic recovery that would absorb all the incremental non-OPEC oil production without eroding OPEC output. This would be a case for a long-term rise in oil prices. Then Agnes came across another article about technological progress in replacing the conventional gasoline engine with something far more energy-efficient. This would be an argument for a long-term decline in oil prices. Then she read still another article by some expert who predicted that the chances of continually discovering new megasized oil fields that are necessary to replace oil being taken out of the ground are getting smaller. Despite technological advances in reducing the probability of drilling dry holes, where does an oil company explore when much of the earth is already peppered with oil wells? With unexplored areas continually shrinking, the world may be exhausting its petroleum reserves, which, of course is an argument for a long-term rise in oil prices.

Agnes was exhausted from this research. One thing she did learn—nobody seems to know what the future holds. Although someone is going to be proven correct, the task of selecting the correct predictor was daunting. Failing that, Agnes decided that she would ultimately have to rely on her own intuition when assessing the future price of crude oil. This is a critical point in the analysis because the future price of crude oil establishes the wholesale price of heating oil, from which follows the retail price that determines the break-even insurance premium.

ASSESSING VOLUME

Agnes realized that the school heating oil bill consists of two elements: the retail price of heating oil and the volume of usage. Volume is linked to the severity of winter weather in terms of wind and temperature. Windy days cause fuel consumption to jump as cold air forces itself into buildings, and, of course, temperature plays a key role. Agnes found degree-day information on the National Climatic Data Center Web site (www.ncdc.noaa.gov) for her particular state. Degree-days for heating purposes are calculated by obtaining an average temperature from a day's high and low temperatures, subtracting 65 degrees, and accumulating the result. For instance, if the high temperature for a day were 50 degrees and the low 30 degrees, the average is 40 degrees. The difference of 25 degrees between the average temperature and 65 degrees is called 25 degree-days. If yesterday's cumulative total were 1,200 degree-days, then today's cumulative total would be 1,225 degree-days. No heating degree-days result when temperatures are above 65 degrees. Parenthetically, there are cooling degree-days calculated in a similar manner when temperatures are above 65 degrees. Cooling degree-days are used as a demand factor for planning electricity-generating capacity required for air-conditioning needs.

Henry obtained the total gallons of heating oil consumed since the 1993/1994 winter season from the school district records. Agnes constructed Table 9.1, linking heating oil consumption to degree-days.

Agnes then set up a scatter diagram of heating oil consumption versus degree-days and obtained the best-fitting curve in Figure 9.19.

Agnes was pleased that the data fell relatively close to the best-fitting curve. But she wasn't pleased with the formula parameters and redid the chart in terms of thousands of gallons and thousands of degree-days. She then obtained the following formula for determining heating oil in thousands of gallons:

$$24.688 * X^2 - 344.01 * X + 1230.3 \text{ where X is degree-days in thousands}$$

Agnes realized that she better be careful to ensure consistency in units when using this equation. More important would be her methodology for determining future degree-days. The first thing Agnes did was plot degree-days with time in Figure 9.20 to see if there was a pattern.

Table 9.1
Heating Oil Consumption versus Degree-Days

	Heating Oil Usage in Gallons	Degree-Days
1993/94	75,066	8,185
1994/95	35,200	7,202
1995/96	90,300	8,516
1996/97	58,000	8,099
1997/98	34,000	6,770
1998/99	30,700	6,763
1999/00	32,400	6,867
2000/01	45,500	7,756

Figure 9.19
Heating Oil Consumption versus Degree-Days

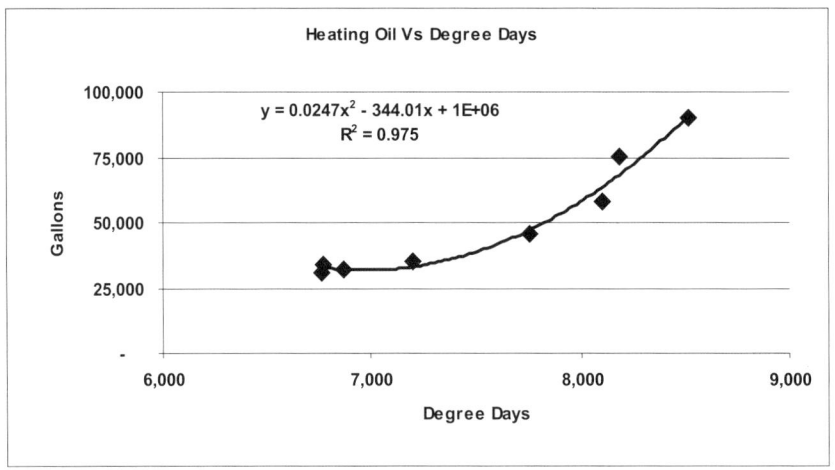

Agnes knew better than to draw a trend line, even though it would support the contention of global warming, which is to her benefit in insuring against high heating bills. She also knew that the weather predictions in *Poor Richard's Almanac* were about as reliable as her prediction of future oil prices. But Agnes noted that degree-days did not appear to be following a normal curve. In fact, they appear to have a more uniform or flat distribution with equal probability of high, low, and medium values within the range of 6,500 to 8,500 degree-days. Agnes did not obtain any data on wind and decided to rely solely on heating degree-days as an indicator of the severity of winter weather.

AGNES' MODEL

Figure 9.21 is the first part of Agnes' spreadsheet model. Column B is degree-days. Agnes decided that there is no relationship in winter weather from one

Figure 9.20
Degree-Days over Time

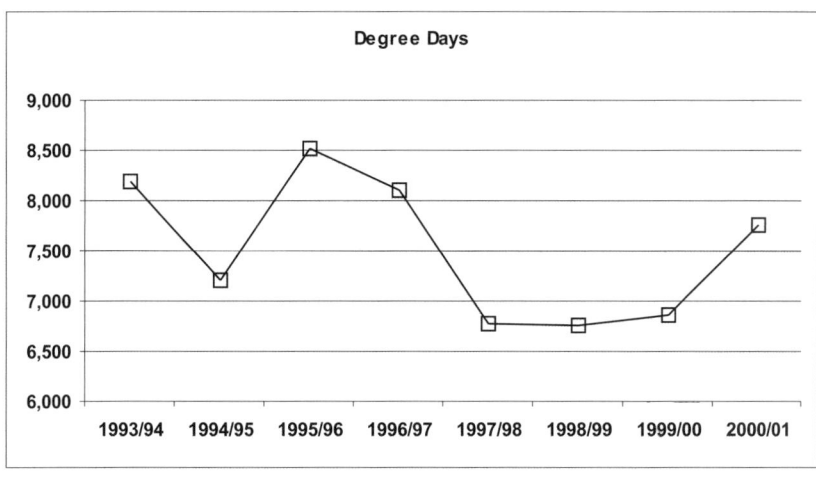

Figure 9.21
First Part of Model

	A	B	C	D	E	F
1	Underwriting Insurance Against Excess Heating Oil Costs					
2						
3					Wholesale	Retail
4				Crude	Heating	Heating
5		Degree	Heating Oil	Price	Oil	Oil
6	Year	Days	Gallons	$/Bbl	$/gallon	$/gallon
7	1	6,572	35,444	$ 26.08	$ 0.71	$ 1.17
8	2	6,958	32,951	$ 23.16	$ 0.66	$ 1.12
9	3	6,920	30,272	$ 22.58	$ 0.62	$ 1.14
10	4	8,077	61,357	$ 22.32	$ 0.57	$ 1.07
11	5	8,471	88,298	$ 30.12	$ 0.83	$ 1.41
12	6	6,816	32,533	$ 24.15	$ 0.72	$ 1.05
13	7	7,461	38,421	$ 30.25	$ 0.75	$ 1.23
14	8	8,059	61,635	$ 31.20	$ 0.96	$ 1.46
15	9	8,357	79,398	$ 28.91	$ 0.74	$ 1.22
16	10	8,392	81,226	$ 25.16	$ 0.67	$ 1.20

year to the next. In other words, degree-days are an independent variable. Her assessment on weather in terms of degree-days was that it would be a uniform distribution between 6,500 and 8,500 degree-days with equal probability of cold and mild winters:

$$=RiskUniform(6500,8500)$$

Column C is the volume of heating oil in gallons expected to be consumed depending on the number of degree-days in column B:

$$=1000*(24.688*(B7/1000)\wedge2-344.01*(B7/1000)+1230.3)+RiskNormal(0,1000)$$

There are two elements in this equation. The first element is the best-fitting line from Figure 9.19 expressed in thousands of degree-days, then multiplied by 1,000 to obtain degree-days. This forms the mean of a normal distribution. The second element is the uncertainty associated with this curve to reflect that not all the data points lie on the best-fitting curve. The uncertainty is expressed in terms of a normal distribution whose mean is zero (the first element of the equation is the mean) plus variation expressed in terms of a standard deviation of 1,000 gallons. Thus, gallons of heating oil consumed will be within 1,000 gallons of the mean two-thirds of the time and within 2,000 gallons of the mean 95% of the time.

Column D is the price of crude oil. Agnes thought the minimum price of $18 per barrel, the most likely price of $25 per barrel with a maximum price of $35 per barrel best models the historical price pattern in Figure 9.18. The Not-So-Random-Walk Price Generator could have been used but Agnes had an alternative idea. Although she felt comfortable with the minimum and maximum prices for oil, she was uncomfortable about the most likely price remaining at $25 per barrel. She thought that the most likely price in a succeeding year would be the now-current price. In other words, if the current price is $20 per barrel, the most likely price next year would also be $20 per barrel. Linking next year's price to this year's price transforms a triangular distribution to an inverted "U" as time progresses as shown in Figure 9.22.

This flattening of the probability distribution increases the probability of having extremes in oil prices, increasing the risk of high oil prices as time progresses. Referring to Figure 9.22, the probability of an oil price above $32 per barrel in year 10 is 8.27%. The probability of an oil price above $32 per barrel in a triangular probability distribution is 5.3%. Flattening of the probability distribution was also seen in generating values using the Not-so-Random-Walk generator. It appears that flattening is a consequence of relating a future value to a current value; in other words, future values are not independent variables, but dependent variables linked to current values.

The price of oil in the second year in cell D8 is:

$$=RiskTriang(18,D7,35)$$

Figure 9.22
Flattening of a Probability Distribution

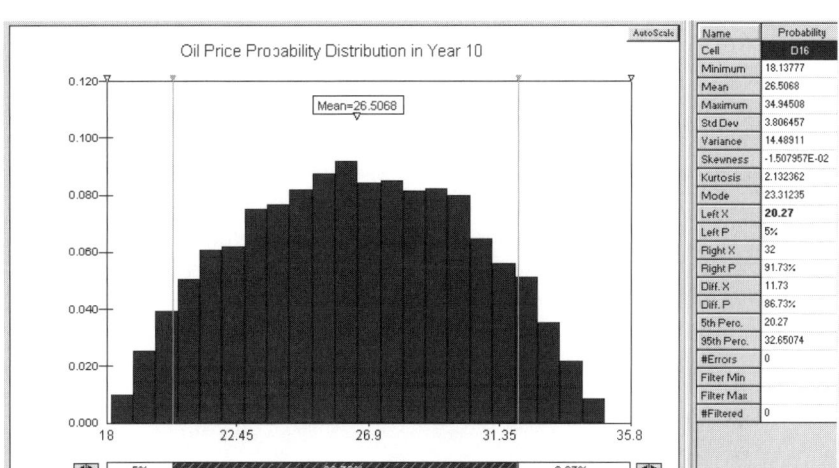

Column I is the wholesale price of heating oil determined by the price of crude oil through the following formula:

=(1.2371*(100*D7/42)–4.287+RiskNormal(0,6))/100+IF(B7>8000, RiskDiscrete({1,0},{0.2,0.8})*RiskUniform(0.1,0.5),0)

This formula has three elements. The first element determines the mean of a normal distribution using the regression equation shown in Figure 9.14. Crude oil prices in $/bbl is translated to cents per gallon to be consistent with the regression equation. The standard error of 6 cents per gallon is incorporated in the second element of the equation as a standard deviation. This assumes that the distribution of values around the regression line is normal. The third element is Agnes' response to the possibility of outliers caused by logistical or operational problems compounded by low inventories during extremely cold weather. Agnes' assessment of the situation is that if degree-days exceed 8,000, then there would be a 20% chance that an additional 10–50 cents will be added to the price of a gallon of heating oil with equal probability.

Column F determines the retail price of heating oil from the wholesale price derived in column E using the formula:

=(1.0365*(100*E7)+51.102+RiskNormal(0,10))/100

The first element of the formula is the best-fitting straight line describing the relationship between retail and wholesale prices shown in Figure 9.16 in terms of cents per gallon. An assessment of a standard deviation of 10 cents per gallon was visually derived by noting that plus or minus 10 cents seemed to include about two-thirds of the data points, or that plus or minus 20 cents seemed to include most (95%) of the data points. This variation is incorporated in the second element of the formula. Figure 9.23 is the remaining portion of the model.

The heating cost in column G is the gallons consumed multiplied by the retail price. Column H is the claim that can be made against Agnes if she underwrote a policy whereby she covers heating costs exceeding $70,000 with a maximum claim of $50,000 as in cell H11. Agnes decided that it would be in her best interests to cap the maximum claim just in case war or natural disturbance sent heating oil skyrocketing to $10 per gallon. In essence, Agnes is proposing that she and Henry foot the school district heating bill with a deductible of $70,000 up to a maximum heating bill of $120,000. The school district pays the portion of the heating bill that is less than the deductible and that portion over $120,000. The maximum claim of $50,000 is embodied in the formula:

$$=IF(G7<70000,0,IF(G7>120000,50000,G7-70000))$$

In Excelese, if the heating oil bill is less than $70,000, there is no claim. If the heating oil bill is over $120,000, the claim is $50,000. The only possibility left is a heating bill between $70,000 and $120,000, in which case the claim is the heating oil bill less $70,000.

The starting reserves are the family treasure nest egg of $250,000 invested in 8% bonds. The cash flow assumes that all proceeds are reinvested at 8%. Cell J18 shows what the next egg would be in 10 years with interest payments reinvested at 8%. If

Figure 9.23
The Rest of the Model

	G	H	I	J	K	L
3			Premium			
4			$ 6,900	69		Heating Oil
5	Heating Oil			Reserves	Income on	Cost Net of
6	Cost	Claim		$ 250,000	Reserves	Insurance
7	$ 41,601	$ -	$ 6,900	$ 276,900	$ 20,000	$ 48,501
8	$ 36,775	$ -	$ 6,900	$ 305,952	$ 22,152	$ 43,675
9	$ 34,469	$ -	$ 6,900	$ 337,328	$ 24,476	$ 41,369
10	$ 65,658	$ -	$ 6,900	$ 371,214	$ 26,986	$ 72,558
11	$ 124,764	$ 50,000	$ 6,900	$ 357,812	$ 29,697	$ 81,664
12	$ 34,277	$ -	$ 6,900	$ 393,336	$ 28,625	$ 41,177
13	$ 47,229	$ -	$ 6,900	$ 431,703	$ 31,467	$ 54,129
14	$ 89,916	$ 19,916	$ 6,900	$ 453,223	$ 34,536	$ 76,900
15	$ 96,699	$ 26,699	$ 6,900	$ 469,682	$ 36,258	$ 76,900
16	$ 97,744	$ 27,744	$ 6,900	$ 486,413	$ 37,575	$ 76,900
17						
18		No Involvement:		$ 539,731		
19						
20		Benefit of Insuring:		$ (53,318)		

INSURING AGAINST BUSINESS RISKS   225

Agnes and Henry do nothing, the $250,000 family nest egg grows to nearly $540,000. This looks quite attractive, but this is a pretax and preinflation calculation. On a posttax, postinflation basis, the true return in terms of purchasing power is not nearly so attractive. Rather than getting sidetracked discussing the true worth of $540,000, 10 years in the future after the taxbite is taken out, the $540,000 will simply be the benchmark for determining the break-even insurance premium. Insurance companies are generally set up in a tax-free or tax-deferred environment to lower their premium quotes.

Reserves grow on the basis of interest earned plus insurance premium income less claims. In the first year of Figure 9.23, the $250,000 earns $20,000 in interest at 8% plus the insurance premium of $6,900 and grows to $276,900 at the start of the second year. With no claims during the first four years, reserves build up to $371,214 at the start of the fifth year. Interest income during the fifth year is $29,697 plus the insurance premium of $6,900 less a claims payment of $50,000 resulting in reserves at the start of the sixth year of $357,812. At the end of 10 years, the ending balance in reserves of $486,413 (cell J16) is $53,318 (cell J20) short of the benchmark of $539,731 (cell J18) of doing nothing. The break-even insurance premium of $6,900 was determined by a RiskOptimizer run with settings shown in Figure 9.24.

As an aside, had Agnes assumed that the price of oil was not dependent on the previous year's price, that is, an independent variable described by a triangular probability distribution with a minimum of $18, a most likely of $25 and a maximum of $35 per barrel, the corresponding insurance premium would have been $6,200. Deciding whether price is truly independent or is linked to a previous price has a major impact on the resulting risk profile and insurance premium to cover that risk.

The objective is for the mean of cell J20 to be as close to zero as possible to establish the break-even rate. This is achieved by varying cell J4 with integer values between 0 and 100. The insurance premium in cell I4 is 100 times cell J4 in order for the premium to be to the nearest $100. The break-even insurance premium will transform Agnes and Henry's nest egg from a certainty of something close to $540,000 to the probability distribution shown in Figure 9.25.

The average of $540,000 is very close to the do-nothing result. There is a 45% chance that the nest egg will suffer erosion in value. The worst case is a nest egg of $229,000, smaller than the original nest egg, representing the highly unlikely case of 10 years of substantial claims. The best of nearly $640,000 represents the equally unlikely event of 10 years of few or no claims. Agnes is risking a severe erosion of the family nest egg for the potential benefit of an additional pot of gold equal to a total of $69,000 in insurance premium income growing by 8% with few or no claims. In the insurance underwriting business, the maximum nest egg is capped by the amount of premium income, but the minimum is not, as it depends on the frequency and amount of claims. This is the nature of the beast when one decides to be an underwriter.

Figure 9.24
RiskOptimizer Menu

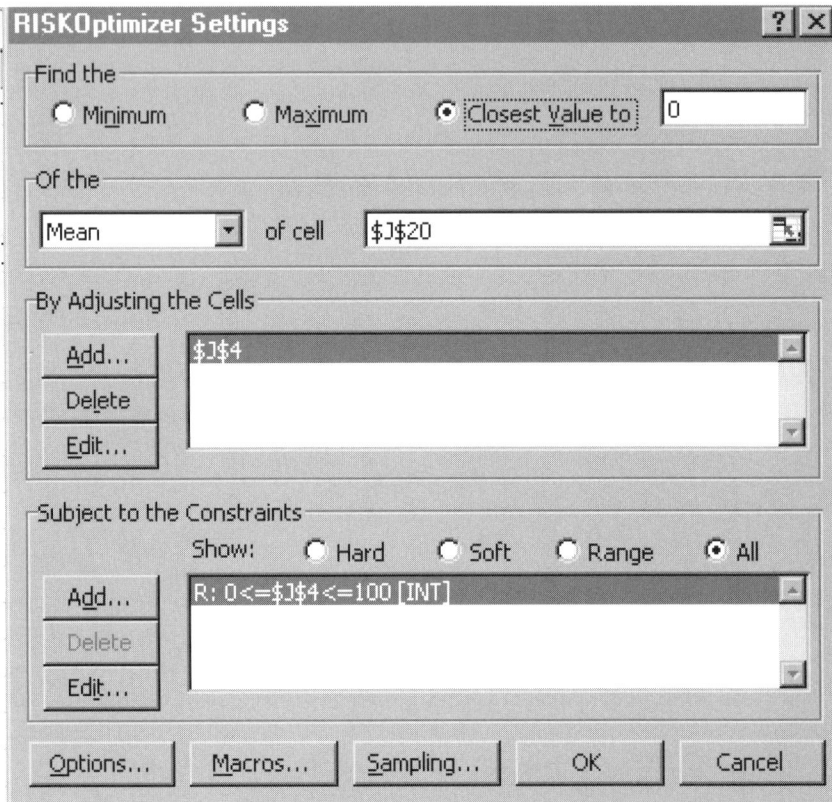

Suppose that Agnes approached the school district about doing this deal with a premium of $8,900, $2,000 above the break-even rate. If the school district accepted her proposal, the family nest egg in 10 years would appear as in Figure 9.26.

As a result of a higher premium, the average return has increased from $540,000 to nearly $570,000, and the maximum has increased from $640,000 to just under $670,000. The chance that the family nest egg will be less than doing nothing of just under $540,000 has been reduced from 45% to 30%.

Before figuring out what Agnes and Henry should do, let's take the position of the school board. Figure 9.27 is the probability distribution of a 10,000 year-simulation of the status quo.

The cost of heating oil before insurance ranges between $23,700 and $192,000 with an average of $60,500. The chance of being above $78,900, the point where Agnes' insurance cuts in plus her premium, is 21%. If Agnes' offer is accepted, the school district will experience heating oil costs shown in Figure 9.28.

Figure 9.25
From Certainty to Uncertainty

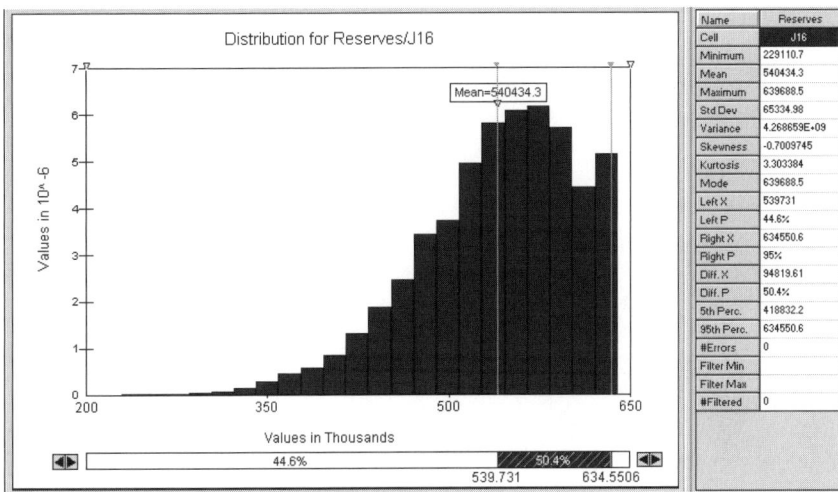

Figure 9.26
Nest Egg with a Premium of $8,900

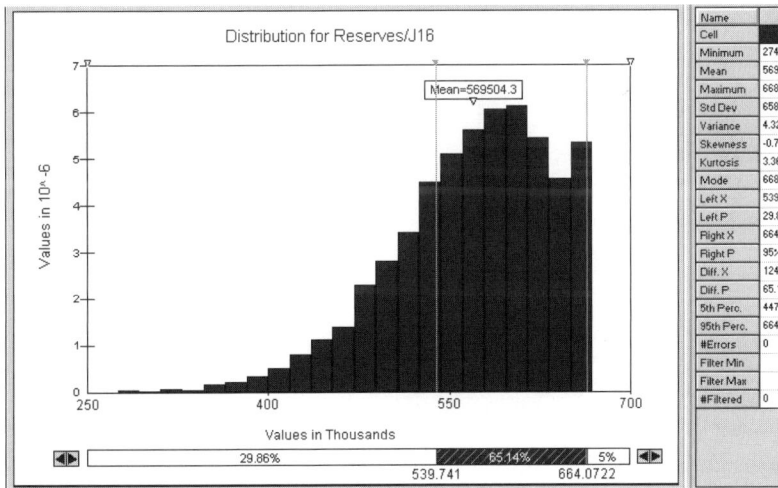

228   CORPORATE FINANCIAL RISK MANAGEMENT

Figure 9.27
Distribution of Heating Oil Costs without Insurance

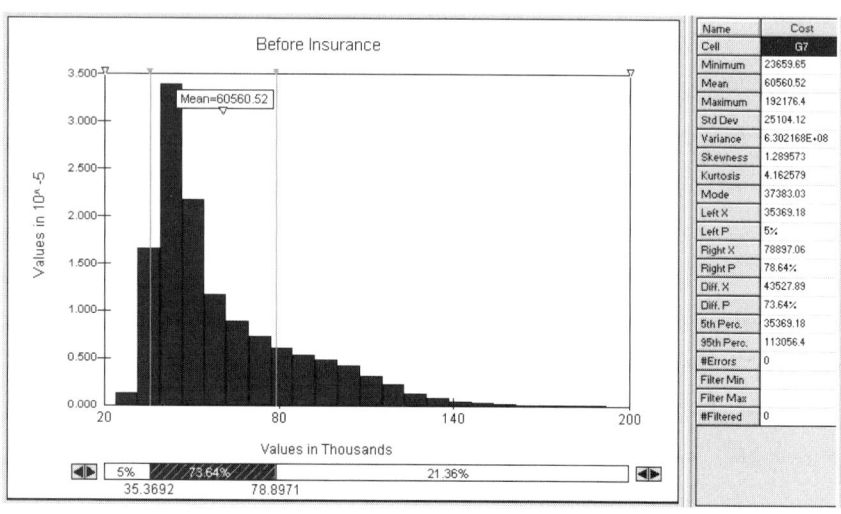

Figure 9.28
Ten Years of Heating Oil Costs with Insurance

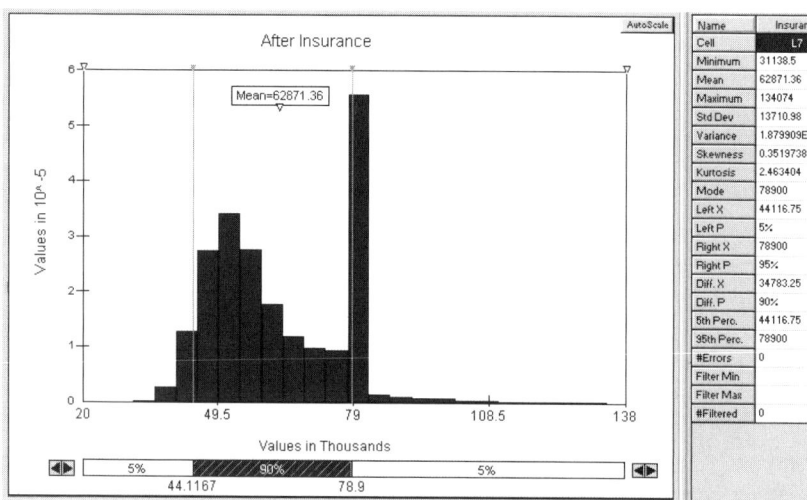

The maximum of a highly unlikely $134,000 is less than the previous $192,000. The average heating bill with the insurance premium of $62,900 is higher than the previous $60,500, reflecting the profit built into Agnes' offer. The chance of the heating oil cost exceeding $78,900, which is the $70,000 where Agnes' insurance cuts in plus her premium, has been reduced from nearly 21% to 5%. The school district might well be interested in Agnes' offer as a means of keeping a cap on heating oil costs for budgetary reasons.

AGNES AND HENRY—SHOULD THEY DO IT?

Henry finally had his say after Agnes explained the situation to him. What bothered him was the change in lifestyles if they became underwriters. Henry pointed out that when a cold Arctic blast was about to descend on them, they'd stock up with food and sit out the storm. If the schools were closed, they would spend most of the day glued to the fireplace munching on butterfingers. As underwriters, they would stay glued to the Weather Channel. They would become experts on the jet stream and its influence on Arctic weather systems. Snow would no longer be something beautiful to behold but a constant reminder that they may be writing a check to the school district. Every time OPEC met, they would remain pinned to the News Channel awaiting developments. Disturbances or political turmoil in the Middle East that could affect oil prices would keep them awake all night.

Did they really want to transform their relatively simple life to one of continual concern about how cold it was, OPEC machinations, and Middle East volatility? For what benefit? Yes, there would be some incremental income in the form of premiums but also some risk that their little nest egg might sustain a major hit. In the end, Agnes had to agree with Henry. It is better to spend a cold winter day baking butterfingers and enjoying the winter scenery through the kitchen window rather than staring in horrid disbelief at how low the mercury in the outside thermometer had sunk or in contemplating the dire repercussions of events far beyond their control.

Another factor played a decisive role: Agnes learned that it was one thing to gamble with one's own nest egg and another thing to gamble with someone else's. Something else escaped everyone's attention. Why doesn't the school board set aside $250,000 in reserves, pay a premium to itself, and self-insure its own heating cost overruns? Agnes would be a prime candidate for managing such a self-insurance scheme.

SUGGESTED READING

Bertstein, Peter L. *Against the Gods*. New York: John Wiley & Sons, 1998.
Byrd, Daniel M. and C. Richard Cothern. *Introduction to Risk Analysis*. Rockville, MD: Government Institutes, 2000.
Campbell, John M., Jr., John M. Campbell, Sr., Robert A. Campbell. *Analyzing and Managing Risky Investments*. Norman, OK: John M. Campbell, 2001.
Conrow, Edmund H. *Effective Risk Management*. Reston, VA: American Institute of Aeronautics and Astronautics, 2000.
Hardaker, J. B., R.B.M. Huirne and J. R. Anderson. *Coping with Risk in Agriculture*. New York: CAB International, 1998.
Newendorp, Paul and John Schuyler. *Decision Analysis for Petroleum Exploration*. Aurora, CO: Planning Press, 2000.
Schuyler, John R. *Risk and Decision Analysis in Projects*. Newton Square, PA: Project Management Institute, 2001.
Shimpi, Prakesh. *Integrating Corporate Risk Management*. New York: Texere, 2001.
Taleb, Nassim. *Fooled by Randomness*. New York: Texere, 2002.

Index

Amazon.com, 94
Argentina, 98
automobile insurance, 2

bias, 162–164
business cycle, 55, 58–59, 62–67, 74, 78

capital expenditures, 113–117
cash management, 121–125
catastrophic loss, 5, 203
circular reference, 91
collar, 191
constraints, 30
continuous distribution, 14, 25
copper, 182–183, 198–199
corporate cash flow, 58–64
correlation, 67–68, 83–85
cost of goods sold, 59
cost–benefit analysis, 180–181, 194–197, 211
credit rating, 117–119

debt financing, 74
depreciation, 60, 63–64
deterministic model, 11
discrete distribution, 14, 25–26
diversification, 3–4, 14, 35–36

dividends, 71–73
dot.com mania, 93–95, 101

Enron, 97–98
Excite@Home, 94
Exodus, 94

factoring, 123–124
financial footnotes, 97–98
financial ratios, 73–74, 77, 91–92
fire insurance, 2–3
funds flow, 93, 96–97, 100–101, 113, 115–119
futures, 197–199

G&A, 60
Gold, 2, 182–183

Hedging, 177–181
Histogram, 8, 16–18

insurance rate, 25–29
insurance reserves, 25–29
internal rate of return, 69–73, 78, 88–89, 148
interest coverage, 77, 79, 115, 117–118
inventory, 126–127, 140, 214–216

judging imponderables, 142–143, 145–146, 149, 154–159, 182–183

kurtosis, 11, 13, 170

life insurance, 3
lognormal distribution, 8–9
London Metals Exchange, 182
Lucent, 94–95, 97

modeling, 108, 153, 220–224

National Climatic Data Center, 219
net present value, 69–73, 78, 88–89, 148
normal distribution, 6–8

OANDA Corp., 186
OPEC, 217–218, 229
Options, 172–175

Palisade Corp., 9, 29
portfolio managers, 103–104
Poten & Partners, 175
Privatization, 62
product development, 141–143, 149
project financing, 55–58
purchasing power, 98–100

random numbers, 7
receivables, 125–126, 137–139
regression analysis, 106–107, 110, 112–113
reinsurance, 4
@Risk, 9–13, 19–23, 134, 168, 192–194, 209
risk averse, 42, 47, 150–151

risk profile, 1–4, 6, 8, 26, 29, 56, 65–66, 80, 170–172, 192, 201–202, 225
risk seeker, 42
RiskOptimizer, 29–32, 121, 132–133, 164–166, 184, 209, 225–226

self-insurance, 45–49, 201–202
shipping ventures, 3–4
skewness, 11, 13
solvency loan, 55, 58, 64, 71–73, 91
stable simulation, 7, 22
standard deviation, 6–8, 11, 41, 108, 116, 139, 223–224
Standard & Poor, 97–98, 102
stochastic model, 11
strategic considerations, 76
swaps, 178–181

taxes, 60–63, 69
threshold of pain, 2, 13–14, 150–151
Titanic, 8–9, 52, 117
triangular distribution, 45–46

U.S. Department of Energy, 212
underwriting risk, 41–45, 225, 229
uniform distribution, 7
utility theory, 42–43

variance, 11

wild cards, 157–159
working capital, 64, 67, 71–73, 90–91, 102, 110–113, 123–125, 190
WorldCom, 98

Xerox, 98

ABOUT THE AUTHOR

ROY L. NERSESIAN is Associate Professor in the Management and Marketing Department, School of Business, Monmouth University in West Long Branch, New Jersey. He is the author or coauthor of five previous books including *Trends and Tools for Operations Management* (2000), *Computer Simulation in Logistics* (1996), and *Computer Simulation in Financial Risk Management* (1991).